101+

ANSWERS

TO THE MOST

Frequently Asked Questions
—— **from** ——
Entrepreneurs

101+
ANSWERS
TO THE MOST
Frequently Asked Questions
— from —
Entrepreneurs

COURTNEY PRICE

John Wiley & Sons, Inc.

New York • Chichester • Weinheim • Brisbane • Singapore • Toronto

This publication is designed to provide accurate and authoritative information in regard to the subject matter covered. It is sold with the understanding that the publisher is not engaged in rendering professional services. If professional advice or other expert assistance is required, the services of a competent professional person should be sought.

Library of Congress Cataloging-in-Publication Data:

Price, Courtney H.
  101+ answers to the most frequently asked questions from entrepreneurs / Courtney Price.
    p.   cm.
  Includes bibliographical references and index.
  ISBN 0-471-31572-9 (pbk. : alk. paper)
  1. New business enterprises—United States—Management—Miscellanea. 2. Small business—United States—Management—Miscellanea. 3. Entrepreneurship—United States—Miscellanea. 4. New business enterprises—United States—Management—Information services—Directories. 5. Small business—United States—Management—Information services—Directories. 6. Entrepreneurship—United States—Information services—Directories. 7. Questions and answers. I. Title. II. Title: One hundred one answers to the most frequently asked questions from entrepreneurs. III. Title: One hundred and one answers to the most frequently asked questions from entrepreneurs.
  HD62.5.P647 1999
  658.4′ 21—dc21   98-40649

This book is dedicated to Ewing Marion Kauffman, founder of Marion Laboratories, Inc., which grew to $1 billion in revenues and $6.5 billion in market capital and had more than 300 millionaires among its staff of 3,400. In the brief time I knew him, he made a dramatic impact on my entrepreneurial philosophies and told me to teach others how to build and grow uncommon companies. He strongly reinforced my belief that hard work, combined with treating others as you want to be treated and richly rewarding those who help create the wealth, are the secrets to personal success, entrepreneurship, and the future of our country. That's the golden nugget of successful entrepreneurship.

Preface

Have you ever dreamed about starting a business, but you don't quite know how to go about it? Are you ready to be your own boss, but you aren't sure how to write a business plan? Do you have an exceptional business idea but can't find any money to finance your new venture? Do you think you have what it takes to be a successful entrepreneur?

Or are you currently operating a business but have trouble meeting Friday's payroll? Do you wonder how to attract venture capital? Are you trying to expand your market?

Then this book is exactly what you need. It addresses the typical start-up and growth questions plaguing many entrepreneurs. I am continually asked these questions by thousands of entrepreneurs from coast to coast. It all began in January 1990 when Deb Goekin, former business editor and now city editor of the *Rocky Mountain News* in Denver, asked me to write a weekly column in the newspaper's business section. Because of the overwhelming response from readers, six months later the column, "Entrepreneurs Ask," was syndicated by Scripps Howard newspapers. After six months' time, I was forced to change the mailing address at the end of the column and rent a separate mailbox because of the hundreds of letters that were pouring in from entrepreneurs. They asked, and 10 years later still ask, a variety of questions about starting and growing entrepreneurial ventures. I quickly realized that founders don't ever know enough about marketing, intellectual property, finance, management, and growing a venture. But I knew that these things could be easily learned.

I knew how critical it was to develop, manage, and grow one's own venture, not only for personal success but also for that of our nation. I knew that entrepreneurs were struggling for tips, strategies, and information on how build new ventures. I also know that entrepreneurs were asking the same questions, and many were making the same mistakes. My experiences owning and managing businesses taught me that business is not hard, but lack of information, planning, and entrepreneurial skills coupled with problems with hiring staff make business difficult. Last, I knew that if I could share my entrepreneurial experiences and know-how I could make a difference. I wanted to share those golden secrets of success that can positively impact the profitability and sustainability of small businesses.

This book comes straight from my experiences running businesses, along with those of others I have consulted or taught with in my 12 year-old Premier FastTrac® entrepreneurial training programs that are disseminated worldwide, with over 30,000 graduates. In addition, I have worked with hundreds of founders in my role as founder of the Entrepreneurial Education Foundation (international FastTrac® headquarters in Denver) and as the first scholar-in-residence at the Kauffman Center for Entrepreneurial Leadership in Kansas City, Missouri. I have written more than a dozen books on entrepreneurship and reviewed thousands of business plans. Through the years, I have learned what works and what doesn't—both the hard way by making hundreds of mistakes myself in my own businesses and by teaching and consulting with other entrepreneurs.

This book highlights typical venture questions and provides a multitude of suggestions that will increase your innovation and help you develop sound entrepreneurial strategies, better organize your venture, manage growth, and build more-successful businesses. You will learn how to better develop and launch new ventures, different ways you can play the entrepreneurial game, how to enter and penetrate the marketplace, and how to evaluate your business ideas so you develop only winning concepts. Entrepreneurial strategies and tactics can be learned. It's up to you. Begin your search by reading the answers to the most common questions from entrepreneurs. Successful entrepreneurs have learned, mostly the hard way, that at the core of a profitable business is ongoing research and a never-ending spirit of inquiry as to how to get it right the first time. They have learned how to distinguish their firms from the multitude of mediocre, "me-too," and just-getting-by ventures that frequently fail. I am convinced that most ventures fail because of a lack of information, knowledge, and planning and not knowing what questions to ask—not from a lack of money.

Join the inspiring and exciting world of entrepreneurship. Release your creative energies, make your dreams into realities, and achieve success by owning your own venture. Never forget that information is sovereign.

Begin here with this book and remember—the greatest job satisfaction, greatest personal development, and freest life comes from being your own boss and being in charge of your own destiny.

Courtney Price

Acknowledgments

I would like to thank Deb Goekin, city editor of the *Rocky Mountain News* in Denver, who gave me the opportunity to write a new column entitled "Entrepreneurs Ask," which resulted in my initial book, *Courtney Price Answers the Most Asked Questions from Entrepreneurs*. Also I would like to thank all my editors at the paper who have worked with me since 1990 and helped shape the direction of my syndicated columns. And a special thanks to Mary Cook, a dear friend and nationally recognized management writer, who encouraged me to take the idea for the first book to New York and obtain a publisher.

This new and updated book would not have been possible without the wisdom and foresight of Michael Hamilton, who agreed to publish it. Mike knew that entrepreneurs needed answers to many questions, and this book gives them those answers.

Next, I would like to thank the thousands of entrepreneurs across the country who read my syndicated column and send me letters asking perplexing and penetrating questions about how to start, develop, and grow new ventures, spurring me to write this book. These questions sent me searching for information and caused me to learn much about many different industries and new entrepreneurial techniques.

A big thanks goes to the thousands of Premier FastTrac® graduates who completed our entrepreneurial training programs and shared their unique business and learning experiences about how to operate successful companies. After 12 years and more than 30,000 graduates, many continue to keep in touch and challenge me with new issues and concerns.

I also want to thank all the people I call on for special expertise, especially my business partner, Mack Davis, who has added thoughtful insights and guidance throughout the years. Don Margolis, patent attorney in Boulder, Colorado, has worked with me on many challenging intellectual properties since I started the column in 1990. Marilynn Force, banking professional and expert on nontraditional financing, has always been an invaluable resource on the latest financing trends for entrepreneurs. Dianne Baker, lending specialist and longtime FastTrac® instructor, has been an inspiration as we have tackled many of the problems facing entrepreneurs. Ted Rice, franchising expert and founder of T. J. Cinnamons, helped craft the answers to technical franchising questions. Small-business attorney and FastTrac graduate Judith D. Judd provided up-to-date information on legal structures. And my dear friend, colleague, and talented author Alys Novak contributed her special nonprofit expertise.

I am particularly grateful to Ray Smilor, vice president of the Kauffman Center for Entrepreneurial Leadership, who not only reviewed my book but suggested that I include a chapter on "The 10 Most-Asked Questions From Entrepreneurs." This idea led me to develop a parallel chapter on "The 10 Questions Entrepreneurs Should Ask But Don't." I knew that the questions that aren't asked are even more important than the ones that are asked. Both of these chapters added a key dimension to the book. I would also like to thank Jeff Timmons for his meaningful comments as well as Dennis Kimbro, Jack Stack, John Bailey, and Greg Loudoun. Thanks also to my dear friend and very successful entrepreneur who always keeps me on track, Barb Grogan.

Additionally I would like to thank Sally Swanson, who spent the summer of 1998 with me at the Entrepreneurial Education Foundation in Denver while completing her MBA at the University of Illinois. Sally researched key information and entrepreneurial resources and helped to update the manuscript. Her grasp of entrepreneurial tactics and techniques I wrote about coupled with her enthusiasm contributed to new cutting-edge strategies in this book. And the final revisions could not have been completed without the help and patience of my outstanding assistant and super editor, Marilee Aust, whom I have worked with for the past eight years.

I also want to thank my mom, Catherine Hart, the greatest copyeditor I know, who read every chapter and sacrificed her own writing career to start and raise our family. Last, thank you to my husband, Gordy, whose heart and wisdom, both in business and in my career, contributed to many ideas for this book, and who as well reads every column I write.

Contents

Introduction, xiii

1 Overview of Entrepreneurship, 1

2 The 10 Most-Asked Questions from Entrepreneurs, 21

3 Starting a Business, 37

4 Legal Structures for Starting a Business, 65

5 Buying a Business, 80

6 Commercializing Technology and Protecting Intellectual Property, 92

7 Marketing Analysis and Planning, 120

8 Market-Penetration Strategies, 143

9 Financing Your Venture, 177

10 Selecting the Best Business Advisers, 225

11 Franchising, 243

12 The 10 Questions Entrepreneurs Should Ask But Don't, 256

Entrepreneurial Resource Checklist, 274
Index, 297

Introduction

The United States was founded by entrepreneurs—those who built our country with small businesses, farms, ranches, and mines. During the Industrial Revolution and after World War II, people began worshiping big business and flocked to the corporate environment, craving stability and job security. These large companies could do no wrong and were profitable regardless of how they operated. At this time our nation was primarily represented by big business, big farms, big ranches, and big mines.

But today, the opposite is true. Our entrepreneurial roots have taken hold and there is an explosion of entrepreneurial ventures driving economic development, reshaping markets, creating new jobs, and playing an important role in our economy, our society, and the global marketplace.

Economic evidence is everywhere: entrepreneurship is truly the megatrend of the twenty-first century. In today's economy, size is no longer the trump card it once was. Size, once considered essential for success, is becoming a liability for many companies.

Since the mid 1970s, small businesses have been the driving force in transforming the American economy. Large dominant companies are no longer the key to a strong American economy. For example, since 1980 the United States created more than 34 million jobs while Fortune 500 companies eliminated 5 million jobs. During 1987 alone, the U.S. Department of Commerce reported that employment in 7 million small firms grew three times faster than in Fortune 500 firms. In 1980, the Fortune 500 employed 20% (one in five) of our work force, but by the end of 1990, they employed only 1 in 14. The downsizing and rightsizing that took place in large companies during the 1990s will continue.

New business start-ups dominate our economic growth at the rate of more than 700,000 per year—double the rate of a decade ago and eight times what it was in the 1950s at the height of the industrial period. Information provided by the U.S. Small Business Association (SBA) office shows that small business provided virtually all new jobs from 1991 to 1995 and comprised 99.7% of all employers in 1993. And according to the Small Business Advocate, today one of every three households includes someone who has had a primary role in a new or emerging business.

The latest statistics report that 1.1 to 1.2 million new American businesses are created annually. Research sponsored by the National Federation of Independent Business estimates the annual number of new start-ups is closer to 3.5 million. This estimate represents millions of uncounted part-time and full-time home-based businesses that have been called the "underground business economy." Home-based businesses have become the fastest-growing segment of the entrepreneurial explosion. It is estimated that there will be 30 million new small businesses by the year 2000. Many experts declare that on average, firms with fewer than 100 employees create the majority of net new jobs in the U.S. economy.

The upheaval of Corporate America will be with us during the next century, and many are starting their second careers as entrepreneurs. Once burned by a big company, people become frustrated working for large companies, wondering if they'll be the next in line to receive a pink slip. Many decide not to go back in the corporate world. Instead they create new ventures or work for an entrepreneurial firm.

Another new trend is the resurgence of the corporate venturing movement, originally labeled intrapreneurship in the 1980s, which is starting new ventures and/or creating new revenue streams under the corporate umbrella. Increasingly we see more and more examples of large companies instilling principles of entrepreneurship in order to survive and to renew. As Jeff Timmons, an internationally recognized entrepreneur educator, states, corporate boards and company leadership, in unprecedented numbers, are launching experiments and strategies to recapture their entrepreneurial spirit and to instill a culture and practice we would characterize as entrepreneurial reasoning.

Entrepreneurship is not only a strong trend in our society that continues to gain momentum, but it is also a global trend in eastern block nations, the new European markets, China, the Pacific Rim countries, India, South America, Australia, and others. Small companies are now turning out a larger portion of U.S. exports from 26.4% in 1987 to almost 30% nearly a decade later—and now nearly $200 billion annually. One reason is the availability of computer technology and the World Wide Web. Competing globally makes small firms more competitive at home also. Exporting is a good strategy, since 96% of the world's consumers live outside America. Entrepreneurship is empowering nations to become independent and more stable. This entrepreneurial trend benefits not only individual business owners, but all of society as well by creating healthy business environments and self-sufficient people.

Women are among the fastest-growing groups of entrepreneurs. According to the SBA, during the past 10 years, the number of self-employed women has increased at six times the rate of men. They are starting businesses at twice the rate of their male counterparts. Projections estimate that women will own over 40% of all businesses by the year 2000. In addition, the National Foundation for Women Business Owners reports that women employ more than 11 million workers—more than Fortune 500 companies.

Entrepreneurs love their work; find it exciting, rewarding, and stimulating; and are eager to create new ventures to bring their ideas to the marketplace. Very simply, they find a need and fill it. Entrepreneurship is a mindset and a total way of life—not just a part-time activity. Today's workers are looking for more self-fulfillment, autonomy, and control over their lives. This is a major reason for the increase in home-based businesses, which give entrepreneurs work options and flexibility to accommodate their lifestyle needs. They have learned that the only job security is that which they create. People are realizing that one of the greatest ways to receive job satisfaction is by becoming an entrepreneur.

Entrepreneurs are changing the way we live, work, think, and learn. That is why many of you are jumping in on this exciting entrepreneurial wave. Now all you need is a telephone, a desk, a customer, and a business plan. Visions of owning your own business and being your own boss can become a reality with proper research, information planning, and entrepreneurial training.

This book is the new release from John Wiley & Sons of the original 1994 sold out *Courtney Price Answers the Most Asked Questions from Entrepreneurs*. It has been updated with the latest (or hottest) entrepreneurial strategies on how to commercialize technology, compete globally, market on the Internet, get involved in E-Commerce, introduce a product on a television shopping channel, and create life-style ventures. It provides the practical information you are seeking and lists business resources telling you where to obtain other critical information. It lists telephone numbers and addresses to help you access the critical information you need. Best of all, the book offers quick, easy-to-find, and common answers to questions entrepreneurs are asking. It is guaranteed to help you produce results and will become your indispensable entrepreneurial reference guide for achieving success.

1

Overview of Entrepreneurship

Overview

A rejuvenation of the U.S. entrepreneurial economy has transformed American businesses, and the adventurous entrepreneur is now revered as the new American hero. The old American dream of owning and managing one's own business is alive and well—stronger now than ever before. Latest statistics show that one out of every three Americans is involved in a new or small business. Many of these businesses are small home-based or virtual companies that are revitalizing the U.S. economy and employing over half of the working population, creating more jobs than are being lost through downsizing. Economic evidence is everywhere that entrepreneurship is the megatrend of our time.

Our economy is no longer dominated by giant corporations, which have restructured, downsized, reduced layers of management, and eliminated jobs. Large American corporations are getting smaller and small businesses are getting larger. Since 1990 most of the United States' employment growth has occurred in small entrepreneurial firms, which have expanded their ventures and created new jobs. When self-employment is included, more than 65% of employees work in small firms.

Entrepreneurship is also going global and affecting countries all over the world. Falling trade barriers improve communications, and expanded markets and the Internet have facilitated new venture creation worldwide. For example, the General Agreement on Tariffs and Trade (GATT), passed in 1995, reduced and/or eliminated tariffs among 117 countries, creating new market opportunities.

This chapter highlights major trends and hot opportunities in the entrepreneurial movement sweeping our country, including those in the computer industry, the service sector, ethnic products/services, health care, biotechnology, and information services.

Many other venture opportunities exist in delivering various goods and services to your customers' doorsteps, such as grocery items, videos, books, wine, flowers, and prepared restaurant meals and services such as auto detailing, pet grooming, and transporting individuals door to door.

Another major entrepreneurial trend is the emergence of home-based businesses, which will continue to grow as our nation shifts from an industrial to an informational base. Currently, 30 million businesses operate out of homes, and the prediction is that this number will increase. By the year 2000, it is forecast that one out of every three people will work full-time from home. Many of these ventures are service businesses. Some home-based entrepreneurs have contracted with large corporations to provide services they now outsource, like computer programming, personnel services, travel management, public relations, and other services. Franchising is another growing trend for entrepreneurs who want to expand their markets or purchase and establish successful businesses.

Women and minority business owners are also at the forefront of entrepreneurship. They are creating entrepreneurial ventures four to six times faster than any other segment in our society. One reason for this trend is that many have reached the glass ceiling and their likelihood of promotion to management and executive levels is almost nonexistent. This chapter offers strategies for women and minorities to take advantage of government and corporate procurement opportunities and obtain disadvantaged business enterprise (DBE) status.

Likewise, many entrepreneurial opportunities exist for the physically disabled, many of whom are discovering that the only way they can do the work they enjoy is by starting a business that accommodates their disability. Many create virtual companies from their homes. Finally, there are more and more entrepreneurial opportunities for talented and motivated executives, particularly those being displaced from their companies, to become more entrepreneurial. Their skills, expertise, and managerial experience make them prime candidates for launching new ventures. As the average human life span increases, so will the number of retiree and second-career entrepreneurs.

Smart Entrepreneurial Strategies

1. When deciding what kind of a business to start, match your skills, contacts, and interests with hot venture opportunities in a growing market.
2. Consider adding delivery services to your product or service line to jump-start your sales and increase your market share.
3. Reassure yourself that starting a home-based business and contracting your services with your former employer can be profitable.
4. To determine if your products or services are suitable for export, attend an overseas trade show to test the market.
5. Include both English and metric units on your international marketing materials and brochures.
6. After you have been put on a government bidder's list, aggressively market your product or service to buyers and end users.
7. Remember that disabled entrepreneurs advance at a rate of success equal to or a little higher than that of nondisabled owners.
8. Know that most entrepreneurs who have hired disabled workers find that these workers usually give back twofold in loyalty and low absenteeism.
9. If you have recently been displaced from your job and are considering starting a new business, question your desire to become an entrepreneur and assess your business skills.
10. If you work for a corporation, discuss new product or project ideas with top management and explore launching your idea inside the company.

Entrepreneurial Trends and Opportunities

New Business Opportunities Abound for Many

Question

I'm interested in learning about hot venture trends since I'm planning on starting a business, but don't know what kind. Where should I look for an entrepreneurial opportunity?

Answer

An abundance of venture opportunities exist in other industries with growing markets such as computer technology, the Internet, children's products, ethnic products, specialty boutiques, and pet pampering.

The computer industry is changing so rapidly that it's impossible to keep up with all the latest and greatest developments. Laptop computers, electronic notepads, CD-ROMs, optical data storage, multimedia computers, robotics, and new software products continue to grow. Computer-related venture opportunities include customized on-site computer training, multimedia content consulting, organizing video-conferences, marketing Internet services, and designing Web sites and innovative software products.

The Internet has become an interactive communication tool, many products are marketed and sold on the World Wide Web. On-line shopping has expanded and is expected to reach over 6 billion homes by the year 2000. Some electronic storefronts are busy taking orders, especially companies that serve narrow markets like those specializing in rare wine, music, china, books, and magazines. Businesses involved in technology, entertainment, publishing, bookselling, accounting, investment, petroleum, utilities, and travel regularly use the Web. Office supplies, small-business equipment, health supplements and vitamins, home-delivered meals, sports equipment, business documents, specialty foods, video games and gaming products, and travel and leisure products have been sold successfully on the Web.

Caution: To be successful, you must have customers who already use the Internet. Or, if you have customers who purchase by mail, then it may make sense to market on the Web. As with any new technology, there will be unexpected pitfalls and no guarantees that potential customers will purchase on the Web.

Two-income families and single-family households with kids have given rise to new ventures that help parents better educate their children, select their furnishings and designs, and transport them to sports events, practices, lessons, and other activities. In addition, more parents are concerned about every aspect of their kids' safety and well-being, from nutrition to physical fitness to improved education.

Many parents have turned to special educational consulting, tutoring, and technology to supplement children's learning. For example, toy stores featuring learning-based play items have sprung up across the nation. The wholesale dollar figure of scientific toys sold in the United States was more than $73 million; educational toy sales topped $30 million in 1994 and are expanding. Niche toy stores have created an entertainment and experiential atmosphere where kids get their hands on computers and brain-teasing toys. Other venture opportunities include juvenile safety products; infant and children's organic food products; kids' fitness centers; kiddie golf; kids' educational software for math, reading, science, and other subjects; CD-ROM encyclopedias; educational games; and children's bookstores.

Many opportunities abound in the design and marketing of ethnically diverse products and services to people from different nations. Asian Americans are one of the fastest-growing, most educated, and affluent ethnic groups in the United States. They are creating new markets for ethnic goods including cafés, restaurants, and food courts offering such hot cuisine items as satay, noodle bowls, and dim sum. Other hot ethnic flavors are Italian, Mexican, and Cantonese-style foods, along with hybrid cuisine like French-Vietnamese.

Besides ethnic restaurants, other opportunities include specialty lines of cosmetics, hair care products, and salons; vitamins and dietary supplements; ethnic grocery stores and cookbooks; and ethnic food mail-order catalogues. Ethnic medicine is another growing market segment, with an increased focus on special dietary, nutritional, and medical needs.

On the opposite end of the ever-larger national retail chains are small specialty boutiques where shopping is more personal, product selection is unique, and there are fewer shoppers to contend with. Clothing boutiques, record and CD stores, bookstores, kitchenware boutiques, gourmet delicatessens, and pet supply stores are some of these hot small retailers.

Opportunities for pet pampering include doggie bakeries, pet hotels, pet grooming and traveling vans, pet home-care visits, pet emergency clinics, old-age homes for pets, pet television and radio shows, doggie day care, cat furniture, clothing stores, and seat belts for pets.

Biotechnology is another growth industry as we expand our knowledge of the human body and other living things at the molecular level. Many new drugs and therapies focus on life extension and improving quality of life. Healthcare futurist Leland Kaiser predicts that during the twenty-first century hospitals will become similar to automobile repair shops, where people will come to replace various body parts. The average life span will be 130 years, creating many new markets for our aging population. Likewise, biotechnology developments and venture opportunities exist in the agriculture and food industries.

Providing personal services is another high-growth industry, with adults spending more hours working outside the home and experiencing less leisure time. They have an increasing need to purchase services such as day care, personal shopping, event and wedding planning, and home-delivery services. Today, working parents have many more unmet needs such as caring for sick children, transporting kids from school to after-school activities, arranging for baby-sitting, and keeping medical appointments.

These are just a few of today's hot venture opportunities. First, determine where your interests lie and match them to your experience, skills, and contacts. Then match your unique talents and experience with an expanding market segment. To write a business plan for your new venture, take one of the Premier FastTrac® business-development programs in your area. Call the Entrepreneurial Education Foundation at 303-338-1740 to learn more about the program and how to sign up.

Cashing In on Home Deliveries

Question

I own an Italian restaurant that has been experiencing a downturn in sales. I was thinking about delivering my meals to my customers as a way to increase my volume. Is home delivery an option I should consider offering?

Answer

It is very probable that you can increase your bottom line by offering home delivery to your customers. Many entrepreneurs are making it easier for their customers to purchase and are expanding their market share by offering home-delivery services for the goods they sell.

The time crunch has made delivery more attractive to many working families and individuals; home delivery can give your customers an extra incentive to do business with you. The biggest users of home delivery are double-income families with children. Many working parents do not want to go out to dinner after they come home from their jobs. They value their time at home and are willing to pay extra to have products and services delivered to their doors. Studies show that at least 40% of all adults order a meal delivered from a restaurant at least once a month. According to some experts, a restaurant that adds delivery service can increase volume by 50% and not take away from its eat-in business.

Also consider offering your delivery services to elderly people in your area. This is an expanding market as the number of older citizens rises and their life spans increase.

In the past, grocery and department stores made home deliveries, before it became too expensive and before women shoppers started driving. Today, most women are employed and drive to work instead of to the store to shop at a leisurely pace. This is one of the reasons that catalogs and television shopping networks have become so popular. Most women just don't have the time and/or the desire to go out shopping. It is looked upon as a major inconvenience.

The home delivery trend is steadily increasing, and such products as grocery items, videos, books, wine, flowers, and meals are being delivered directly to consumers' homes. Multitudes of services are also being sold and delivered to homes, such as auto detailing, pet grooming, and transporting people door to door. Some chain grocery stores provide delivery and pickup services in response to telephone, computer, and fax orders.

In addition to individual restaurants that offer home delivery services, firms have sprouted up that publish menu guides from local restaurants and transmit orders to them. The meals are then delivered to the customer's doorstep. These companies generally require that a restaurant sell to them at a 25% discount.

Businesses delivering a service directly to the home often add a $10 to $20 delivery fee. Customers seem willing to pay extra for this convenience. Home-delivery services are especially attractive in climates that experience inclement weather.

If you can make it easier for your customers to purchase your Italian food, you could ultimately increase your profit share while creating goodwill. You have a good chance to expand your market share by delivering and reaching an untapped market segment in your community.

Home-Based Business Opportunities

Question

I have two small children at home and would like to return to work. However, with all of the corporate downsizing taking place these days, I think I will have a difficult time finding another data processing job. I am thinking about working at home and contracting with my former employer. What do you think about home-based business opportunities as a viable option?

Answer

Home-based business opportunities are rapidly increasing as more and more people try to balance work with family commitments. Recent studies show that one out of three new businesses in the United States is run from the home. Today there are over 30 million home-based businesses, and by the year 2000 there will be approximately 40 million.

John Naisbitt and Patricia Aburdene in *Megatrends 2000* explain that much of this growth is due to the availability, affordability, and reliability of technology such as computers, specialized software, fax machines, modems, and voice mail, along with both 800 and 900 phone numbers.

Adding to this trend is the number of women, like you, who want to work but have small children at home. According to the National Center for Policy Analysis, women run 70% of home-based businesses.

Both physically disabled people and seniors citizens are also discovering the joys of starting their own home-based businesses. The American Home-Based Business Association reports that 15 percent of home-based businesses are run by retirees. As the average life span in our country increases, so will the number of senior home-based entrepreneurs.

One of the key benefits in starting a home-based business is that it is an inexpensive way to test the market and prove customer acceptance. You can gradually start your new venture and grow it slowly to fit your needs.

By operating a home-based business, you will receive the precious gift of time. You will no longer waste time commuting to and from work and will avoid messy traffic jams. You can use your household resources for your business and thereby avoid lease expenses while greatly reducing your child-care expenses. Other benefits include setting your own hours, being your own boss, becoming independent, and reducing your wardrobe expenses.

You should determine whether you are a good candidate for operating a new venture from your home. It takes certain skills, experience, and marketing knowledge to launch and operate a profitable home-based business. Take advantage of the many helpful books and magazines available, as well as governmental assistance and college courses, to help you start your business in your home. Review *The Best Home Businesses for the 90s* by Paul and Sarah Edwards. Just because a business is being run from your home doesn't mean it should be operated any differently from a freestanding venture.

International Opportunities

Question

I am a small manufacturer who is considering exporting to Mexico and South America. How can I get more information about selling my goods abroad?

Answer

Many opportunities exist to do business internationally, and many informational sources are available to get you started. Many entrepreneurs expand their markets by exporting since the international marketplace is more than four times larger than that of the United States alone. In addition, the North American Free Trade Agreement (NAFTA) has made it easier for companies to export to Mexico and Canada by eliminating trade barriers.

Even though exporting opportunities are great, there are also risks involved, and not all entrepreneurs are positioned to sell abroad. For example in most situations exporting should not be considered when first starting a new business. It is hard enough to get a new venture profitable in the United States without adding the problems associated with exporting.

In addition, you must be able to offer a quality product or service at a competitive price. Therefore it is essential to know your competitors and their strengths and weaknesses. You also need to distinguish your goods in the marketplace. There are thousands of separate markets, and each has its unique characteristics that require different market-penetration strategies.

There are other costs and risks involved with exporting. You must weigh the potential benefits against the commitment of time and extra resources.

Before deciding to export, take steps to determine your export readiness. First, look internally and evaluate your firm's commitment and ability to enter into the global marketplace. Exporters should be prepared to take a long-term view of this process. Firms can be successful in attracting some international sales and distribution the first couple of years. But long-term success takes more perseverance and planning for the additional time and costs involved with international transactions.

The initial costs of setting up an exporting arm can be substantial. You should justify your export costs and include additional financing costs. Currency fluctuations could ruin your company. Collections can be time-consuming and expensive.

Initially, you could probably service up to a dozen foreign markets with existing staff. But if you add more foreign markets, you will need to expand your staff. There are detailed paperwork and bureaucratic barriers to overcome when conducting business in other countries.

Explore alternative ways of selling your goods overseas. You could use an export marketing or trading company, or overseas distributors who are responsible for all aspects of marketing and distributing your products in their country. You need to explore these alternatives and take your time when selecting an international partner.

Consider obtaining assistance from export service providers to develop an international marketing plan. For more information, contact the Trade Information Center at 800-USA-TRADE (800-872-8723), an international clearinghouse on exporting. Ask for the desk officer who specializes in your industry for country-specific information.

Seek out exporting assistance in your local community. Many places offer exporting help for little or no cost. Start by contacting your local chamber of commerce and the international department of your bank. You could also contact your local small business development center (SBDC), a freight forwarder, a local international trade club, or a local entrepreneur group.

Your state Department of Commerce, the Small Business Administration, and the U.S. Department of Commerce also provide exporting assistance. Commercial attachés in U.S. embassies abroad can help you find and meet foreign dealers and representatives. Any of these sources can help you or can refer you to private consultants and agencies that have expertise in your particular exporting needs. Lastly, there are about 60 world trade centers in the United States that can provide information about and assistance in exporting your product.

There are also several exporting hotlines. The Department of Commerce's Trade Information Center, at 800-USA-TRADE, has a directory of governmental export assistance programs. The Small Business Foundation of America, at 800-243-7232, offers market analysis, referrals, trade fair information, and assistance in licensing, customs distribution, options, and other areas. It's free, except for customized services that cost from $15 to $40. Finally, 800-USA-EXPORT offers a fax-retrieval service 24 hours a day that covers 50 industries and 78 countries. Its electronic directory can help you promote your products and services to buyers and suppliers in Canada and Mexico. Ask for the Exporters Kit.

Minority and Women Entrepreneurs

Special Minority Programs for Entrepreneurs

Question

I am a minority who owns a small printing firm. I am interested in finding out about procurement opportunities. Does the Small Business Administra-

tion or government offer any special procurement opportunities for women and minority business owners?

Answer

Generally, contracting opportunities with the federal government are available to any business, but there are special programs to encourage participation by small businesses, small disadvantaged businesses, and women-owned businesses. Often the government will limit competition for contracts to small or minority-owned firms. An increasing number of awards are also limited to women-owned businesses. These are called set asides. Most federal procurement contracts valued under $25,000 are also reserved for small businesses.

To take advantage of these opportunities, become familiar with your local government agencies. All have target goals for contracting with small and minority-owned firms. One of the biggest myths about doing business with the federal government is that all you need to do is to get on a government bidder's list and wait for a call. In reality, the government, like any other customer, does business with people it knows. Therefore, it is essential that you continually market, market, and market your services with the buyers and end users.

There are numerous places to obtain further information and assistance for getting involved with government procurement. Each government agency has a small-business specialist available to assist small-business owners interested in doing business with that agency. These individuals should be your first contact point to identify a buyer or end user for your product. A useful reference book is *The Entrepreneur's Guide to Doing Business with the Federal Government.*

The Department of Defense also funds Procurement Technical Assistance Centers (PTACs) in most states. Call your local Defense Logistics Agency officer for information or check with your local Small Business Development Center.

Your local SBA office should also have a procurement-assistance program. To locate the nearest office, call the SBA Answer Line at 800-827-5722. Also available to minority firms is the SBA's 8(a) program. This is a business-development program that lasts nine years in which the SBA assists in a firm's business growth. Government contracting is a portion of this program, but any 8(a) firm is encouraged to vigorously pursue commercial business. Participants in the 8(a) program can receive assistance in business-plan development, leads on government contracting, and some financial aid, including help with bonding and advance payments under contracts to maintain cash flow during contract performance. The SBA Answer Line can direct you to your local SBA office for more information. Request Fact Sheet 35, which explains this special program.

✔ COURTNEY'S SMART TIP

8(a) certification is *not* necessary to be recognized by the federal government as a disadvantaged business.

Federal work is self-certified, which means that the small or small disadvantaged business owners state they meet the required criteria as outlined by the SBA. Special certification is not needed.

Finally, many public utilities and corporations, especially those that have large government contracts, set annual goals for women- and minority-owned business participation. Each company has a different certification process. Call the small-business liaison officer for valuable assistance on how to become a certified contractor. To pursue procurement opportunities, you most likely will have to supply information on your company's ownership, financial backing, history, expertise, list of clients, and so on. Presenting your business plan is also helpful.

How to Become a Disadvantaged Business Enterprise

Question

I am a minority entrepreneur who has recently started a small travel agency. I heard that I could qualify to become a disadvantaged business enterprise and be eligible for special loans or grants. Is this true, and how can I receive this type of certification?

Answer

You may be able to become a certified disadvantaged business enterprise (DBE) if your venture meets certain criteria and you submit a completed application form. However, becoming a DBE does not qualify you for special loans or grants. This is a big misconception among many minority and women business owners. The purpose of becoming a DBE is to have the opportunity to compete for various federally and locally funded projects that have certain goals established to award a portion of their work to certified DBEs.

Because of federal legislation, the Department of Transportation provides money through the Federal Highway Administration, the Federal Transit Administration, and the Federal Aviation Administration for state and local transportation projects. A minimum of 10% of money granted to state and city agencies must be contracted with certified DBEs.

To become a DBE, you must be a small business concern that is 51% owned and controlled by one or more minorities or women who are involved with day-to-day operations and who also meet other eligibility criteria.

First, you must submit an application for certification as a DBE through your local certifying agency. When your completed application is received, it will be reviewed to ensure that all the proper information has been included. DBE certification requires that an on-site interview be conducted. During this meeting you will be asked questions to determine if you are eligible to become a DBE.

After a completed application is received, it takes an average of 60 days to determine if you are eligible to be certified. Once certified, you will be allowed to participate as a DBE on Department of Transportation (DOT) financially assisted projects. Most minority business owners claim that it *is* worth the time and trouble to obtain DBE certification.

A number of public agencies in every state have minority- or women-owned business goals on various governmental projects. Check with your state's Department of Transportation, Transit Agency, and Board of Water Commissioners. Also contact city governments and other local agencies.

To be eligible for DBE certification under DOT guidelines, you must be a citizen or lawful permanent resident who is socially and economically disadvantaged. The following classes of people are presumed to be disadvantaged: black, Hispanic, Portuguese, Asian American, American Indian, and Alaskan Native; women and members of other minority groups; and other individuals found to be economically and socially disadvantaged by the Small Business Administration under section 8(a) of the Small Business Act.

Usually, out-of-state firms must first be certified in their home state before certification can be granted in another state. Proof of home state certification must be included when applying for certification in another state.

DBE firms are subject to an annual renewal process. Renewal applications and financial information must be submitted prior to the certification expiration date. Financial information is required to ensure that firms continue to meet the small-business size standards as defined by the Small Business Administration. If ventures undergo changes in ownership and control of the firm, a new application may be required.

If you are denied certification, you may appeal the decision directly to the Secretary of the Department of Transportation or through your state's hearings process. Firms may correct deficiencies in their ownership and control and then reapply for certification at any time.

Becoming a certified DBE firm allows you the opportunity *only* to bid on certain contracts.

✔ COURTNEY'S SMART TIP

Even when you qualify as a disadvantaged business enterprise (DBE), it is crucial to aggressively market your firm with governmental agencies.

Since there are many competing firms, obtain further assistance in securing these contracts by contacting the Minority Business Development Center in your region or the National Minority Supplier Development Council, 15 West 39th Street, New York, NY 10018, 212-944-2430.

Challenges and Opportunities for Women Entrepreneurs

Question

I'm a woman who owns a small retail business, and I have found that women face some unique and frustrating barriers and attitudes as business owners. Are there any support organizations that have information or articles that could address my problems and concerns?

Answer

Women business owners are attracting considerable attention, and many opportunities are available to this fast-growing group. Women business owners are a driving force in our economy and owned 35% of all firms in 1996. The Small Business Administration estimates that women-owned businesses will increase to 48% by the year 2000.

Between 1987 and 1996 the number of women-owned businesses grew 78%. Women are looking for ways to balance family commitments and professional aspirations.

Despite their increasing numbers, women do experience both more problems and different kinds of problems than men. Women entrepreneurs are more likely to fail than men. Typical barriers include lack of access to capital and a lack of basic business skills, entrepreneurial training, and marketing expertise.

Research has shown that the disparity between women's and men's roles in the business world is rooted in childhood. For example, men and women are socialized differently from the time they are born.

Boys are taught to be competitive and encouraged to learn team sports. Girls are taught to follow the rules and avoid risks.

This disparity continues when they become teenagers. Girls tend to lose more of their self-esteem and self-confidence. They tend to focus on family activities with parents, while boys focus on competitive team sports. By the time girls go to college, they are not prepared even to think about running their own business, and most often do not have the skills required to do so.

Studies indicate that women business owners use less-formal and more-participative management styles than men. They define their business goals more broadly to include customer satisfaction as well as profit and growth. They start their ventures with less than half as much capital as men.

Several different resources could be helpful to you. The National Education Center for Women in Business (NECWB), located at Seton Hill College in Greensburg, Pennsylvania, began in 1993 to promote women and business ownership nationwide. The center is devoted to research, education, and information about women entrepreneurs, who are often overlooked in academic and business circles. This nonprofit organization's mission is to help women who are currently growing their businesses as well as to help the next generation to be more prepared to become entrepreneurs.

NECWB publishes a free quarterly newsletter, and offers women-oriented educational programs across the United States, books, and videos.

To find out more about NECWB's resources, call 724-830-4625.

Another resource is the National Association of Women Business Owners based in Chicago (312-922-0465). Last, Joline Godfrey, in her book *Our Wildest Dreams*, discusses the unique problems facing women entrepreneurs. She is also cofounder of An Income of Her Own, a San Jose, California, company that offers entrepreneurial education to women.

Physically Disabled Entrepreneurs

Group Aids Disabled Entrepreneurs

Question

I recently became disabled and cannot continue in my current job, although I have great working experience in desktop publishing. I'm thinking about starting my own business. Is there an organization that helps disabled people start a new business? Are there special loan programs, grants, or low-interest loans for disabled entrepreneurs?

Answer

Technological advancements have made it possible for entrepreneurs to start a business from their homes, resulting in an increase in the number of disabled people starting their own businesses. This may be the only employment option for individuals with disabilities.

One organization that assists the disabled in starting new ventures is the Disabled Businesspersons Association (DBA) in San Diego. This group reports that entrepreneurship by the disabled is the fastest-growing segment of business start-ups today. The DBA estimates that 60% of small businesses are owned and managed by persons with disabilities. It offers a variety of services, most of them free, and publishes a quarterly newsletter. Contact Urban Mirares, president of the DBA, at 619-594-8805.

For information about adaptive advice to help you work at home, contact your state office of rehabilitation. Other resources include the IBM Special Needs Information Referral Center in Atlanta at 800-426-3333.

No special federal funding sources for disabled entrepreneurs have existed since the SBA's Handicapped Assistance Loan program was canceled. Grants, on the other hand, are usually awarded to not-for-profit organizations. Sometimes a for-profit organization can qualify for a grant from a private foundation depending on the purpose of the request, the type of business, the business location, and other related factors.

For information about foundations, contact the Foundation Center in New York City at 212-620-4230 or the Council on Foundations in Washington, D.C., at 202-466-6512. In addition, many states publish foundation directories that contain local grant sources. Entrepreneurs rarely rely on grants to launch or grow their ventures.

With regard to low-interest commercial loans, there may be opportunities for obtaining special low-interest loans from some microlenders. Typically, microlenders represent institutions or nonprofit organizations that either receive grant money or purchase or borrow money from lending institutions at favorable tax rates to make small commercial loans.

There are over 400 microlenders in the United States, and each establishes its own lending criteria. Most charge the going rates for loans since they incur the same loan-processing fees whether the loan amount is $2,000 or $100,000. They usually loan to microenterprises, which they define as businesses with one to four employees, gross annual sales under $1 million, and net worth under $250,000. Most home-based businesses fall within this definition. They provide short-term, fixed-interest-rate loans between $1,000 and $25,000. Some loan only to existing businesses, to ventures in a designated economic development area, or to a specific group of individuals.

To locate microlenders in your area, ask your banker or contact your chamber of commerce. Other resources to help you launch your venture include a variety of SBA programs and SBDC centers. Call the SBA Hotline at 800-827-5722 or visit the SBA Web site at http://www.sbaonline.sa.gov for more information.

Obtaining adequate funding could be a challenge since some lenders consider making business loans to disabled entrepreneurs an added risk compounding the already risky proposition of business itself. Many have discovered that the disabled show just as much grit as their nondisabled counterparts. Entrepreneurs need to be extremely determined and persevere in the midst of adversity, just as the physically disabled do.

Executive Entrepreneurs

Entrepreneurial Opportunities for Retirees

Question

I am 64 years old and bored. I took advantage of an early retirement opportunity after working 30 years for an insurance company. I have always been interested in running my own business, but don't know what kind of business to start. What do you suggest?

Answer

Many retirees are starting new enterprises, since they still want to work but cannot find suitable employment opportunities. They have several advantages over other entrepreneurs, such as retirement dollars to invest in a business. Another advantage is having already established a long-term banking relationship with a personal credit history, demonstrating credit-worthiness and some available assets to use as collateral.

You have many options to consider as to what kind of venture to start. First, examine the skills, expertise, and hobbies you have that are transferable to a business venture. What have you done in the past that either satisfies a current market need or solves a problem for a potential customer? Taking advantage of your skills and interests is the starting point.

Are there contracting opportunities with your previous employers that you could explore? Is there some type of project or new product or service that they might be interested in starting? If so, maybe you should establish a joint venture with them.

Consider the following questions:

Could you start this venture on a part-time basis to test the need and feasibility of your idea?

Could it be started as a home-based business, thus reducing start-up costs?

Are there existing businesses for sale that you might be interested in buying?

Would you be interested in starting a franchise, for which the success rate is much higher than for a new start-up venture?

Are there any agreements available through which you could—for a small fee—be licensed to represent an existing product or product line?

Once you have identified a definite need in the marketplace, consider your competitive advantage. Avoid becoming a "me-too" business that just duplicates a successful concept. Determine how you could differentiate your venture, carve a niche, and capitalize on your competition's weaknesses.

Interview owners of existing businesses you might be interested in starting. Ask them questions about the problems they encounter as well as growth opportunities. Contact the national trade association in your industry and ask for information on starting a business in that industry. Or go to work full- or part-time for a business you are interested in starting.

Check Network Marketing Offer at Many Levels

Question

I recently retired and am looking for a business opportunity. I considered franchising but don't want to spend all my savings purchasing a franchise. I cut out an ad for a network-marketing opportunity, but my friends and family have told me to avoid multilevel marketing companies. What do you think about them? Should I pursue this opportunity?

Answer

Network-marketing, or multilevel-marketing, companies have gotten a bad name because of reported pyramid scams or Ponzi schemes in which people made money by recruiting others instead of selling goods. Front loading, where distributors compel new recruits to purchase lots of inventory that they probably cannot sell, is an illegal practice. Companies that make money whether or not any product is sold at retail are subject to prosecution and should be avoided.

However, there are many legitimate network-marketing companies. Today it's an over $15 billion industry that offers aspiring entrepreneurs a chance to start a home-based business with minimum costs. This rapidly growing industry has been fueled by lifestyle issues, computer technology, and a desire for personal freedom.

As with any business opportunity, it is crucial that you thoroughly investigate the company's history as well as its financial and legal records. Look for pending lawsuits, allegations of misconduct, or other types of business complaints. Check with the Better Business Bureau in your area. Obtain a credit report from a respected credit-reporting agency like TRW. Ask your banker to help you conduct a background investigation. Some banks provide a company's credit report to its customers.

Call suppliers and ask about the company's payment record and its reliability. Go to the library and search for articles written about the company. If the company looks good, respond to the ad and review the information provided. Ask the firm for names and phone numbers of its attorney, banker, and accountant. If it has nothing to hide, the company should respond to your request.

Start with the banker and ask how long the company has been a customer. Check whether it has applied for credit and if it was granted. Does it pay on time?

Next, contact the accountant and check if the company is having financial problems. Ask for a profit-and-loss statement, and ask whether there are any state or federal tax liens.

Then call the attorney and ask whether the company has been or is currently a plaintiff or defendant in any litigation. If so, what kind? How often? What was the final disposition of the suit?

Obtain a litigation history on the company and its founders by contacting a background investigation firm in the country in which the company is registered. Another good source for background information is Prentice Hall Legal and Financial Service. Compare all of the responses you have gathered with this information. Look for any trends and patterns of abuse. This due diligence should cost you under $200 as well as some time, but it is well worth it. If the company checks out, it is time to evaluate the market for the product and its profit potential, and to write a feasibility plan to determine if this is a sound business opportunity and whether you should start this type of home-based business.

Pitfalls to Avoid

1. Starting a new business offering the same services you performed in your corporate job without continually marketing the business and looking for additional clients.

2. Failing to operate a home-based business professionally and not treating it as a separate business venture.

3. Exporting products that are not distinguishable from those of the competition.

4. Thinking that if you get on a government bidding list, purchasers will contact you.

5. Assuming that becoming a disadvantaged business enterprise will qualify your venture for special loans and/or grants.

6. Thinking that entrepreneurship is too risky for disabled people.

7. Starting a new business because you have recently been displaced and cannot find other employment.

8. Thinking that your corporate skills are directly transferable to starting a new business.

2

The 10 Most-Asked Questions from Entrepreneurs

Some entrepreneurs dream about starting a business but don't quite know how to go about it, while others have an existing business that is barely breaking even or just making a small profit. Both categories of entrepreneurs have many questions about the world of entrepreneurship. That is why I was asked to write a weekly column in the business section of the *Rocky Mountain News*, now syndicated by Scripts Howard.

In the column, entitled "Entrepreneurs Ask," entrepreneurs were asked to send their business questions to me. I was immediately flooded with over 100 letters asking a myriad of questions, from "Do you think I have what it takes to be an entrepreneur?" to "How do I go about writing a business plan?" to "How can I attract venture capital to fund my business?" I continue to be deluged by letters from entrepreneurs across the country asking thousands of questions about starting and operating entrepreneurial ventures. Many ask the same questions over and over again. Here are the "10 Most-Asked Questions from Entrepreneurs" who have been responding to my column for the past 10 years. The answers are concise, helpful, practical, and present cost-efficient strategies. They are intended to help entrepreneurs grow more profitable ventures and to positively impact job creation and economic development.

10 Most-Asked Questions from Entrepreneurs

1. I'd love to start a new business, but I don't have a great idea. What kind of business should I start?

2. I want to open a business in my home. What do I need to do to get started?

(Continued)

(Continued)

3. How do I approach a banker to get a loan to start my new business?

4. Where can I find a venture capitalist to finance my new venture?

5. How do I go about obtaining a patent for my new software program?

6. I have already patented a new invention but need to find a marketing company to distribute my product. Where can I find one?

7. How can I increase my sales and find new customers?

8. Since I don't have much money to market my business, where should I advertise?

9. How can I successfully market my product with a limited budget?

10. What kind of franchise should I purchase?

In this chapter, each question is discussed at length.

Question #1

I'd love to start a new business, but I don't have a great idea. What kind of business should I start?

Answer

I would do people a great disservice if I tried to recommend what type of venture they should start. People are successful if they are doing what they truly love to do. Entrepreneurs should combine their likes and desires with potential venture ideas.

You do not need a great idea to start a new business. If you wait for that phenomenal new idea to strike, you may never find it. Having the best idea is not the critical element in launching a successful venture. The truth is that many successful entrepreneurs decide to start a new business first and then go looking for a product or service to offer. Seldom does a successful founder start a new venture with a great idea.

✔ COURTNEY'S SMART TIP

It is far better to start a new business because you find an unmet need in the marketplace with a competitive advantage that matches your experience, rather than because you come up with an idea that will revolutionize the marketplace.

Consider many laid-off workers who have spent 10, 15, 20, or more years in the corporate environment and are in the process of starting new ventures because they cannot find comparable jobs. Many do not have a great idea but search for products or services to offer that match their experience and expertise.

You begin the venture hunt by assessing your personal criteria to determine what kind of business will fit your lifestyle requirements. Ask yourself about the type of business that would satisfy you and your lifestyle. Then consider the following list of soul-searching questions:

Entrepreneur's Venture Checklist

1. What do you like to do?

2. What are your interests and hobbies?

3. What are your areas of expertise?

4. Do you have any special skills or talents?

5. What industry are you most interested in?

6. What are your financial needs?

7. How much financial risk are you willing to expose yourself to?

8. Would you be more comfortable with running a small business with few employees or a larger business with many employees?

9. How many years do you want to work?

10. Will your current physical condition withstand the pressures and stresses that come with starting a new business?

11. Where do you want to live and work?

12. How many hours per week are you willing to work?

Entrepreneurs must identify and evaluate what is important to them in starting a new venture. The key is to assess your personal desires and then decide which business venture matches your personal criteria and represents a significant marketing opportunity. Read several of the entrepreneurial magazines that feature new venture ideas, like *Success*, *Entrepreneur, Inc.*, *New Business Monthly*, and *Fast Company*.

Once you have found products or services you want to offer, don't forget to calculate the opportunity costs involved in starting a new venture. Should you spend your time, effort, and money doing something else? If you have the talents to grow a successful business, these talents will also be highly valued by other corporations. And building a venture takes more time than you think. Should you consider other alternatives?

If you don't have the right skills for that business, sign up for entrepreneurial courses or seminars to develop your business skills. Reading this book and others like it can also help prepare you for launching and/or growing a profitable venture.

Question #2

I want to open a business in my home. What do I need to do to get started?

Answer

There is a growing trend for men and women to start and operate successful small businesses from their homes. Recent studies show that one out of three new businesses in the United States is run from the home. Currently there are over 30 million home-based businesses, and by the year 2000, there will be about 40 million.

Before starting a home-based business, assess your capabilities and abilities to run a business from your home by taking the following quiz. The more yes answers you have, the more likely it is that you are suited to start a home-based business.

Home-Based Business Quiz

1. Do you have adequate living space to devote a section of your home to a business without disturbing your family?

2. Will your family refrain from interfering with you while you work on your business?

3. Are you comfortable operating independently?

4. Can you organize your time well, set aside the necessary hours to run your business, and stick to it?

5. Can you make decisions on your own?

6. Are you a self-starter?

7. Will you leave your home and go out to make customer calls?

8. Do you tend to complete projects on time?

9. Do you have sufficient funds to start a home-based business?

10. Are you willing and able to acquire the right equipment to operate a home-based business?

11. Will your local zoning rules and regulations permit you to run a business in your home?

12. Are you willing to research your home-based business idea and write a business plan to make your dream a reality?

✔ COURTNEY'S SMART TIP
Run your home-based business as if it were located in a separate office.

Next, consider whether the type of business you want to start lends itself to working at home. If location is not important to your venture, then a home base might be perfect. One of the benefits of operating a home-based business is the attendant economies of scale—that is, getting started with minimal capital and overhead expenses. In addition, you have more time to work because you no longer need to drive to and from an office location.

Be sure you establish a network of professional contacts, since running a home-based business can be lonely. Take advantage of the many available home-based resources, support groups, and professional associations. Get a copy of the *Complete Guide to Owning a Home-Based Business* by *Entrepreneur Magazine* or *Homemade Money* by Barbara Brabec. Contact the SBA office in your area and obtain a copy of "How to Start a Home-Based Business."

Question #3

How do I approach a banker to get a loan to start my new business?

Answer

This is one of the most frequently asked questions by entrepreneurs who have the misconception that a bank is the first place you should go to finance a new venture. Just the opposite is true. Most first-round financing for new ventures comes from family and friends. When looking for start-up capital, first talk to your family, friends, and relatives about investing in or loaning you money for your venture. Next, look to some of the alternative sources of financing discussed in Chapter 8.

Many entrepreneurs do not realize that the available sources of capital change dramatically depending on the stage and rate of the venture's growth. Most debt and equity financial sources are not available until the venture progresses beyond the early stages of growth.

Many commercial banks do not need or pursue small-business clients. By the same token, owners need the support of banks and their services to deposit checks, process credit card transactions, obtain lines of credit, and so forth. Therefore, establishing a banking relationship is extremely important to all entrepreneurs. However, it is difficult to obtain a small-business loan unless you have a significant amount of initial equity money, including both a primary and a secondary source of repayment. In addition, banks prefer to lend to businesses that have at least a three-year operating history, with accompanying financial statements. *Banks lend almost exclusively to existing businesses with identifiable cash flow and capital.* Typically a loan officer will require the following documents before considering a loan request:

Banker's Lending Checklist

1. Current interim balance sheet and income statement.

2. Cash flow projections.

3. Pro forma balance sheet, income statement, and cash flow.

4. Fiscal year-end financial statements.

5. Three-year historical balance sheet, income statement, and cash flow statement.

6. Business tax returns for the past three years.

7. Current accounts receivable.

8. Current accounts payable.

9. Inventory, furniture, fixtures, and equipment lists.

10. Business plan.

11. Current personal financial statement.

12. Personal tax returns for the past three years.

Generally, a start-up venture is able to provide only a business plan, pro forma or financial statements, a personal financial statement, and personal tax returns. Bankers know that the younger the company, the riskier the investment. Remember, banks and risk do not mix. Bankers feel that start-ups have little if any proven capability of a strong management team, much less an ability to generate sales and subsequently pay off short-term debt.

✔ COURTNEY'S SMART TIP

Establish a banking relationship before you ever need to borrow money. Finding the right banker is more important than finding the right bank.

The first step in establishing a banking relationship is to get a referral for specific loan officers at several different banks from business associates and other business owners. Ask your referrals to call ahead and let the loan officer know that you will be calling to set up an appointment. The following checklist of questions is provided for you to use when interviewing and selecting the right banker:

Checklist Questions to Ask Bankers

- What type of commercial loans does the bank make? Does it prefer loans under $500,000? Over $1 million? Does it secure loans by assets of the company, such as accounts receivable, equipment, or inventory? Or does it prefer to use real estate and personal assets of the owner? Do they offer term loans that amortize, or revolving lines of credit?

- What type of repayment options are available? Interest for only 6 to 12 months? Principal and interest payments due monthly, quarterly, or semiannually? One-year term? Five-year term?

- What criteria are considered when the loan is first submitted? What documentation is required?

- Ask what documentation will be needed when the loan matures and you wish to renew.

- What will be the interest rate and all other fees?

- Are the interest rate and fees open to negotiation?

- What determines rates and fees?

- How long does the process usually take from application to closing?

- What other business services does the bank offer? What types of deposit accounts are offered and how is interest paid? Does the bank offer credit card deposits? Are money bags supplied to make deposits in? What are the related fees?

- May the applicant (or applicant's attorney) review all loan documents prior to signing them?

- Does the bank have an advertising program where businesses can put ad coupons in the statements mailed to bank customers?

- Ask if the bank can use your services.

- How long has the bank been open? Under its current management?

- How long has the loan officer been with the bank? In banking? Determine if he or she understands your business and its needs.

- Find out how, in the event of a temporary downturn in your business, the bank will work with you.

- If the bank would be unable to help you at such a time, could it recommend a bank that might be able to?

An excellent resource for start-up financing is Lawrence W. Tuller's *When the Bank Says No!* It contains an extensive appendix for financing assistance.

Question #4

Where can I find a venture capitalist to finance my new venture?

Answer

Very few start-up businesses can qualify for venture capital funds. Most research shows that less than 14% of investments made by venture capitalists are in start-up ventures, and most of these investments are for new product development. Venture capital firms are not a good source of financing for start-ups.

To begin with, a very limited number of venture capitalists are interested in funding raw start-ups. Although venture capitalists frequently invest in high-risk ventures, usually through an equity purchase, they look for a 20% to 30% annual return on their investment—and, if successful, 10 times their investment in about five years. They are interested in the strong cash flow and profits that a business can generate. Like bankers, they prefer to see several years of operating history before they consider investing. They also have stringent criteria for their investments and fund less than 1% of the deals that come across their desks.

For their financial help, venture capitalists usually get a healthy percentage of ownership in the business. It is not unusual for venture capitalists to take up to 75% ownership of a start-up high-technology venture. They want a hand in managing the company, usually through active participation in management decisions and/or through board seats—either as directors or as advisers.

In addition, they prefer to invest in companies that will go public within a reasonable time period, usually five years, at a share price high enough to give the venture capitalist a significant gain on the investment and an exit. Last, they usually invest in certain types of industries like computer hardware, electronics, and health care.

If you think your start-up business can qualify for venture capital, look in the Yellow Pages, *The Wall Street Journal,* and *Venture* magazine. To better understand the venture capital world, read *Venture Capital at the Crossroads* by William D. Bygrave and Jeffry A. Timmons. You can also get a listing of venture capital firms from the National Venture Capital Association, 1655 North Fort Meyer Drive, Suite 700, Arlington, VA 22209.

Instead of looking for a venture capitalist to fund your new business, look to informal sources of venture capital, such as family, friends, private investors or angle networks (groups of independent investors interested in lending to entrepreneurs), professional advisers, business acquaintances, successful entrepreneurs, customers, suppliers, and prospective employees. It has been estimated that over 95% of capital for new businesses comes from these sources.

Question #5

How do I go about obtaining a patent for my new software program?

Answer

Many investors do not understand the field of intellectual property, the need to become more familiar with it, and how to protect their ideas. Overall, there is much confusion about how to protect intellectual property and the differences between a patent, a trademark, a copyright, and a trade secret. Determining the form of protection to pursue is critical before marketing your invention. See Chapter 6 for more detailed information on different types of intellectual property and how to obtain protection for them.

To begin with, software programs can now be both patented and copyrighted. A patent may be obtained for a new and usable process, machine, manufacture, or composition of matter or any new and useful improvement. A patent gives the inventor the right to exclude others from making and selling the product for 17 years, provided that maintenance fees are paid every $3\frac{1}{2}$ years. A patent keeps others from using or selling the patented invention and is in a sense a legal right to litigate against those who infringe on the patent.

To apply for a patent, you must file an application with the U.S. Department of Commerce, Patent and Trademark Office, Washington, DC 20231. Although you can do much of the legwork yourself, I strongly recommend that you consult with an intellectual-property attorney to assist in this process. Become knowledgeable about the process before you begin. Also read *Patent It Yourself* by David Pressman.

If your creation involves any written or artistic matter that includes a symbol, word, shape, or design, you can qualify for protection under trademark law. Trademarks are used by a manufacturer or business to identify goods and to distinguish them from other goods. Service marks are slogans or phrases used in the sale of advertising of services as opposed to products. A trademark can be easily obtained by attaching the letters TM to your mark (or SM for a service mark). It is advisable to register with both your state and federal trademark offices. Unlike patents, trademarks have an indefinite life when used properly. Federal trademarks are issued for a period of 10 years and can be renewed if still in use. For the appropriate forms and information to register a trademark federally, write to the Patent and Trademark Office, Washington, D.C. 20231.

A copyright includes any book, poem, speech, recording, computer program, statue, painting, label, cartoon, dramatic or musical work, pantomime, choreographic work, motion picture, video, map, game board, packaging design, or instructions. Copyrights offer legal protection just like patents and trademarks but are much easier and less costly to obtain. To give notice of your copyright, write "Copyright," followed by the year the work is completed, along with your name or company name. You can also use © as an alternative to writing "Copyright." It is advisable to register your copyright with the U.S. Copyright Office, Washington, D.C. 20559.

Trade secrets include techniques, designs, materials, processes, and formulas that are not known by the public and can be licensed in the same way as a patent. Trade secrets last as long as you keep them secret. To qualify as a trade secret, the information must have economic value and be a secret; also, you must attempt to protect it. It is strongly recommended that you stamp all such information "confidential" and use a confidentiality or nondisclosure agreement for information you consider to be a trade secret.

To remember the differences between patents, trademarks, and copyrights, think of Coca-Cola:

- The artwork on the can or bottle can be copyrighted.
- The way it is expressed can be trademarked.
- The formula for Coca-Cola is a trade secret but could have been patented.

Martha Blue's *Making It Legal* includes an extensive section on patents, trademarks, and copyrights.

Question #6

I have already patented a new invention but need to find a marketing company to distribute my product. Where can I find one?

Answer

Don't bother looking for one. The problem with most invention marketing companies is that they promise you the moon but deliver little.

Many of these companies advertise in entrepreneurial and invention magazines looking for investors with novel ideas who want to take their invention to the marketplace.

For an initial fee, usually $500 to $800, these companies will research your invention to determine its marketability. You will receive a boilerplate research report that indicates an exceptional potential for your invention that will bring in thousands of dollars and make you rich and famous.

Next, these companies will entice you to send in more money—this time between $2,000 to $8,000—to produce an in-depth report on how to market and sell your invention. The second report, like the first one, promises a huge success and forecasts spectacular earnings for the invention.

The problem is that few if any invention-marketing firms deliver on their claims. According to *The Wall Street Journal*, fewer than 1% of investors ever get a penny from their inventions, despite the high fees they paid up front. Many of these companies are being investigated by the Federal Trade Commission. See Chapter 8 for further information and hints on how to investigate invention-marketing firms.

✔ COURTNEY'S SMART TIP

Research the market potential for your invention. Write a business plan to determine if the invention could be profitable, and then learn how to market your product yourself.

Question #7

How can I increase my sales and find new customers?

Answer

Add sales to your business by first concentrating on developing and expanding your current customer list. Many entrepreneurs spend the majority of their time looking for new markets instead of trying to cultivate their current customer base. They make the mistake of responding to the many different market segments without successfully penetrating any of them. Also, they forget the 80/20 rule: 80% of sales come from 20% of customers. Your marketing goals should be to concentrate on the 20% who generate most of your business. Remember that new sales and spinoff products or services often come from customers and employees.

Pinpoint your best customers and then work at increasing their individual orders. Here are the advantages of developing your own customer list:

1. It is probably the most inexpensive marketing strategy you can use.
2. You can increase your ability to accurately measure the results of your marketing efforts.
3. You can zero in on this target market and personalize your message.
4. You will receive the highest response rate from this group.
5. You can experiment on different marketing strategies and receive feedback on what works best.
6. You can increase your sales to proven customers.

Seasoned entrepreneurs have been compiling their own mailing lists of current and potential customers since opening their ventures. Research your customer base and develop a detailed customer list containing such information as your customers' backgrounds, how they discovered you, purchasing history, buying preferences, and specialized needs. Look for common customer characteristics and purchasing trends. Use the following tips to increase your sales.

Smart Customer Marketing Tips

1. Send postcards announcing an upcoming sale.

2. Send an informal newsletter or a "For Your Information" memo to keep customers informed about new products/services or special offerings.

3. Send a fax about a special promotion.

4. Send a direct mailing about items customers might be interested in purchasing.

5. Call customers at various times during the year when they make their biggest purchases.

6. Try using coupons and track which ones are redeemed.

7. Send an attractive promotional one-page flyer.

8. Follow up after customers have purchased from you to determine if everything was satisfactory.

9. Visit customers at their offices and ask about how you could improve your product/service.

10. Take people out to lunch to keep them informed about your business and to inquire about their future needs.

11. Send a thank-you note after people have purchased from you.

12. Ask your customers for new customer referrals.

13. Ask your best customers for testimonial letters you can use to solicit new customers.

14. Experiment with Internet marketing.

The more you find out about your current customers, the better able you will be to increase the amount of business you get as well as to receive referrals for new customers. Develop creative ways to stay close to and continually communicate with your customers. See Chapter 7 for more information.

Question #8

Since I don't have much money to market my business, where should I advertise?

Answer

First, consider whether advertising is the best market-penetration strategy for your business. Many entrepreneurs take the easy way out and just place an ad in a newspaper or magazine without first determining whether that type of advertising will bring in more sales. Using ads and mailing brochures is a lazy marketing strategy that usually does not bring about desired sales. You may reach many people, but how many will take action and purchase your product or service? Ask yourself if advertising is the best marketing method to use.

According to *Marketing Without Advertising*, more than two-thirds of profitable businesses operate successfully without advertising. There are several reasons that advertising may be inappropriate for your business:

- It may not be cost-effective.
- Directly reaching your target market is more important than reaching a large audience.
- Advertising may not establish a sound customer base with repeat sales.

Instead, develop a sound marketing plan that evaluates several different market-penetration strategies and the costs of each, then identify which types of media should be used to obtain the greatest amount of response and sales. Each type of media has its own particular strength and should be selected for its ability to meet your marketing goals and fit your marketing budget.

Entrepreneurs have been experimenting with many new marketing tools during the last decade: bumper stickers, postcard decks, buttons, T-shirts, contests, skywriting, 800 telephone numbers, personal letters delivered via overnight mail, movie and theater advertising, and so forth. There are many choices.

Start by analyzing each market-penetration method and determining which ones will reach your target customers, whether you can use the method properly, and whether you can afford it. Read Chapter 7 to get more ideas about developing a marketing plan. Another resource to help plan your marketing strategy is *Guerrilla Marketing* by Jay Conrad Levinson.

Question #9

How can I successfully market my product with a limited budget?

Answer

Be creative and develop a marketing plan. Begin by developing a marketing plan that includes identifying your best target markets and then developing a strategy for penetrating each. First, study your markets and determine who your best customers are or could be. Prepare individual profiles on all your current customers, listing important demographic and lifestyle information.

Next, identify your target markets. Prioritize them according to profitability, size, and the share of your market they represent. Pick the markets that will produce the most sales and are easiest to penetrate. Then observe your competitors to determine what kinds of marketing tools they utilize. Look at which marketing methods work well and which kinds do poorly. Try to learn from others' mistakes. Attend your industry trade shows and professional meetings. Ask other owners what works well for them and which pitfalls to avoid.

Consider the various market penetration methods available:

Direct sales force	Direct mail
Manufacturing representatives or sales agents	Infomercials
	Distributors
Telemarketing	Franchising
Trade shows	Licensing

Consignment sales	Exporting
Media advertising	Interactive computer disks
Flyers	Internet and E-mail
Signage	

Look for cost-saving ways to use each of the preceding market-penetration methods. For example, buying remnant space in magazines can reduce your media costs. Writing feature stories about your business is another cost-free way to obtain media coverage. Look for additional innovative marketing tools. Evaluate each market-penetration method and its costs. Then match these strategies with your markets.

Successful entrepreneurs use multiple market-penetration methods. They begin by trying to determine which methods will be most successful and then experiment with a few. Your market research will indicate which methods are likely to be the best ones for you to pursue. Remember that your market-penetration methods will change as your business matures.

Finally, write a marketing plan that outlines realistic short- and long-term goals. Include a marketing calendar. Stick to your marketing plan; evaluate its effectiveness and the results of your marketing efforts. Revise your plan accordingly. Flexibility is important. Remember, most entrepreneurs severely underestimate the amount of money it takes to successfully penetrate just one target market.

Question #10

What kind of franchise should I purchase?

Answer

Franchising is one of the hottest new entry strategies for entrepreneurs. This is especially true in light of the increasing number of displaced workers who have lost their jobs but have substantial separation packages. Many of these displaced workers purchase franchises as their entry strategy.

Purchasing a franchise eliminates many of the headaches associated with starting a new venture from scratch. Also, proven franchises offer lower risks of failure than unproven franchises or new start-up businesses. *Inc.* magazine has reported that 38% of start-up businesses fail within the first year, while less than 4% of franchises experience failure in the first 12 months.

However, I could not recommend a specific franchise operation for an entrepreneur. Considerable due diligence should be exercised in evaluating and choosing a franchise before ever entering into a franchise agreement.

First, visit your library to review franchise handbooks that contain information about existing franchises and their parent companies. Write for a copy of the *Franchise Opportunity Handbook,* published annually by the Superintendent of Documents, U.S. Government Printing Office, Washington, D.C. It is extremely helpful and contains more extensive information on franchises than any other publication. The handbook costs about $10.

Next, ask the librarian to assist you in locating some of the electronic databases that contain financial information and disclosure statements on franchises. It is critical that you evaluate the financial strength of the parent companies. These databases contain annual reports, quarterly financial statements, and other detailed financial information.

While at the library, obtain copies of anything written about the franchises you are interested in pursuing. Also examine the various magazines that publish annual listings of franchise opportunities. For example, each year *Inc.* magazine publishes a list of the 100 best franchise operations.

During your evaluation process, compare the different front-end fees, royalty payments, expenses, and so on. Franchising can offer an easier alternative to starting a new business, but entrepreneurs must carefully assess and analyze each opportunity.

✔ COURTNEY'S SMART TIP

Most entrepreneurs think that purchasing a franchise is a turnkey operation. In reality, much due diligence, research, and up-front work is necessary.

Potential franchisees who think this is a slam-dunk business venture have been misled. Instead, finding the right franchise to purchase, locating a site, negotiating a lease, finishing the tenant space, obtaining the equipment, putting together the management team, and hiring the right staff take much time and effort. Read Chapter 11 for more detailed information on how to evaluate different franchise opportunities.

3

Starting a Business

Overview

One of the most frequently asked questions I receive from my readers is, "What kind of business is easy to start and guaranteed to be successful?" It is impossible for me to offer a winning business idea, since launching a successful venture is so dependent on the entrepreneur, venture trends, and economic trends worldwide. Other entrepreneurs want to know where to look for a novel idea that will revolutionize the marketplace. Most successful ventures come not from novel ideas but from gaps in the marketplace or problems that people encounter. Prospective entrepreneurs should begin by assessing their abilities, business acumen, motivations for getting into business, and proposed business strategy. It is critical for them to evaluate their talents, skills, experiences, and contacts and then to determine if these could be translated into a successful venture.

Another frequently asked question is, "Do I have the right stuff to start and run my own business?" Many prospective entrepreneurs are perplexed, since they recently lost a job or are going nowhere in their current position. They are seriously thinking about starting a business of their own. They are a little frightened of taking a risk and failing. The risk of starting a new venture is significantly reduced when you thoroughly research an idea and prove that there is both a market for the product or service and potential customers who want to purchase it.

Others frequently ask about how to start a home-based business, wondering if it is possible to operate a business from their home and what type of licenses are required. Still other readers inquire about whether it makes sense to locate a new venture in a business incubator. Incubators nurture and help new and young businesses grow by providing space where owners share offices, professional services, shipping, warehousing and other facilities. There are advantages and disadvantages to both approaches for starting new ventures.

Sometimes, readers ask me to recommend a consultant to do all the legwork and research their business concept to determine if it is feasible. Some ask me for consultants who could write a business plan for them. I caution readers that it is critical that they research their business idea and learn about the flaws in their business concepts and the weaknesses of their venture idea. They will not discover the venture's pitfalls if they hire someone else to write their business plan. Besides, most entrepreneurs cannot afford to pay someone to write their plan. It would cost too much, since it takes many hours of research and pounding the pavement or talking to everybody from potential customers to suppliers to determine if the idea is feasible.

Readers often question whether it is even necessary to write a business plan. Why can't they just open their doors for business? In most instances, they have just talked with a potential lender or investor who wants to review their business plan before deciding whether to approve a loan request or invest any money in the venture. The importance of writing a business plan cannot be overemphasized. Developing one is the first step in deciding whether to start a new venture.

This chapter includes the questions that readers of my column ask most frequently about start-up issues. I hope you find this information helpful to use in deciding whether to start a new business.

Smart Strategies for Starting a Business

1. In determining whether to start a new business, analyze your personal criteria, interests, knowledge, and skills.

2. Be sure to prove that there is a market for your new idea before embarking on the venture.

3. Remember that your experiences and know-how are key to starting and operating a successful venture.

4. Be aware that starting a new venture from scratch takes time, market research, seed capital, and a sound business plan.

5. Before starting a new venture, conduct a feasibility analysis to determine whether to pursue your business idea.

6. Consider becoming a creative imitator versus trying to find a unique idea for starting a new venture. Imitators often have a tremendous ad-

vantage over innovators. Imitators already know there is a demand for the product or service.

7. Study the strengths and weaknesses of potential competitors. Improve upon their weaknesses and avoid trying to compete against their strengths.

8. Looking for a market gap or solving a problem for potential customers will produce sound venture ideas.

9. Become a trend spotter. Look for trends that are just beginning to unfold and take advantage of your window of opportunity by getting to the marketplace quickly.

10. Write a business plan to prove your venture concept and develop your business strategy while researching the industry and your competition.

11. Consider the advantages of locating your new venture in a business incubator if location is not important to your business concept.

12. Operate your home-based venture as if it were in a separate business location. Be professional at all times.

13. Carefully research and evaluate potential retail locations by studying the trading area, reviewing customer demographics and traffic patterns, talking to other tenants, and contacting a competent commercial real estate company.

14. Always negotiate the terms and conditions of a commercial lease for your venture.

15. Home-employment schemes are one of the oldest types of classified-advertising frauds.

Do I Have the Right Stuff?

Question

I am in a dead-end sales job and seriously thinking about quitting and starting my own business. But I don't know if I have the disposition or the right characteristics to become a successful entrepreneur. I am not a big risk taker, but I am self-motivated. How can I determine if I have the right stuff to start my own business?

Answer

The most common entrepreneurial traits include a strong desire to be your own boss, the drive to implement your ideas, and a thirst to control your own destiny. Entrepreneurs are inordinately determined to be successful and persevere in the midst of adversity. They thrive on ambiguity and prosper in a world that is confusing and has few answers.

✔ COURTNEY'S SMART TIP

If you cannot accept and operate in the ambiguous world of entrepreneurship, you would be wise to avoid it.

Running your own business is an ongoing puzzle, a long series of problems to be solved. If you do not like constantly solving a multitude of problems, then an entrepreneurial career might be difficult. Much of your time will be spent troubleshooting, pinpointing problems that are plaguing the business, and trying to solve them. As soon as you solve one problem, others spring up.

Almost invariably, successful entrepreneurs have the creative capacity to recognize and pursue opportunities. They possess strong selling skills and are both persuasive and persistent. They persuade others to lend them money, work long hours, buy new products or services, and sell products on favorable terms. They are constantly promoting their company, its products or services, and new ideas. Entrepreneurs are visionary and get others excited about and committed to their vision.

Entrepreneurs have high energy levels, are impatient, and can't sit still for a minute. They continually think about their business and how to increase market share. Most have experience in the type of venture they start and are confident about launching and operating the firm. Research shows that the role of experience and know-how is central to successful venture creation. If you lack experience, consider working as an apprentice for someone in a business similar to the one you want to start.

Overall, successful entrepreneurs develop essential business skills, know-how, and contacts. Evaluate your talents. Question whether your skills, contacts, and experience are transferable to the business idea you want to pursue.

What about support needs? Many people are surrounded by staff ready to support their activities and are accustomed to having people attend to their needs. Entrepreneurs do not have the luxury of hiring staff support, especially when starting a venture. Instead, they wear many different hats, performing tasks ranging from opening the mail in the morning to emptying the trash at night. They do everything that needs to be done by themselves.

Risk is involved in making any entrepreneurial venture successful. Entrepreneurs take calculated risks and reduce the risk factor by thoroughly researching their business concepts, industry, and market. One way to reduce risk is to start small—at home—and test your business concept by asking potential customers to buy it. Don't ask friends if they think your venture idea will work. Instead, ask customers to give you a letter of intent to purchase which forces them to seriously think about whether they would buy it. If you are unable to obtain a letter of intent, you may not have a viable idea.

If you have the drive to research the industry and your market and write a business plan, you have significantly increased your chances of starting and operating a successful venture.

Question

I am looking for a business idea with high success potential. Where can an aspiring entrepreneur find a good business idea?

Answer

Examining some entrepreneurial myths can lead to discovering a good business idea.

Myth 1

The best product or service will be successful. This myth comes from Ralph Waldo Emerson's frequently quoted statement that if you build a better mousetrap, the world will beat a path to your door. Ralph probably would not have made a successful entrepreneur. Thousands of potential entrepreneurs have been sidetracked, even ruined, by taking Emerson's advice to heart.

Unfortunately, just the opposite is true. Regardless of the superiority of your product or service, customers do not beat a path to your door. Producing the best-quality item does not guarantee market share. It simply means you may have an edge over your competition. Successfully penetrating your market is key. The entrepreneur who demonstrates this superior mousetrap to the world and convinces people to buy it is successful.

Myth 2

At the core of every successful new enterprise is a novel idea or invention. Granted, a completely original idea or new technology has a good chance of succeeding. The fact is that very few new business ideas are truly novel. Instead, they are modifications or improvements of already-existing products or services. Many aspiring entrepreneurs make the mistake of searching for a completely new idea and never find one. Focus on improving or enhancing proven venture ideas. Inventors design new products, but entrepreneurs seek out new opportunities anchored by customer needs, a competitive edge, and good timing.

Myth 3

Great ideas make successful ventures. There is an enormous difference between good ideas and doable ideas. Ideas that are feasible may have a potential market. Entrepreneurs observe new trends and market opportunities. They continually listen to customer concerns and complaints. Potential ideas come from customers who are willing to tell you about the deficiencies and inadequacies of the existing product or service. What do people want that they cannot find? What are they unhappy about? What new products or services are they excited about? Discovering customer dissatisfactions is a great way to find a new venture idea.

Idea Resource Guide

Use your experience factor to generate new business ideas. Many studies reveal that the common denominator among successful start-ups is the founders' knowledge of the marketplace, new technology, and the industry in which the bulk of their apprenticeship and managerial experience has been acquired.

Read. Successful new venture ideas come from a multitude of sources, such as trade magazines, patent magazines, business books, journals, and newspapers. Look for emergent themes, changing values, and new habits.

Observe demographic changes. Research local, national, and worldwide demographic trends that might identify new markets. Examples include the growth of the Hispanic population, the increasing numbers of working women, the "graying of America," and new opportunities in foreign markets. Read *American Demographics* magazine.

Monitor society, industry, and market changes. Are people's tastes, routines, lifestyles, or habits changing? Pick up a copy of *Clicking or The American Forecaster Almanac,* published annually, to learn about emerging trends.

Watch the Information Superhighway. Surf the Internet to spot new trends, exchange information on electronic bulletin boards, and shop various cybermalls. A great source for the latest information in your industry is online information.

How important is power? Would you be more comfortable operating a venture or taking directions from others? Some people crave power while others find it distasteful.

How old are you, and how many years of hard work can you look forward to? If you are in your thirties, you can undertake ventures that might be more difficult for someone older. If you want to move quickly because you are aging or plan to retire, you will need to find a venture that you can launch and grow quickly. At times it may be necessary to look for an injection of outside capital or find a management team that will speed up your rate of growth.

Are you healthy? Can your physical condition withstand the pressures and stresses associated with starting a new venture? Or will spending long hours daily on your venture during the first several years hurt your health? Health considerations will dictate what type of business an entrepreneur can undertake.

What role does—or will—your family members play in the business? Will they work in it? Will they eventually take it over? These decisions will affect the type of venture you start and your business strategy.

Where do you want to live and work? How many people work hard all their lives so they can retire to Hawaii, Arizona, or Florida? Why not locate your business in one of these areas and get there quicker?

Do you plan on investing any money in the venture? Decide early on about the extent to which you are willing to expose yourself to financial risk. Many entrepreneurs refuse to invest much money in their own ventures. Instead, they use their brains and somebody else's money.

Your attitudes about these personal criteria will determine which type of venture you should pursue. Whatever business you decide to start—be passionate about it.

Talk to your industry contacts and editors of your association journals. Venture ideas can come from suppliers, wholesalers, and distributors who have an acute awareness of strengths and weaknesses of existing products. Ideas also come from competitors whose products or services can be improved upon.

Attend a trade show. Over 60% of those attending a trade show are there to buy. Trade shows covering the industry you are interested in may provide a wealth of potential doable ideas.

The real challenge for the entrepreneur is (1) to look for venture opportunities, (2) to identify doable ideas, and (3) to implement those ideas with a proven market and growth potential.

What Factors Should Entrepreneurs Consider Before Starting a New Business?

Take the Time to Find the Right Name for Your Business

Question

I'm starting a business and don't know whether to use my own name or come up with a different name for my business. What do you suggest?

Answer

Although many founders begin operating their businesses under their own names, it makes such businesses look small and unprofessional. Therefore, I recommend you decide on a trade business name and register it.

The choice of your company name is important because as with location, a business name is recognizable and can serve as a form of advertising. It is part of the total package you are selling and will promote familiarity and confidence in your product. Your company name should be appropriate to your product, easy to read, and easy to remember.

Since you'll spend considerable time and money launching and operating your business, protect its name. Before you order business cards, stationery, or a brochure design, check with your county or city clerk to ensure that no one else is using the name you decide on. If you choose a trade name that no other business is using, you can register it. If someone else is using the one you select, you will have to choose another one. Have several alternative names ready in case the one you want is already being used. Check the Yellow Pages of your telephone book to see if anyone locally is using the name you are considering. In most states, you file a trade business name statement with the county or city clerk and publish a specially worded notice in the legal section of your local newspaper. A majority of states provide the form for filing, publish the notice, and file the required affidavit; some require that you register a company name.

To register your company name, you will fill out a form, sign it, get it notarized, and pay the required fee. Fees range from about $10 to $60. Ask when you must renew your name registration.

If you decide to use your own first and last name, you will not need to register it. However, if you add words like *co.* or *associates*, or if you change your own name in any way, it is considered a trade name and should be registered.

In some states, sole proprietorships and partnerships are registered at the state level rather than the local level. Corporations are always registered at the state level with the secretary of state. I recommend that you register your name with the state department of commerce to prevent its use by any corporate entity.

Someone outside your local area could be using the name you select. To protect your company name and to obtain national rights, register it with the U.S. Patent Office. To register the name as a national trademark, the company must first use it on the product in interstate commerce and then file it with the Patent Office.

Unlike a patent application, a trade name application can be made on a government form. Issuance of the registration can take up to a year and is good for 20 years, after which time it can be renewed for additional 20-year periods. If international rights may have some value, there are ways to register your business name in a foreign country.

Some consultants specialize in developing company names, and some attorneys specialize in researching the registrability of company names. Services that maintain databases on business names can also be used to search names. Names in use can be found in the *Trade Names Dictionary* and the *Thomas Register* available in the reference section of your local library.

Other good references are *Brand Names: Who Owns What*, which lists 15,000 brand names of about 750 firms, and *The Name Game: How to Name a Company and Product*.

Your company name is an integral part of your intellectual property and should be properly protected.

Question

I have recipes for good dill pickles, sweet pickles, and pickle relish, and an excellent spaghetti sauce that I would like to sell to a large manufacturer. I don't have the funds to market them myself or the time to do it. What do you recommend?

Answer

Probably, you should continue making your pickles and spaghetti sauce for friends and enjoy them yourself. You may have great ideas for several new tasty food products, but you may not have anything worth selling at this stage.

There are millions of recipes for these types of products, and hundreds of varieties are already in the grocery stores. Why would someone want to buy yours and pay you a royalty each time a jar of your pickles or spaghetti sauce is sold? Unfortunately, many aspiring entrepreneurs have great ideas but nothing proprietary to sell. You could copyright your recipes. However, someone could just substitute a few ingredients, and then you would have nothing of value to sell.

Customers purchase food items for both the taste and the name. Usually, they buy the name first and the taste secondarily. You do not have an established, recognized name, like Heinz or Kraft. Recognition in the marketplace will be difficult to achieve. Even if your spaghetti sauce is better than Paul Newman's spaghetti sauce, customers will most likely choose his product. Why? He has a recognizable name that sells in the grocery stores.

Most investors, other entrepreneurs, and larger manufacturing companies do not buy ideas. Instead, they buy proven concepts that have established sales in the marketplace. Consider the following questions:

- Have you thought about a name for your products?
- Have you thought about carving a distinctive niche for your products?
- What distinguishes your pickle products and spaghetti sauce from others in the market?
- What is unique and different about them?
- Why should a customer switch from buying Heinz dill pickles to yours?
- What steps have you taken to protect your proprietary interests— that is, your recipes?
- How will you mass-produce these products?
  How much will it cost you?
  Can you competitively price your products?
  Who will carry your products?
  How will you obtain shelf space in grocery stores?

- How will you market these products?
  Will you use coupons?
  What types of licenses and governmental approvals will you need to obtain before making and selling food products?

Hundreds of questions like these need to be researched and answered before you can produce and sell these items yourself or find someone to purchase and sell your products.

If you are serious about building your pickle products and spaghetti sauce into a business, you should first write a feasibility plan that proves your concept and proves that your business ideas could be feasible and profitable.

A feasibility plan includes an executive summary and a description of the product or service, market, price and profitability, and plan for further action. Obtain a copy of *The Entrepreneur's Planning Handbook*, which will take you through the phases of writing feasibility and business plans. Ideas are usually not sold, but proven business concepts with sound business plans could be sold and marketed. (See "What Type of Preplanning Is Necessary" later in this chapter.)

✔ **COURTNEY'S SMART TIP**
Without researching the feasibility of your concept and developing a feasibility plan, you will find it difficult or almost impossible to obtain a potential investor or corporate partner.

Work-at-Home Come-ons Often Too Good to Be True

Question

I retired early and I'm interested in pursuing a work-at-home business opportunity. I have discovered many advertisements in magazines. Recently, I was sent some information about a home-based opportunity that looks too good to be true. But after attending their seminar, I think this is a great business opportunity. They want me to give them a $2,000 up-front fee. Should I proceed?

Answer

While some work-at-home plans may be legitimate, many are not. Home-employment schemes are one of the oldest classified-advertising frauds. Con artists can be found everywhere and market their products through direct mail, in magazines, and over the Internet, among other places. As you have found, entrepreneurs are being bombarded daily about "extraordinary business opportunities" through mass mailings, classified ads, seminars, informational demonstrations, telemarketing, TV and radio infomercials, and trade show booths. The problem is separating the legitimate ventures from the outright scams.

The offers are usually too good to be true and contain statements like, "Make easy money—even while watching television in your own home! Make money so fast you can hardly count it . . . have the time, freedom, and money that most people never have working for someone else! Accept this exclusive invitation . . . only a limited number of men and women in this area will be allowed to share in this exciting business opportunity . . . make people line up and beg you to take their money."

Key words and phrases found in most of this type of advertising usually promise a thriving market that will bring extraordinarily high returns for very little investment or effort almost immediately.

✔ COURTNEY'S SMART TIP

Look for these tip-offs to fraudulent work-at-home schemes: Promises of unrealistically high profits; claims of a high market with great demand for the product or service; the "no experience is necessary" statement and the "exclusive invitation" offer.

A common scheme is an advertisement that entices entrepreneurs to pay a high fee to receive information that usually can be found, free of charge, in any public library.

State and federal regulators report that the largest categories of fraudulent or troublesome enterprises involve the following:

1. The purchase and installation of coin-operated machines.
2. Highly specialized home businesses such as ostrich farming, customized computer software, clearance (liquidated) merchandise, gemstones, or precious metals.
3. Person-to-person direct sales of unproven and weakly regulated products.
4. Anything new or unfamiliar in the telecommunications industry.

The companies often do not tell you about the up-front investments and hidden costs involved, such as buying the envelopes, paper, stamps, and other supplies required to do the job. Some people who have invested money in product-assembly kits are told their work is unsatisfactory when they return the finished products. Both money and time are wasted, and only the company gets rich selling its bogus kits.

Several companies hold seminars and "informational demonstrations," like the one you recently attended, in large hotels to sell business opportunities. Their presentations and materials are very professional, promising money-back guarantees and company support.

The company usually wants a decision before you leave, along with an up-front investment (anywhere from $150 to $5,000). They urge you to act quickly—today—because your opportunity might vanish or it might, in their words, "cost you more each day you delay." Some companies have organized home-based business associations that make their activities appear like friendly nonprofit support systems.

Their advertisements and infomercials tout glowing success stories, but typically very few consumers who purchase their business opportunities earn a substantial income or even recoup the costs of the up-front investment. Money-back guarantees may or may not be honored, and in most situations continued company support is nonexistent.

First, ask specific questions about what you will be responsible for and how you will get paid and by whom. Ask what supplies, equipment, or membership fees are required. Specify that you want these answers in writing.

Next, ask for a copy of the presale disclosure document. The Federal Trade Commission (FTC) requires that sellers of business opportunities, including franchises, provide information on 20 items, including names and phone numbers of other franchisers. Ask your business attorney, accountant, or both to review this contract and answer questions you have about the details of the agreement.

Then ask for the names of others who have purchased the company's home-based business opportunity. Be aware that the names the company gives to you might be insiders who work for the company. Therefore, personally check out their operations and observe them in action. Inquire about their annual sales and net sales. Ask if you can see their business records.

Check several different sources for information about this home-based business opportunity. The company may list memberships in trade groups and chambers of commerce to make it appear legitimate, so search beyond this list. Here are some additional agencies and organizations that can assist you:

The Better Business Bureau (BBB) can tell you if this company has had complaints registered with it. Be aware that the BBB might not have information on new companies or those that operate under a variety of different names.

The attorney general's office in either your state or the state where the company is located can tell you if you are protected by any state law regulating work-at-home programs.

The U.S. Postal Service investigates fraudulent mail practices and can tell you if complaints have been made against the company. Contact your local postmaster.

The National Fraud Information Center (NFIC), a project of the National Consumers League, focuses on telephone frauds. NFIC provides information, referral services, and assistance in filing complaints. Call its hotline at 800-876-7060 and ask for the booklet *Schemes, Scams and Flim-Flams: A Consumer's Guide to Phone Fraud.*

The Federal Trade Commission (FTC) can take action if there is evidence of a pattern of deceptive or unfair practices.

The Direct Selling Association can't tell you if it has received complaints against a specific company, but it will send you valuable information on how to check on companies selling home-based business opportunities. Call 202-293-5760.

Remember that home employment schemes are one of the oldest types of classified-advertising fraud. If the offer seems too good to be true, it probably is. Research all home-based business opportunities carefully. Be cautious, and when you have doubts, walk away.

What Type of Preplanning Is Necessary?

Question

I want to start a catering business but work full-time, go to school at night, and have only one day off. Therefore, I have no time to research the market before I open my doors for business. I cannot quit my job, since I am my sole means of support. Do you know of any inexpensive consultants who would do the necessary groundwork for me?

Answer

No. There are many small-business consultants who could help you get started, but since you are so stretched for time and money, you probably would run out of both before opening your doors for business.

Consider working for a catering company that might be interested in selling the business at a later date. Look for a partner who has the time and money and whose skills balance yours. Contact the catering industry association for leads. Launching a business from scratch takes time, market research, seed capital, and a sound business plan—all of which you lack.

Although catering is one of the easiest businesses to start, it is beset by stiff competition, poor management, improper market testing, and lack of sufficient capital. The failure rate is shocking. Many industry experts claim the reasons for this high failure rate include poor planning, not running the venture as a business, and failing to carve a distinctive market niche.

Being an excellent cook is just one ingredient for operating a successful catering venture. Experience in the industry—coupled with enough cash to get through the first year and differentiating your services—is your biggest challenge. Discovering a promising idea that matches your expertise and has potential for success is the starting point. Although you already have the idea, 90% of the work involved in launching your new enterprise remains, and it is unrealistic that you can find someone to do the rest.

Your next step is to conduct a feasibility analysis to see if your catering idea could be profitable. A feasibility analysis consists of researching your business concept—its workability, marketability, and profitability—and assessing your capability. The analysis will help you guard against an unworkable concept that does not fit the market, takes too many resources, cannot compete with other companies, and is not worth your time and effort.

Choosing the business you want to start and then making it work takes considerable research, trial and error, and refinement. You must be willing to do much of the legwork, follow-through, and market testing yourself.

Question

I have created a delicious raspberry salsa that I want to produce and market. Since I don't have enough money to lease a kitchen, what can I do to start producing it in large quantities?

Answer

Your specialty food item is in a market where there is plenty of room for new products and strong growth potential. This market is growing rapidly due to consumer demand for high-quality, exotic, unusual, and healthy foods, including ethnic specialties.

However, start-up costs for food products are high, ranging from $25,000 to well over $100,000 per year for the first few years. Start-up costs include labor and leasing production facilities along with packaging, labeling, marketing, and distribution.

Because you don't have enough money to lease a kitchen and because it will be difficult to attract start-up capital, look for a licensed kitchen to rent on a part-time basis. Many licensed catering, restaurant, church, and school kitchens charge vendors monthly rent for commissary privileges.

Initially, your volume will be low and will not justify the cost of leasing a separate kitchen. Renting kitchen space is an excellent, more cost-effective alternative.

Rents usually range from $150 to $2,500 a month depending on the food product, the amount of time required to produce it, and the kind of kitchen equipment needed.

If your volume does not justify a month's rental for a licensed kitchen, inquire about a per-use fee until your volume warrants further expansion. You might also check to see if any kitchen incubators exist in your area. There are several around the country; you can locate these by contacting the National Business Incubation Association at 614-593-4331. Or call your local college or university food science or home economics department.

Laws require vendors who produce foods for sale to use a licensed commercial kitchen. Local health departments inspect these kitchens regularly to ensure they meet stringent health specifications and codes.

Even if you rent a licensed kitchen, you must be licensed to make food products and are required to have a sales license. Also, some states require registration of your product before you can sell in that state; contact your state health department for further information. In addition, you should obtain product-liability insurance. Product recall insurance is also available. Your insurance agent will be able to help you with these issues.

Renting a commercial kitchen gives you the opportunity to test your product in the market to determine the strength of customer demand with minimal investment. I recommend you test your product locally before trying to sell nationally.

Conduct tasting sessions at retail outlets and farmers' markets. Consumer feedback will give you information about your product's strengths, and the potential demand will determine whether you should proceed. By testing your product, you'll learn quickly whether it will sell while competing with other brands.

To expand your knowledge of the salsa market and gather market research, visit food trade shows, especially those sponsored by the National Association for the Specialty Food Trade (NASFT) in New York City, the largest U.S. association representing and promoting specialty food and confectionery products. Call the organization at 212-482-6440 and ask for a membership packet.

While at these trade shows, talk with customers, producers, distributors, brokers, and retailers. Learn about competing products, test your pricing, and identify food trends.

By researching national trends and competing products, renting space in a licensed kitchen, and initially testing the local market, you can launch your salsa smartly and cost-effectively.

Question

I have a great idea for starting a new business, but my banker is insisting that I have a business plan before proceeding with the loan request. Do I really need to write a business plan? Are there small-business consultants who would write a business plan for me?

Answer

Entrepreneurs constantly fight the battle of writing good and sound business plans that will attract financing for their new ventures. Most often they delay writing business plans because they are uncertain of how to write and prepare the planning documents essential to operating a successful venture. A business plan forces you to consider every facet of your proposed business and places funding decisions on paper, where they can be evaluated and considered by everyone involved.

On the basis of my experience reading thousands of business plans, I suggest that you begin with the following outline, or a similar one.

Outline of a Business Plan

1. Cover page
2. Table of contents
3. Summary and executive overview
4. Management and organization
5. Product or service plan
6. Marketing plan
7. Financial plan
8. Operating and control system
9. Growth plan
10. Appendix

This outline was taken from a book I coauthored entitled *The Entrepreneur's Planning Handbook*. The book features a question-and-answer format. After answering the questions in each section, you will have essentially written your business plan. The book also provides formatting tips and lists subtitles for each section. Other recommended books for writing a business plan include *How to Prepare and Present a Business Plan* and *Business Plans That Win $$$*.

Developing financial statements for the business plan is a difficult task. Your accountant or bookkeeper can help you develop these documents. But it is still necessary for you to study your industry and market carefully. This research forms the basis for making realistic and meaningful projections. You might also consult the *Business Planning Guide*, which has a lengthy segment on developing the financial section for the business plan. Refer to *Robert Morris Studies*, available in most libraries, when preparing your financial documents. This reference book lists industry statistics and financial ratios for every industry.

There are companies or consultants who will prepare your business plan. However, most of the benefit of writing a business plan is lost if another person writes it. Sitting down and developing the plan, section by section, forces you to think critically, evaluate, and plan. Without exception, entrepreneurs who have written their own business plans report that they were compelled to rethink many aspects of their venture when it became apparent that there were some serious flaws in their thinking.

If you need assistance developing your business plan, ask your local college or university about courses on writing a business plan. Or call your local chamber of commerce, small-business development center, or FastTrac headquarters at 1-800-689-1740. The best news about developing and writing your own business plan is that once you have been through the process, additional plans take half the time to write. Also, you have learned valuable planning skills that will be critical to your success as an entrepreneur.

Should I Locate in a Business Incubator?

Question

I have heard a little about business incubators that offer shared services with adaptable space that entrepreneurs can lease on flexible terms and at reduced rates. How do I determine if I should locate in one, and where can I obtain further information?

Answer

Business incubators were started in the 1970s, and today there are over 600 in the United States. The goal of business incubators is to launch new ventures and improve their chances of success by providing low-cost space, overhead, and ancillary administrative services.

Most business incubators are private, nonprofit organizations sponsored by government, nonprofit, university-related, or privately sponsored agencies whose mission is to spark job creation and economic growth in the community. What distinguishes incubators from shared office space is free in-house management consulting and technical consulting. Essentially, they offer shared support such as financial, managerial, technical, and administrative services.

No two business incubators are alike. Their orientation depends on the particular needs of the region where they operate and their mission statement. Incubators are driven by local economic needs. Thus, if technology transfer is of prime importance, the business incubator facilitates this mission. Incubators can be technology based, service based, retail based, or manufacturing based. Kitchen incubators are for start-up catering ventures that prepare specialty foods like salsa, cookies, breads, burritos, and soups.

Interestingly, incubators are opening at faster rates in rural areas than in suburban and urban locations. Nearly 36% of the country's incubators are located in rural areas. The largest number of business incubators are urban facilities (45%), while 19% are suburban incubators.

The benefits of locating in an incubator include affordable rental space on flexible terms, no building-maintenance responsibilities, sharing of equipment and services, access to various types of financial and technical assistance, and networking opportunities. On the average, incubators offer rents 15% to 50% below market. Locating in an incubator gives a start-up venture legitimacy, a business address, a functional location, and access to an entrepreneurial resource network. Basic secretarial and bookkeeping services are part of the rental package, and an array of office equipment is available, including computer technology.

Another benefit is the opportunity to network with other entrepreneurs who conduct business in the incubator facility. They begin sharing ideas, referring customers, participating jointly on specific projects, and experiencing personal enrichment and growth as business owners.

The potential disadvantages of an incubator are geographic limitations, poor neighborhood image, and the public's perception of the incubator's location. Incubators vary according to their mission, services, costs, and managerial expertise.

Before locating in a business incubator, investigate whether the in-cubator has an established track record. Determine how successful its previous tenants have been. Interview both the director of the incubator and several key tenants to discover whether this is the right setting for your new venture. To find various types of business incubators, contact the National Business Incubation Association, One President Street, Athens, OH 45701, 614-593-4331, www.nbia.org.

How Do I Select a Retail Location?

Question

I am in the process of starting a small vacuum-repair service business. I live outside of Denver, but I would not mind opening up my new store somewhere in the city if the location was right. What criteria should I consider in choosing a location for my business?

Answer

There is no ideal location. In most cases there are just compromises. You must compromise some ideas for the sake of finances or your personal preferences. But that's the fun of being an entrepreneur. You can put your business where you want it, as long as you can afford the space.

Several different factors need to be considered before a specific location is chosen. The decision will depend on whether the business is a service or involves manufacturing. Since your venture is a service business, I will discuss the factors you should consider in selecting a retail location.

First, the location of retail stores is an art unto itself. The value of a piece of property depends almost entirely upon its location.

✔ COURTNEY'S SMART TIP

For the retailer, the key to business success rests in the selection of a good location. A particular location can make or break a retail business.

You should consider the following factors before deciding on a specific area of the city to open up your business.

1. *State of incorporation.* Since the majority of retail businesses are incorporated, you must decide in which state to incorporate. The corporate statutes of most states are similar, but there are some differences that may be important. For example, some states give stockholders

more rights than others. The laws of the state in which you incorporate establish the ground rules under which you must operate your business.

Delaware is a popular state for incorporation because its laws allow management maximum control over the business with a minimum of interference from minority stockholders. If you incorporate in a state other than the one in which you are doing business, you must file as a foreign corporation in the state in which you are doing business. The matter of determining the state in which you should register as a foreign corporation is complex, may have tax consequences, and requires legal counsel. If you are doing business in several states, legal counsel might advise setting up separate corporations in each state. The general rule to follow is to incorporate in the state in which the business will be operating.

2. *Taxes.* The success of the southern states in attracting new businesses demonstrates the effect that low taxes have on locational decisions. In some situations, however, you may be better off paying higher taxes and selling more goods for a higher price. There are many places to locate and enjoy tax relief, but you may have difficulty generating a profit there.

3. *Costs.* The best location for your business may be in the newest local mall. But the cost of the space may prohibit you from locating there. You may be forced to go where you can afford the rent or where you can operate more efficiently.

4. *Security.* Many retailers avoid certain areas of a city because they fear for their safety and property. Customers might also be leery of driving to these types of locations. Choose a site where you will feel both comfortable and secure.

5. *Availability.* Many entrepreneurs locate where there is available space at the time they wish to open. Expediency does have its virtues, but consider the long-term effects of your immediate decision. Don't be shortsighted.

6. *Infrastructure.* Sometimes location decisions are based on selecting an area where a large infrastructure is ready to help you get into business and serve your continuing needs. For example, computer businesses often locate in an area where materials and parts are readily available.

7. *Personal considerations.* The location of your business may depend on how far you want to drive to and from work each day. Family commitments may prohibit you from locating in a more desirable area that requires considerable driving time. Your personal happiness is an important

factor as well. Once you have considered these elements, it is time to focus on the selection of a specific area for your retail location.

Question

I am in the process of opening a frozen yogurt store and need some advice about selecting a retail location. What factors do I need to consider?

Answer

After deciding on the general area for your business, consider the following nine major factors to select your retail location:

Smart Tips for Selecting a Retail Location

1. Determine the trading area.

2. Look up the demographics of your trading area.

3. Observe traffic patterns.

4. Evaluate the ease of entry and exit.

5. Evaluate available parking.

6. Study community growth patterns.

7. Pinpoint the competition.

8. Look for an anchor store.

9. Contact a reliable commercial real estate company.

1. *Determine the trading area.* Every location has a trading area from which the venture derives its business. The trading area may be only a few blocks surrounding the store, or it may have a five-mile radius. Each type of store draws customers from varying distances. To determine your particular trading area, start by locating on a map your potential site and your competitors' stores. Everything being equal, customers trade at the place most convenient to them. If location is important to your business, survey the license plates of cars parked in or around your proposed location to determine where they come from.

2. *Look up the demographics of your trading area.* Determine the sizes of the families living in the surrounding area and the average family income. This information will be helpful in forecasting the sales potential for the proposed location. Can the people living in your area afford your product? Evaluate the buying habits and profile of potential customers in your trading area.

3. *Observe traffic patterns.* Where does the traffic come from and where is it going? Are cars just zooming by on the way to or from work? Is public transportation accessible? Ask nearby residents about their buying habits. Approach a local merchant to find out where his or her customers come from. Don't be fooled about the number of cars passing by your site hourly. Vehicular traffic may not stop at this location. The key is to assess the quality of the people exposed to your proposed site, not just the quantity. Both are important, but the quality outweighs the quantity.

4. *Evaluate the ease of entry and exit.* Are there any major freeways, one-way streets, traffic patterns, or other physical characteristics of the area that directly influence where people go to shop? Some locations appear to be excellent but on closer inspection prove to be quite difficult to get to. Keep in mind the principle of convenience.

5. *Evaluate available parking.* Does the location you are considering have enough accessible and convenient parking? Is the location so busy that customers cannot find a parking place? Adequate parking is essential to selection of a good location site.

6. *Study community growth patterns.* You might want to consider locating in an area targeted for significant growth and expansion as opposed to situating in a well-established center. To obtain a prime space, you may need to anticipate the direction of growth in an area and locate a store in this path before adequate sales volume is realized. Smaller merchants usually need immediate sales volume and cannot risk betting on growth. You must have sufficient money to wait until the market develops.

7. *Pinpoint the competition.* Is there any competition located close to your proposed site? You may want to locate your store near a competitor with an established clientele that you hope to attract. Or you may want to locate where there is no close competition to capture the market in the immediate area.

8. *Look for an anchor store.* Retailers often locate in shopping centers where there are popular anchor stores, such as established chains. You can live off the existing traffic flow and offer a selection of goods the shopper cannot find in the anchor stores. Entrepreneurs can use the promotional efforts of larger stores to help build their traffic and customer base.

9. *Contact a reliable commercial real estate company.* Some real estate companies have trained salespeople who are familiar with the availability, traffic patterns, demographic information, and busy centers in your city.

Selecting a location is one of the most critical elements to your success. Base your decision on facts rather than on subjective perceptions. Research the area well. The rewards your business will reap are the direct result of the time you spend today investigating various available locations.

There are also several pitfalls to avoid when selecting a retail site. Entrepreneurs are often too eager to get the door open. They want the business to be open right away. Selecting a retail location is a complex process that often takes considerable research and much time.

First, you get what you pay for. The bottom line is that good locations cost more money than less-desirable locations. Many retailers simply do not have the money to invest in a good location. Three main factors contribute to operating a successful store: location, location, location.

Rents are not a function of costs; they represent how much money can be earned from the space. A small location in a large shopping mall can cost more than a larger space in a smaller mall. However, large shopping malls attract more people per square foot than do smaller malls. Entrepreneurs pay for the people the mall delivers to their door.

Remember the Law of Landlords: They are in business to make money. Often they are reluctant to risk the successful image of their shopping center or mall by renting to an unknown retail operation when they can obtain prospective tenants from a host of well-known, well-established national retailing organizations. Some landlords may not want to risk renting their space to you. They may fear that your business will eventually fail, leaving their lease virtually unenforceable. You must compete with large retail chains for prime space.

Beware of so-called deals. Don't get lured into a vacant store location by landlords seeming to offer the bargain of the century. They may offer you a few rent-free months until you get settled or a lower-than-average price per square foot. Be careful of space that is consistently vacant. Maybe the location is tucked away in the corner of the shopping center, and the store cannot be seen unless the sign falls on a passing customer. Find out which other tenants have occupied the space and for how long a time. Don't fall prey to such great deals. Instead, thoroughly research the center.

Be careful of unsubstantiated claims. Landlords are anxious to rent available space in their centers and tend to be overly optimistic about the virtues of their location. Verify every piece of information they give you. Talk to other tenants in the center. Ask lots of questions about the location, customers, and traffic and the policies enforced by the landlord. Locate other business owners who closed their shops to determine what problems they encountered.

Researching any site location is essential. In-depth research can mean the difference between selecting a really superior site or finding one that merely appears to be good. You can learn much about the feasibility of a location by both subjective and qualitative observation.

Negotiating a Lease

Question

I have decided to open a dry-cleaning business in a new shopping center. I have selected the location, and I'm confident there will be enough traffic and potential customers to make my business successful. I am getting ready to negotiate a lease with the landlord. Can you give me any tips?

Answer

Negotiating a lease with a landlord is similar to negotiating the purchase of a car. Get as much information as you can in advance of your negotiations.

Determine competitive prices and market conditions in your area. Ask other tenants in the shopping center, as well as other business owners, about the terms and conditions of their leases.

You may want to consider working with an experienced real estate broker who specializes in commercial leases. Leases can be extremely technical. They're difficult to interpret. A broker can help. Usually a broker's fee is paid for by the landlord.

Second, realize there are no standard leases. Most landlords or rental agents will say they use only a standard lease that cannot be altered.

✔ COURTNEY'S SMART TIP

One common rule in entrepreneurship is that everything is negotiable, especially when it comes to leases.

This principle is really applicable when there is an overbuilt commercial real estate market.

It is helpful to have your business attorney look over your lease before you sign. Make sure you understand all the conditions in the lease. The money you pay for a legal opinion is money well spent.

Smart Tips for Lease Negotiations

1. Negotiate the length of your lease.

2. Negotiate one or two renewal options.

3. Negotiate the initial lease rate with a renewal rate.

4. Understand all the conditions concerning your monthly rental.

5. Determine whether a gross or net lease is better for your business.

6. Find out about every tenant obligation in the lease.

1. Negotiate the length of your lease so it will allow you to remain in the same location for a reasonable length of time yet give you flexibility if the business is unsuccessful. Most shopping center leases run from two to five years.

2. Negotiate one or two renewal options in your lease. After the initial term of your lease expires, it should be your option to stay or to leave if business is not meeting projections.

3. Negotiate the rate of the initial lease along with a renewal rate. When the occupancy rate is low, many landlords offer free initial rent as an incentive.

4. Be sure you understand the conditions concerning your monthly rental. Landlords may ask for annual increases. If this is the case, negotiate a reasonable and competitive rate. If you can agree to a fixed annual increase, you will know exactly what your rent expense will be in subsequent years. Be careful not to agree to an annual increase that may rise above the market rate in later years.

✔ COURTNEY'S SMART TIP

Agree that the rent may be raised according to the cost of living in your area as determined by government statistics.

---

5. Determine whether the lease will be a gross or a net lease. With a gross lease, the landlord pays for taxes, insurance, janitorial services, and utilities. This is more advantageous for entrepreneurs. A net lease means tenants are partially responsible for these expenses.

6. Find out your exact obligations as a tenant. Once into a lease, you may find you are responsible for trash or snow removal.

Pitfalls to Avoid

1. Don't think that all good ideas are opportunities and will make successful ventures.

2. Don't let others tell you what kind of business you should start.

3. Don't conclude that lack of competition means you have a wonderful opportunity. It might mean there is no market for your product or service.

4. Don't search for a business concept that will revolutionize the world.

5. Beware of friends and family telling you what they think of your business idea.

6. Don't start a business that does not match your image and personal goals.

7. Don't open a me-too venture—a direct copy of an existing business.

8. Don't fool yourself into thinking that good food recipes are easy to sell and market.

9. Don't forget about securing the required licenses for starting a home-based business.

10. Don't overlook business insurance for your equipment and inventory—even if it is a home-based business.

11. Don't start a business without writing a business plan.

12. Beware of business consultants who offer to write your business plan for a reasonable price.

13. Don't assume that all business incubators offer the same level of management expertise and consulting services.

14. Don't try to save start-up costs by locating your retail business in a less-desirable location.

15. Don't get lured into a vacant store location by a landlord who offers an unbelievable deal.

16. Avoid paying up-front fees to companies that are selling home-based business opportunities.

The Good News

If entrepreneurs are willing to exercise a little patience, thoroughly research their venture idea along with the potential market, and write a feasibility and/or business plan, their chances for success will be greatly improved. Learn from other entrepreneurs in similar industries by studying their successes and failures. If you lack business experience, read entrepreneurship books and take an entrepreneurship course or seminar. Business is not risky, but starting one without researching your industry and strengthening your entrepreneurial skills is.

4

Legal Structures for Starting a Business

Overview

Typically, entrepreneurs launch new ventures without much fore-thought about which legal structure is best for their enterprises. They don't stop to consider key issues about ownership, control, liability, management, decision making, and capital. Yet these key issues directly affect income taxes and the future success of the venture.

The four major forms of business ownership are sole proprietorship, partnership, LLC, and corporation. If the entrepreneur owns and operates the business as an individual and does not have large capital needs, the informality of a sole proprietorship may be appropriate. This is true only if business liability is not an issue or sufficient liability insurance has been purchased to protect the founder. During recent times, the limited partnership and LLC have become more popular.

Of prime importance to a new venture is assessing financial needs, legal risks, and liability. Overall, the corporate structure provides the liability protection that founders need. If corporate profits are paid out in salary and/or commissions, the problem of double taxation can be avoided. In addition, the corporate structure makes it possible to raise capital that would be extremely difficult, if not impossible, for an entrepreneur to raise. For these reasons, most entrepreneurs select the corporate structure.

It is not unusual for entrepreneurs to create a corporate shield but act as a sole proprietor. They neglect to follow corporate requirements and fail to hold board meetings, take minutes, file a corporate report with the secretary of state every two years, and follow other procedures.

Some choose to form S corporations to avoid the double taxation involved with incorporating. However, while the S corporation may be ideal for new ventures and for businesses that are losing money, it may not be the best legal structure when profits are realized.

To avoid the requirements of a corporation, some entrepreneurs select the partnership form, in which owners pool their resources and share control. Others choose to operate as a limited liability company, which combines the advantages of a corporation and a partnership.

Still other entrepreneurs start charitable nonprofit organizations, designated as 501(c)(3), which qualify for exemption from federal income tax. With a nonprofit organization, the entrepreneur identifies a need in the community that is currently not being addressed. An example is an organization that solicits contributions to form a loan pool for minority and female business owners who have difficulty accessing capital.

Selecting the legal structure for an enterprise is a critical decision that takes considerable forethought and planning. The decision should always be discussed with an accountant, since ever-changing tax laws affect business owners differently according to their personal financial situations.

Smart Strategies for Legal Structures

1. Evaluate and select the most appropriate business structure for your new venture, taking into consideration ownership issues, liability, tax ramifications, and your ability to raise capital.

2. Consider working with a potential partner on a trial basis before giving away equity.

3. Incorporate your business and limit your liability by protecting your personal assets.

4. Don't conduct business without limiting your personal liability or obtaining liability insurance.

5. Keep separate records for your business, regardless of the type of legal structure you choose.

6. Preserve the corporate shield by following all the corporate rules, regulations, and reporting requirements.

7. Don't become a general partner if you have the majority of personal assets. You are jointly liable for all the debts of the business regardless of how the partnership agreement defines ownership.

8. Purchase key-partner life insurance, which provides money for the corporation to buy out the shares of any partner who dies.

Should I Worry About What Kind of Legal Structure to Choose?

Question

I have just started a carpet-cleaning business and was wondering if I should remain operating as a sole proprietorship. Also, do I have to file any special papers for my new business?

Answer

A sole proprietorship is the easiest legal structure to start (and terminate), since there are relatively few formalities and legal restrictions. Also, you have complete control of the business and are the sole recipient of any earned profits. For tax purposes, the IRS treats you and your business as one, and your reporting goes on the Schedule C of your 1040 tax form. If the business ends up losing money, you can deduct these losses on your tax return against any other income that you may have earned during that year. For these reasons, the sole proprietorship is the form most used by small businesses.

In a sole proprietorship, you are fully liable for all business debts and actions. If your business is unable to meet its financial obligations, creditors can pursue your personal assets, including your home and car. Your personal assets are not protected from lawsuits. You can lessen the risk of liability in the case of physical loss or personal injury by purchasing business owner's insurance.

Another major obstacle in operating as a sole proprietorship is your ability to raise capital. If you borrow money for your business, the bank will usually require you to sign personally for the money and pledge your personal assets. You will be required to make periodic loan payments regardless of whether your venture is making money. Therefore, risking your personal assets is an important factor to consider.

Another disadvantage of running a business as a sole proprietorship is that the life of the business terminates with the life of the proprietor. Obviously, severe problems can arise here with estate planning and disposing of the business. Also, the sole proprietor cannot deduct many expenses that are deductible to corporations, like defined-benefit pension plans, insurance expenses, and health-care benefits. Last, it is difficult to attract good management to a sole proprietorship, and this can severely hamper the business's growth and performance.

Since you have already begun your business as a sole proprietorship, you need only file whatever licenses are required in your area. If you are operating the business under a name other than your own, you must register the business as a trade name with your state's revenue department.

✔ COURTNEY'S SMART TIP
Given the realities of the business world, the corporation is the best legal structure for those entrepreneurs who intend to grow their business and raise money from outside sources.

Key considerations in choosing a legal form of business include your income and tax implications, your ability to raise capital, and your need to limit your liabilities. If you are in business alone and will not need much capital, then the informality of a sole proprietorship might be appropriate.

Should I Form a Partnership?

Question

I started a small limousine service a couple of years ago. My business has grown substantially, and I now have four limos. However, as my business has grown, my capital has shrunk. I can't borrow any more money from the bank and am thinking about getting a partner who has some money to invest. Is this a good strategy to follow? Will I need to become a corporation, or will becoming a partnership be better?

Answer

What are you really looking for—a true partner who will share investing in and operating your venture, or an investor? If you are just looking for an investor, you don't need a partnership. If you are looking for someone who will contribute money and share in the management of the business, then consider forming a partnership.

A partnership is a tricky proposition. Finding someone with cash, similar goals, the expertise you need, and a style you can work with is difficult. It is akin to finding a marriage partner. You must choose wisely or bear the consequences. Many partnerships end up in disaster under the pressure of a crisis. Crises and chaos are typical environments in entrepreneurial ventures. Conflict seems inevitable when the founder has a need for autonomy.

The advantages of taking on a partner include companionship as well as the enhanced ability to raise money and recruit and motivate key people. The disadvantages include losing control of your venture, losing wealth, being stuck with other owner(s), and having to account to others. The most common reason that entrepreneurs add partners is to raise money; acquiring needed expertise is secondary.

Issues that need to be addressed include deciding who will contribute the most money; how much equity you will give up for additional investment; what kind of exits will be available; who will make the spending decisions; who will sign checks; and who will hire, supervise, and fire staff.

✔ COURTNEY'S SMART TIP
Select a partner who complements your skills and then structure a partnership agreement that addresses both the division of ownership and buyout provisions.

Try to find a partner who complements your strengths and weaknesses rather than one who has a similar background to your own. Look for someone who specializes in your weakest area. Seek out someone you can trust, are compatible with, and can communicate with easily. Be sure to evaluate whether a potential partner exhibits the ability to compromise.

Be wary of partnering with family or friends. Most often you will end up gaining a partner but losing a friend. Consider a trial period before settling on a partner and giving ownership in your venture.

Many investors consider a venture team more advantageous than a single founder. They like to see a balance of talents among the members of the management team. There are many functional areas involved in operating a business, and it is unlikely that someone will be highly competent in all aspects of the venture. Instead, strengthen your business by either adding partners or hiring staff who will balance your management team. Entrepreneurial wisdom affirms that it is very difficult to run a business on your own.

If your business is currently a sole proprietorship, you could become a partnership immediately. The terms do not have to be written down, especially if you become equal owners. However, it is better to have the terms of the partnership detailed in a formal agreement.

There are two legal forms to consider: the general partnership and the limited partnership. In a general partnership, the owners are liable for all business debts, even if the partnership agreement specifies a certain split in profits. Each partner is 100% responsible for all liabilities.

Personal assets of the partners may be attached to cover the partnership's liabilities.

In a limited partnership, one general partner runs the business and remains personally responsible for all the partnership's debts. The limited partners are liable only up to the amount of their investment in the business. They do not contribute to the day-to-day operation of the venture. To create a limited partnership, you must file a certificate of limited partnership with the secretary of state.

If one partner dies or withdraws, the partnership terminates. For tax purposes, the income of the business is considered the income of the partners. The partners are individually responsible for the taxes on their personal income tax return. Profits and losses may be divided in any way agreed to by the partners. If the partners are operating the business under a name different from their legal names, the business must be registered as a trade name with the state department of revenue.

Incorporation is another option to consider. It requires formal paperwork and documentation but offers the advantages of limiting the owners' liability, existing as a separate entity from the individual owners and generating certain tax options. The corporate structure is usually more attractive when partners share control and management of the venture. Most founders wisely select the corporate structure as their business grows.

How to Structure Buy-Sell Agreements

Always Include a Buyout Agreement in Legal Structures

Question

Should entrepreneurs always include a buyout agreement in their legal structures?

Answer

Yes. There should always be a buyout agreement, whether you have formed a partnership or a corporation. Clashes between partners are inevitable, and some provision should be made for separation if the dispute cannot be resolved. Either the partnership agreement or the corporate bylaws should stipulate that any owner must sell back shares at a predetermined price upon separation. This is known as a buy-sell agreement.

It is also recommended that the buy-sell agreement include a shoot-out clause stipulating that a partner who wishes to buy out another must offer to sell at the same price at which he or she wants to buy. Then the other partner must agree either to sell at the offered terms or to buy at those same terms.

The trick with this type of agreement is how to price the shares. There are two approaches you can take. The first is to set a predetermined price that is agreeable to the partners. The problem here is that as the venture grows, the value of the shares will change. The other approach is to agree to make a yearly evaluation determining the price of the shares for that year. The evaluation could be made by the partners or by an outsider, or it could be mediated or arbitrated.

✔ COURTNEY'S SMART TIP
Develop a provision regarding how and when the shares of the venture will be priced for buyout.

The buy-sell agreement also makes provisions for the death of a partner. Typically it provides for redemption by the company of that person's share, possibly paid for by a life insurance policy carried by the company. Or it provides for cross-purchase of the person's shares by the surviving partner(s), possibly paid for by insurance carried by the surviving partner(s). The best arrangement depends largely on tax considerations. Consult your lawyer and accountant about a buy-sell agreement suited to your particular situation.

A valuable adjunct to the buy-sell agreement is key partner life insurance, which provides money for the company to buy out the shares of any partner who dies. An advantage of purchasing this type of insurance is that the premiums are tax-deductible expenses for the company.

Consideration should also be given to insure key employees of the business whose loss could have substantial financial consequences. The loss of a key person could mean the loss of key customers, loss of services or special skills provided by that person, or loss of capital. Many entrepreneurial ventures purchase key employee life insurance, which pays compensation to a business on the employee's death, or key employee disability income insurance, which pays compensation caused by permanent and total disability.

Incorporating a Business

Should I Incorporate?

Question

I have been thinking about starting a gift-basket service business and was wondering if I should incorporate. What do you think?

Answer

Let's look first at the various advantages and pitfalls of becoming a sole proprietor. When you operate as a sole proprietorship, all the profits are yours, as well as all the losses. The liabilities are also yours, which means they are unlimited and a major disadvantage in this litigious age. This form of business provides no shield for your home, car, or other personal possessions.

Further, operating as a sole proprietorship makes it difficult to raise money from lenders, since if anything happens to the owner, the venture could go down the drain. Sole proprietors borrow funds on either their personal signature or collateral. Life insurance is usually required to cover the amount of the loan in case something happens to the founder. Owners are severely restricted in their ability to raise money, and growth is limited. The death of the founder means the end of the business.

For these reasons and others, most entrepreneurs are strongly advised to incorporate their ventures. A corporation is a legal entity that exists separate from its founders. You create it by filing articles of incorporation with the secretary of state. The company is owned by its shareholders and run by a board of directors elected by the shareholders. You can become a one-person corporation, the sole shareholder, and the only director. However, you cannot be both the president and the secretary of the corporation. You must appoint another person to act as the secretary, but you are not required to give this person any ownership.

Three primary characteristics distinguish a corporation from other legal structures. First, a corporation limits a stockholder's liability to the amount of investment in the business. Second, if shareholders are active in operating the business, they are considered employees and must be paid a reasonable wage subject to both state and federal payroll taxes. Finally, a corporation must pay tax on income as a separate legal entity. If profits are distributed to shareholders as dividends, these profits are subject to taxation as part of the shareholder's income.

Corporations shield shareholders from the claims of creditors and contractual relationships, unless the shareholders sign personally instead of as officers of the corporation. The corporate shield does not protect any shareholders against personal negligence, civil wrongs, or torts.

✔ COURTNEY'S SMART TIP

Preserve the corporate shield by strictly following all the legal requirements and reporting procedures that pertain to corporations.

Great care must be given to protect the corporate shield and keep the affairs of the corporation at arm's length. This means the shareholders must adopt bylaws, file separate corporate tax returns, hold regular shareholder meetings, record minutes of the proceedings, maintain corporate records, and file a report with the state every two years. Following these procedures takes time, effort, and money.

Compliance with all such requirements is mandatory if you wish to maintain the corporate shield and receive limited liability protection. For example, shareholders should always identify themselves as officers of the corporation and keep the affairs of the corporation separate from their personal lives. Shareholders should never pay corporate debts personally and should never pay personal debts from corporate funds. If shareholders follow legal procedures to keep the corporate shield intact, their personal assets should be protected.

The main disadvantage of operating as a corporation is the double taxation—that is, the corporation pays a tax on its profits, and those receiving salaries and/or corporate dividends are taxed again. A way to overcome this problem is to take any yearly corporate profits in salary, commissions, or both. Entrepreneurs seldom pay corporate dividends anyway. Therefore, under our current tax law, the tax advantages favor the corporate structure.

One of the best resources available for making the job of incorporating easier is *The Do It Yourself Incorporation Kit* by S. J. T. Enterprises. Also, check with your state about its business start-up kit for new business owners. Many states provide these kits free of charge.

For information about corporations, obtain copies of Internal Revenue Service Publication 589, "Tax Information of S Corporation," Publication 334, "Tax Guide for Small Business," and Publication 910, "Tax Information and Assistance." Request these by calling 800-829-3676.

How Does a Regular Corporation Differ from an S Corporation?

Question

For the past six years I have been running my gardening business as a sole proprietorship. Because my business is growing, I am thinking about incorporating to protect my personal assets. Should I form a regular corporation or an S corporation?

Answer

Whether you should form a regular corporation or an S corporation depends on your financial condition, your assets, and your tax bracket. The S corporation was designed for the lower-income enterprise, since profits or losses are reported on a shareholder's 1040, as in a partnership. Income or losses pass through the corporation to the shareholders in the same form as they are in the corporation. Few entrepreneurs operating small companies ever pay out corporate dividends.

S corporations are not actually separate legal structures, as are corporations, but constitute a special tax status granted by the IRS. S corporations do not pay corporate income tax; rather, expenses and income are divided among its shareholders. Shareholders report profits and losses on their personal income tax returns. You need to find qualified tax counsel to answer your specific question and take advantage of the tax law's provisions.

Most entrepreneurs form S corporations to avoid the regular corporation's double taxation. This should not be the primary reason for forming an S corporation.

✔ COURTNEY'S SMART TIP

Avoid double taxation by taking corporate profits as salary and/or paying bonuses or commissions.

There are several restrictions on the organization and activities of an S corporation. First, it must be a domestic corporation. It may have only one class of stock—common stock—issued and outstanding. However, common stock can be issued with or without voting rights.

An S corporation may not earn more than 25% of its gross receipts from passive investment income (royalties, rents, dividends, interest, etc.) during any three-year period. It must have a tax year that ends December 31. It cannot have more than 75 shareholders, and all shareholders must be citizens or residents of the United States. Last, all shareholders must agree to elect S corporation status.

To become an S corporation, you must file articles of incorporation with your state's secretary of state before applying to the IRS for S status. Then your corporation should file Form 2553, Election by a Small Business Corporation, to indicate it chooses S corporation status. Generally, the election must be filed by March 15 to be effective for the current tax year. The S corporation status remains in effect until the shareholders revoke the choice or until the corporation no longer meets the qualifications. If the corporation reverts back to be taxed as a regular C corporation, it must wait a full five years to once again make the S election.

Although the S corporation can be ideal when the venture is losing money, problems may occur when profits are realized. Stockholders must pay income taxes on these profits while no cash is passed on to pay the taxes. This is one compelling reason for obtaining qualified tax counsel to assist in the S corporation decision.

Before you decide to become an S corporation, give careful consideration to the amount and type of income your company might generate in the future, other income or losses you might earn independent of the company, and whether you plan to sell either the assets or the entire company in the foreseeable future. An S election can be a viable tax-saving device in certain circumstances. It provides a way to operate the business as a proprietorship or partnership for tax purposes and still benefit from the protection of the corporate shield.

For example, if you do not have many assets or do not anticipate your revenues to be over $300,000 per year, usually it is better to form an S corporation. While the S corporation can be ideal when the business is losing money, problems may occur when profits are realized and passed on to the stockholders. They must pay income taxes on these profits while no cash is passed on to pay taxes. This is one compelling reason to consult a qualified tax accountant or lawyer to assist you with this decision.

For more information about S corporations, request a copy of Internal Revenue Service Publication 589, "Tax Information on S Corporations," by calling 800-829-3676.

Should I Form a Limited Liability Company?

Question

Some of my business associates are thinking about buying a business and are considering a limited liability company. What are the pros and cons of this type of entity?

Answer

The limited liability company (LLC) is neither a corporation nor a partnership. It is a relatively new type of business entity that, when properly structured, combines the benefits of liability protection afforded to shareholders of a corporation with the favorable tax treatment provided to partnerships and their partners.

In many states, LLC owners are called members, and people who operate the business are called managers. Managers are elected by members. (There must be at least two members to form an LLC.) The exact number of members may vary among states. Corporations are usually eligible to become members of an LLC.

The principal advantage of an LLC is that, unlike a C corporation, it pays no federal income taxes. Instead, as in a partnership, the income or loss of the LLC is passed directly through to its members and reported on their respective tax returns. The principal advantage over the partnership is that, unlike with general partners (in both general and limited partnerships), the members' liability for the debts of the LLC is limited to the extent of their investment in the business. In addition, in an LLC all owners may participate in management, a right once available only to general partnerships. Last, the LLC offers the same limited liability of the corporate structure.

Because of these advantages, along with the flexibility it offers, the LLC may be a better choice of legal structure than the S corporation. It is not subject to the cumbersome and often confusing rules relating to electing S corporation status. S corporations are inhibited by strict limitations on who may be shareholders (only U.S. citizens, resident aliens, and certain types of trusts). S corporations are also limited to issuing only common stock, and the allocation of profits and losses must be proportionate to shareholders' ownership. In contrast, the LLC provides tremendous flexibility in distributing and allocating profits and losses.

Forming an LLC is like forming a limited partnership. Articles of organization must be filed with the state secretary of state. In addition, there must be an operating agreement, akin to a partnership agreement, that spells out the details of how the business will be operated and how the profits and losses will be shared. Consult a business attorney to pre-pare the LLC's articles of organization and operating agreement.

The LLC has disadvantages as well. Unlike the corporate arrange-ment, unanimous written consent of all members is required to admit new members or to transfer a member's interest, since this structure is treated like a limited partnership. Additional restrictions are imposed on transfers of interest and upon an LLC's ability to continue if a mem-ber withdraws. These restrictions are tax-driven, since they provide the pass-through tax advantage of a partnership.

It is not clear whether states that do not yet have LLC legislation will respect the liability protection afforded to its members. As of 1997, 46 states permitted LLCs. Since it has been publicly ruled in Wyoming that LLCs are treated as partnerships for tax purposes, many founders form their LLCs in Wyoming, where this form of ownership has been in operation for many years.

Another disadvantage of the LLC relates to legal costs. It is more expensive to start an LLC than a corporation, since there are no stan-dard documents to use as a model. The operating agreement must be tailored to each venture and requires the services of an experienced at-torney. No boilerplate kits are available as with corporations.

Despite its disadvantages, the LLC is a good planning tool. It is an attractive legal structure because it creates tax savings, shields busi-nesspeople from personal liability, and provides almost unlimited op-portunity to participate in the management of the venture. Its simplicity and flexibility make it attractive to closely held businesses that operate in a state with LLC legislation. This legal entity is ideal for many real estate ventures as well as oil, gas, and mining businesses.

✔ COURTNEY'S SMART TIP

As your business grows, change your legal structure to accommodate changing tax laws and the individual situations of your members. Al-ways consult with a tax accountant and/or business attorney first.

Forming a Nonprofit Company

Question

I want to start a day-care center, and I am interested in incorporating as a nonprofit business. I want to fund my venture from tax-deductible donations or by applying for a grant. What do I need to do to become a nonprofit cor-poration?

Answer

First, research whether it is likely that private individuals, foundations, and/or corporations would consider making charitable donations to your nonprofit corporation. Today, the demand for charitable donations is extraordinarily high and increasing. Competition for funding abounds among nonprofit corporations.

Question whether your venture will be seen as meeting a critical need in the community and therefore deserving of contributions. True, day-care services are vital in most communities, but your venture will be serving relatively few residents and thus may not attract enough funds. Fundability is a key question that must be answered before proceeding.

Developing a constituency of potential donors takes considerable time and effort. Michael Seltzer's *Securing Your Organization's Future* offers a comprehensive workbook approach on how to acquire funding for nonprofit corporations and how to identify potential donors. Two good funding resources are your state's community resource center and Junior League. Also, check to see if your state has an association of nonprofits or a council of foundations. The United Way agency in your city could assist you with contacting such organizations.

Obtaining funding for nonprofit organizations is a challenge. You must write a sound and professional proposal to be considered for funding. This can be a long process, since many donors review proposals only at certain times during the year. Their response is not immediate, and it may take from 6 to 18 months to secure funding.

Consider direct-mail solicitation. But remember that it takes time to build a constituency. Response rates tend to be low, averaging 1% to 2%.

Once you determine that your venture provides a needed service in the community and that it is feasible to obtain funding, you can begin the process of forming an independent 501(c)(3). This organizational structure qualifies your venture for exemption from federal income tax and enables donors to make their donations tax-deductible.

You can register as a nonprofit corporation with your secretary of state. Registration does not grant your corporation tax-exempt status, however. A separate application must be made to the IRS. Numerous forms and documents must be created and completed. The IRS fees depend on the size of the proposed project. In addition, it takes from three to six months to receive the 501(c)(3) designation. Call your local IRS office to determine how to obtain your application packet.

Because of the technicalities and complications involved in obtaining 501(c)(3) status, legal assistance for nonprofits is essential.

Contact an attorney who specializes in nonprofit incorporation and taxes. The cost ranges between $2,000 and $10,000. You can reduce these expenses by doing much of the legwork yourself and having your attorney review your efforts.

Contact some of the organizations in your state or community that provide both management consulting and training to nonprofit corporations.

Pitfalls to Avoid

1. Choosing business partners who do not complement your strengths and weaknesses.

2. Not thinking through the ownership issues, management concerns, liability issues, and tax consequences of the various types of legal structures for your venture.

3. Failing to require a written partnership agreement that specifies all the agreed-on terms of the business.

4. Operating as a sole proprietorship when the venture has potential liabilities for which you would be personally responsible.

5. Mixing personal and business expenses on your financial statement.

6. Paying corporate debts personally and/or signing personally on corporate business.

7. Piercing the corporate veil by disregarding the rules, regulations, and requirements for maintaining the corporate structure.

8. Using an attorney who does not specialize in nonprofit incorporation and taxes.

9. Emphasizing a community service that is already being provided by another nonprofit.

10. Failing to have a buy-sell agreement that provides for business separation.

The Good News

Entrepreneurs can benefit from spending the required time and effort to research the right legal structure for their ventures. Legal structure and tax implications affect all founders differently, depending on their personal situations. Carefully consider all the alternatives, and seek advice from the infrastructure about what kind of legal entity to form.

5

Buying a Business

Overview

The entrepreneurial trend is growing; it's here to stay and expanding worldwide. However, a new model of entrepreneurship is emerging—the buyout entrepreneur. This individual buys a business instead of starting one from scratch. Many entrepreneurs are finding that big returns come from the growth and revitalization of existing businesses.

The number of businesses for sale is increasing, and so is the number of buyers, including corporate acquirers, larger corporations (based both in the U.S. and overseas) that are looking for smaller companies to provide innovative products in new markets. In addition, the impact of downsizing by larger corporations will be felt for years. Today, displaced workers are more receptive to becoming entrepreneurs, and a good proportion of them find buying a business more appealing than launching a new one.

The often-quoted statistic that 6 out of every 10 new businesses fail during the first five years tells of the risk that is involved in starting a new venture. Overall, a successful business needs an operating history of five to eight years to sufficiently prove its concept, market, prices, location, and management.

In a start-up venture, all operational aspects are unknown. There is a high degree of uncertainty in starting a new venture from scratch. Some entrepreneurs estimate that they will break even in 6 months. However, it might take 18 to 24 months, during which time they need unanticipated operating capital. Typically, penetrating a market takes two to fives times longer than originally projected.

However, buying an existing business is different. One can equate the differences to those involved in buying a house versus building a house. With new house, owners worry about everything—just like someone starting a new business. With the purchase of an older home, however, less risk is involved—just as in the acquisition of an existing business. When you purchase an ongoing business, its reputation, customer base, suppliers, equipment, leases, and cash flow already exist. The infrastructure and management team are also in place.

Many entrepreneurs are more successful as turnaround artists—building ventures rather than starting them. They are not creator types with ideas that could revolutionize the marketplace. Instead, they recognize good business opportunities and make an existing venture more profitable. One successful entrepreneur claimed that he had only two failures out of 10 ventures—the two businesses he started from scratch. The other business successes were all ventures he had purchased and grown.

Buying an existing business is a good entrepreneurial strategy when you have thoroughly evaluated and analyzed the business opportunity. It may take up to a year to find the right purchase. It is also a wise strategy to match your interests and industry experience with an opportunity to purchase a business.

Smart Strategies for Buying a Business

1. Reduce the time involved in planning, organizing, and launching a new start-up by buying the right business.

2. Negotiate with the seller to carry back debt and give you good terms so that the business can generate enough cash to buy itself back in five years.

3. Ask the seller to continue working in the business for three to six months to help you make the transition and provide training.

4. Seek outside help from accountants, lawyers, and bankers to assist you in assessing opportunities to purchase a business.

5. Always ask for audited financial statements for the past three to five years.

6. Present yourself as a fully qualified businessperson so you will receive a positive response from a seller or broker.

7. Hire the owner of a similar business outside your competitive area to help you evaluate purchase opportunities.

8. After analyzing historical sales and profits, prepare your own projections of future profitability and growth potential.

✔ **COURTNEY'S SMART TIP**
Business failure costs the seller money since you can negotiate a lower price.

Making the Purchase Decision

Question

I have a choice between purchasing a business that has been in operation for several years and starting one of my own. Which route would you recommend?

Answer

Many entrepreneurs feel that purchasing an existing business is like buying a used car. You inherit all the problems and headaches that someone else has caused. However, purchasing a business can be an attractive alternative to starting one of your own. There are six good reasons for buying a business instead of starting one from scratch. They include time, finance, existing operating systems, lower risk, management training, and lower asset costs.

Starting a business from scratch takes considerable time and effort, usually requiring several years to get it to a level of profitability. You can own a profitable business from the beginning by purchasing it. Buying an existing business is a quick way to obtain ownership of a mature business that is generating profit.

What if the business you are interested in purchasing is losing money? Should you still consider purchasing it? Buying this type of venture is still a quicker way to get to profitable operations than starting a new business. Turning around a business can be an experience that is both profitable and rewarding. Many failing businesses are just poorly managed. An astute entrepreneur may be able to immediately generate a profit.

Perhaps the most compelling reason for buying a business is to make use of the seller's invested capital. Most sellers ultimately finance a large part of the sale to help sell the business and to obtain a higher selling price. Sellers are the purchaser's biggest financing source.

Typically, the seller's money is the lowest cost of funds available. Sometimes, the seller will finance the entire transaction if he or she has faith in the buyer. Many times, the seller does not need cash immediately but instead wants assured income.

Most sellers will ask for all cash up front. However, they often have to give more lenient terms to make the sale. It all depends on the buyer's persuasive powers and the seller's alternatives and needs.

Remember, the selling price of the business is not the most important aspect. Instead, the terms for purchasing the business are key to making the deal work. Also, bankers and other lenders are more willing to lend to an established business with several years of performance to evaluate. It is a known quantity.

✔ COURTNEY'S SMART TIP

Terms are everything when buying a business; the selling price is not.

The entrepreneur who starts a business spends considerable time, money, and effort building an organization and developing an effective operating system. The buyer of a business already has one in place and can avoid the pitfalls of start-up.

Most often, some changes are needed. It is usually easier to make changes in the operating systems than to begin from nothing. Some of the value of an existing business comes from the fact that it is a going concern. All its parts are functioning. One of the most valuable parts of the operating system is the venture's current customers. Customers are gold. It takes a substantial amount of time and effort to build and maintain a good customer base.

Another important part of a venture's operating system is its sales force and distributing system. It is one of the most significant values of an existing business that does not appear on any balance sheet. A well-trained sales force combined with an effective distribution system is a most valuable asset and one well worth acquiring.

Advantages of Buying an Existing Business

Question

I am going to be laid off in the next several months, and I have an opportunity to buy a rental business that a friend of mine owns. Is this advisable?

Answer

Overall, the risks associated with entrepreneurship are less in buying a business than in starting a new business. There are many advantages to buying an existing business, especially if you know the owner and his or her business. Consider these advantages of purchasing a business—lower risk, management training, and lower asset costs.

It is often easier to assess the risks involved in buying a going business than those inherent in developing a new venture. You can evaluate a known quantity with an existing location and current customers, staff, suppliers, and reputation. The first two years of any business are the riskiest. Survival is key during this period and the failure rate is the highest. It can take two or three years to reach the break-even point with a start-up and another five years to become stable and successful.

Two major factors help limit risks. First, the buyer has better information on both the operating characteristics of the venture and its established market than the entrepreneur would have with a start-up enterprise. Much of the market speculation and sales forecasting are eliminated, since the business already has a track record. Therefore, better and more accurate forecasts can be made.

Second, and perhaps more important, the buyer can usually invest fewer dollars when purchasing an existing business. This relates back to the seller financing the majority of the venture. The more the seller is willing to carry back as debt, the more he or she can expect to sell the business for to a prospective buyer.

As previously mentioned, this is usually the least expensive cost of funds available. Negotiated terms can be better than those available from any other type of lender. The buyer should be more concerned with how the purchase can be structured than with the actual price involved.

Management training provided by the seller is another advantage of buying an existing business. Often, the seller will teach the buyer how to run the business. Much inside knowledge and expertise can be exchanged. Consequently, the buyer of an existing business may not have to learn those important start-up lessons the hard way. In addition, a financially involved seller is motivated to hold the buyer's hand for a longer time.

✔ COURTNEY'S SMART TIP

Ask the seller to work with the new owner for the first six months after the sale.

Finally, it is usually cheaper to acquire assets by buying a business than it is to purchase them new. You can often purchase the building and equipment for 10% to 20% of what it would cost new. Some businesses are purchased just for their location or for the lease they have with the building owner.

Frequently, the assets of an existing business are not worth much, except as to how they are used in that particular business. Thus, an entrepreneur may be able to get into this type of business with less capital than by starting a new venture. In essence, you are purchasing used equipment at an attractive price. This happens more often when you acquire a firm that is in trouble.

An entrepreneurial tip to remember is that the business success a seller has achieved costs the buyer more money. Likewise, business failure costs the seller money.

Disadvantages of Buying an Existing Business

What to Look For when Buying a Business

Question

I have an excellent opportunity to buy a business from someone who is moving. Because of the business's existing client base and positive cash flow, I think this would be a good investment for me. What should I look out for?

Answer

Many businesses for sale aren't worth buying. The advantages of buying a business usually outweigh starting one from scratch. However, there are some disadvantages of buying existing businesses that you should consider before deciding to buy.

Many businesses for sale should be avoided. Primarily, these businesses can be grouped into the following six categories:

1. Inadequate market potential.
2. Serious competitive problems.
3. Technological problems.
4. Disadvantageous cost characteristics.
5. Seller backing out.
6. Nothing worth buying.

Let's take a look at each of these disadvantages. First, many businesses are not going anywhere because there is nowhere for them to go.

The founder is doing everything possible and the business is still losing money. Essentially, the market potential is just not there.

Second, the business is experiencing serious competitive problems. The market is saturated with similar ventures, and the cost of the product has become very competitive. There are just too many businesses chasing after the same consumer dollar. It is a dog-eat-dog industry where it is difficult to enter into the marketplace.

Some businesses become technologically obsolete. Would you purchase a business that makes silent movies or 78 rpm records? Sometimes the product can no longer compete technologically in the marketplace because of new inventions.

Astute entrepreneurs may realize that they are losing their technological edge. They quickly place their business for sale before this situation becomes apparent to the general public. In acquiring any business with a technology base, take great care to assess what is happening to the technology in that industry. Are new products being tested that will replace yours? It is essential that you determine whether the business has the ability to compete in the new technological arena.

It is also difficult to make money if your competition has a cost advantage over you. You will always be vulnerable to price wars. Moreover, your cost disadvantage comes right out of your profits. Unless you have an idea of how to rectify the cost problem, be careful.

Sometimes you will negotiate with a seller for several months. Then, just as you get ready to sign the deal, the seller notifies you that he or she has decided not to sell the business. Often, sellers become too emotionally attached to let go of the venture. Yet you have spent considerable time and money performing due diligence, doing research, securing financing, and negotiating the deal. In addition, you have paid legal and accounting fees that are unrecoverable, plus the incalculable opportunity costs.

Last, some businesses are just not worth buying. They are going nowhere fast. Their products may be inadequate, defective, or both. The inventory is old and outdated. The business is on a downswing and experiencing a negative cash flow. Overall, it is difficult to find one good feature about the business, except the sales price. When this situation occurs, it is easier to start a new venture than purchase an old one.

Be careful when you find an owner who is trying to sell the business in a short time. He or she may be trying to bail out quickly before the market turns sour. When speed replaces price as the primary goal, beware. You might be able to get a good deal, but the business is or will become unprofitable.

Where to Look for a Business to Purchase

Question

I am a corporate refugee who is looking for a business to buy. I don't want or feel qualified to start one from scratch. Where do you suggest I look?

Answer

Avoid a hasty decision and try not to get too excited about a good potential business until you have spent enough time evaluating it and analyzing its marketplace. Many experts say that you should count on spending at least a year to find and evaluate a business that you would like to purchase. Use the following guidelines as a starting point in your search.

1. *Newspapers.* The easiest place to start looking for a business to buy is in the classified section of newspapers under "Business Opportunities." The Sunday edition usually has the most listings. Look in the "Mart" section of *The Wall Street Journal* on Wednesdays and Thursdays. *The New York Times* Sunday edition contains several pages of diverse businesses for sale. There are also specialized business opportunity newspapers, such as *The Business Opportunity Journal*. Check with your librarian for similar publications to review.

2. *Industry trade magazines.* Many industry magazines and trade papers contain a classified section with business opportunities that are industry-specific.

3. *Banks.* Some banks, such as the First National Bank of Maryland, publish newsletters of business opportunities. Call 800-842-BANK. There may be a charge for some of the newsletters and/or catalog listings. You may also ask banks in your area if they have lists of businesses for sale. Bankers can be helpful in your search, and establishing a relationship with them early on is a must. It might not be long before you'll be asking them for lending assistance to help finance your venture.

4. *Business professionals and members of the infrastructure.* Talk with attorneys, accountants, venture capitalists, investment bankers, insurance agents, salespeople, and other members of the entrepreneurial

infrastructure. These professionals often know of business opportunities that are never advertised.

5. *Business brokers.* Brokers have extensive lists of businesses for sale. They work for business owners and are paid a commission to market and sell businesses. A business broker's fee typically runs between 5% and 10% of the purchase price. Your response to an ad may very well be to a business broker. Try to negotiate a buy-broker agreement in which the broker agrees to seek out companies for you. Look in the Yellow Pages of your telephone directory for listings of business brokers. You can also obtain a brokers' list of those who belong to the International Association of Business Brokers by calling 617-369-5254.

6. *Business owners.* Look for businesses you might be interested in purchasing and contact the owners. Ask them if they are interested in selling. On the average, about 3 out of every 10 calls attract some interest. If owners are not interested in selling, they might be able to refer you to someone else.

7. *Chambers of commerce.* Some chambers of commerce maintain buying and selling services for businesses in their area.

8. SBA *and state or county economic-development agencies.* These organizations frequently know of businesses for sale and can give you referrals.

9. *Trade sources.* Check with suppliers, vendors, distributors, manufacturers, and trade associations about potential businesses for sale. They are excellent resources for industry-specific businesses.

10. *Business bankruptcy listings.* Most local business journals publish a list of businesses that have filed for bankruptcy. If you feel you have skills to become a turnaround artist, these listings may produce good leads.

11. *Friends.* Your friends have a wide network of contacts. Let them know what kind of business you are looking for, and ask them to notify you of any opportunities they discover. You might want to consider offering an incentive to get people to give you qualified leads. Paying people for their time and effort is a good business practice.

When answering an ad, present yourself as a fully qualified businessperson so you will receive a response back. You will probably be asked some qualifying questions to see if the owner or broker wants to continue the process. This list is a starting place and demonstrates that there are many sources for you to tap during your search. A successful search requires diligence and hard work.

Checklist for Buying an Existing Business

Question

I have recently taken an early retirement benefit and received a cash bonus. I have been thinking about buying an office-supply store instead of looking for another job. What factors should I consider before buying this business?

Answer

There are personal considerations as well as business factors to analyze and evaluate when thinking about buying an existing business.

Identify your personal goals for purchasing the business. Will the business you are considering match these goals?

Think about your expertise. What are your strengths and weaknesses? Do they complement the venture? Will your knowledge and skills be of help in operating the business? No one is strong in all areas of entrepreneurship.

Consider your lifestyle. There is prestige in owning your own business. Does this business fit your status and image needs?

Decide about location. Is the location convenient for you and does it have enough traffic flow? Is the location convenient to your target customers?

Determine the location history. How long has the office-supply store, for example, been in that location? Have other businesses failed and frequently turned over in that location? Sometimes a location carries a stigma and should be avoided. On the other hand, sometimes entrepreneurs purchase existing businesses just for the location and the lease.

Look at the surroundings and physical condition. Is any remodeling needed? If so, estimate the costs for such remodeling.

Consider your financial needs. How much money do you want to make? How much money will you need to purchase the business?

After identifying your personal criteria, make an in-depth venture analysis. You will need assistance in investigating the office-supply store from various business experts, including an accountant, an attorney, and a banker.

✔ **COURTNEY'S SMART TIP**
Hire a successful owner of a similar venture in another community, someone who is not a competitor, to consult with you. The owner's wealth of experience can help you detect areas of concern that you might otherwise overlook.

Ask for historical and projected profit and sales figures. Ask for the past three to five years of audited balance sheets, income statements, and cash flow statements. Have your accountant review them.

Review the venture's operating ratios. How do they compare with industry ratios from the Robert Morris studies, which is a reliable source of statistics and financial ratios on every industry? If there are significant deviations, ask the owner to explain identified differences.

Ask for a list off current assets and liabilities. Examine the age and condition of assets. Evaluate debts and other liabilities. Are there any pending legal actions? Count the number, amount, and ages of the receivables. Review how many receivables were written off as uncollectible each year for the past three years.

Review corporate tax returns. Remember that a seller won't exaggerate the business's worth to Uncle Sam. If the seller cannot provide financial information for the past three years, this is an indication that something is amiss.

Run a background check. Contact the local Better Business Bureau to determine if customers have filed a complaint about the business. For a fee, Dun & Bradstreet will give you an estimate of the worth of the business. Look for a local office in the Yellow Pages.

Assess the current staff. You are buying not just the company but also the employees. Who are they? Is there good chemistry among them? Do they appear to be ethical and honest? Check their personnel files and look for any disciplinary actions and poor evaluations.

Evaluate local economic and political conditions. What are the industry trends for this business? Is the market increasing or decreasing? What is the growth potential? What is the competitive environment? Is the market overcrowded with competition?

Meet with customers. Determine their level of satisfaction with the business. In any walk-in business, always talk to customers who come into the store. Also, talk to former customers and find out why they are no longer buying from this store.

Choose the right seller. The owner should be both cooperative and willing to disclose all the financial, personnel, customer, and legal information related to the venture. If the owner is resistant to sharing this information, you have reason to be concerned.

These are just some of the key issues to raise and information to analyze when considering purchasing a business. A good reference is C. D. Peterson's *How to Leave Your Job and Buy a Business of Your Own.*

Pitfalls to Avoid

1. Purchasing a business without thoroughly evaluating the venture and its financial statements.

2. Accepting nonaudited financial statements.

3. Purchasing a business with a shrinking market.

4. Purchasing a business in an industry with many competitors.

5. Thinking you can manage the business better than the owner without any prior business experience in the industry.

6. Buying a business when the owner is trying to sell it in a short time.

6

Commercializing Technology and Protecting Intellectual Property*

Overview

Entrepreneurs have millions of great ideas that are commercialized every day, for the right product idea can create a profitable company. But many don't think about protecting their intellectual property, which can consist of extremely valuable proprietary rights and assets. Intellectual property covers patents, trademarks, copyrights, trade secrets, and trade names. Astute entrepreneurs not only protect their intellectual property, but they also may be able to obtain an injunction against infringement and compensatory damages. The costs associated with obtaining such protection are well worthwhile.

The amount of time it takes, the associated costs, and the particular agency with which to register your intellectual property to obtain protection for intellectual property differs. You can register patents and trademarks by filing an application with the U.S. Patent and Trademark Office. The greatest benefit of a patent is the U.S. government's grant of the right to exclude others from making, using, and selling the invention in the United States for 20 years from the filing date of the application after it is issued, so long as the patent is maintained. Patents and pending patent rights can be licensed for royalty payments and are also assignable for valuable consideration.

Many inventors fall prey to paying invention-marketing companies high up-front fees for commercializing their inventions only to discover that they have been taken advantage of. Most of these companies are long on promises but short on delivery. Few inventors ever earn a penny from these companies. Inventors should avoid

*Note: Don Margolis, a patent, trademark, and copyright attorney in Boulder, Colorado, contributed and reviewed many of the articles on intellectual property.

using them or should diligently research them before signing a contract.

If your idea includes any written or artistic matter that includes a symbol, work, shape, or design, and you use this mark as a brand name, service mark, or trade dress, then using the trademark letters (TM) is strongly recommended. You can easily obtain a common-law trademark by using the mark with the goods or services. By using the letters TM or SM, you can show your clear intent to use your idea as a registered trademark. You can also register it with state or federal trademark offices. Trademarks are an important marketing tool for distinguishing the owner's goods or services from those of competitors. They add value to a venture as intellectual property and assist in raising capital.

A copyright is the legal right to control specific uses of art, sculpture, books, music, motion pictures, videotapes, photographs, software programs, and other types of original material. It is a low-cost procedure administered by the U.S. Copyright Office. According to current copyright law, a copyrightable work is automatically protected from its creation whether it is marked or not. However, it is best to include a copyright notice on the material in the form of the full word "copyright," the abbreviation "copyr," or the small circle ®, along with the year of completion and the owner's name.

Trade secrets are any proprietary information used in the course of business to gain an advantage in manufacture or commercialization of products or services. They can be formulas, devices, patterns, techniques, customer lists, sales forecasts, databases, manufacturing processes, or compiled information that has a specific business application. They must have economic value, they must be secret, and the owners must take steps to attempt to protect them. Trade secrets are an important part of an entrepreneur's intellectual property, and often owners either are not aware of these rights or just don't bother to protect this proprietary information that is critical to operating their ventures.

Protecting intellectual property takes time, effort, and money but is well worth it. Finding an experienced intellectual-property attorney to assist you in protecting your proprietary rights is essential.

Caveat

All government fees quoted are correct as of this writing but may be (and probably will be) increased annually. When submitting fees to the government, avoid the delay and disappointment of having your papers rejected on the technicality of an improper fee by contacting the appropriate agency and verifying the fee.

According to business start-up data and income tax returns, more than 250,000 individuals a year lose money on new technology-based products. Many spend over $50,000 without ever getting a product to market. Others have spent under $1,000 and raised over $1 million from investors to have successfully launched technology ventures. There are more similarities than differences between introducing a technology-based product with money and doing so without money. The challenges of commercialized technology and protecting intellectual property are highlighted in this chapter.

Smart Strategies for Protecting Intellectual Property

1. Use a logbook to document and describe in detail your invention, recording your ideas in ink. Then date and sign these pages as you go along, mark them "confidential," and have at least one noninventor witness and date them as "read and understood."

2. Conduct a novelty search at a library with a patent depository to determine if your idea or a related idea has already been patented, or engage a patent professional (not a marketing company) to provide such a search.

3. To obtain a valid patent in most other countries, file your U.S. foreign patent application before making any nonconfidential disclosures of your invention, and then file your foreign patent application within one year.

4. Before you disclose your ideas, protect them by having others sign a confidential disclosure agreement.

5. Protect your customer lists by treating them as a trade secret and requiring employees and agents to sign a confidential information agreement.

6. If you have an innovative or high-technology invention, consider trying to license it to an established company and collect royalties.

7. Establish a working relationship with a potential licensee before sending a blind solicitation letter or confidential disclosure agreement.

8. Buying the licensing rights to a well-known product or name can be a good way to start a venture.

9. To protect your invention while marketing it, after filing a patent application, use the words "patent pending" to warn others not to start copying your product during the patenting process.

10. Trademarks add value to your venture as intellectual property and also assist in raising capital.

11. Use a copyright notice to alert others that your material is not in the public domain.

12. Trade secrets can be sold or licensed and used as a financial strategy for increasing revenues.

13. Protect your proprietary information by stamping all relevant information "confidential." Keep it secure and advise others that it is confidential.

Patents and Inventions

How to Protect a Patent

Question

I have developed several patentable ideas for new products. I would like to know how to protect these ideas before I apply for or receive a patent, since I know this will be a very expensive process. I understand that if I don't protect my rights, they could later be lost. How should I proceed?

Answer

Keeping a patentable idea confidential until a patent is obtained is not an easy process. Protecting your patent rights is extremely important, especially before you take any ideas to the marketplace. The following five steps will assist you in protecting your patent idea:

1. Reduce your idea to writing and drawings, in ink if appropriate, by preparing clear and concise descriptions of the invention. Photographs may be used. Sign and date these documents.
2. Immediately mark all the documents "confidential." Each page should contain the word "confidential" on them. It is your responsibility to inform people that your idea is secret and confidential. Your state's trade secret laws will provide you with the necessary protection; but even so, do not disclose trade secrets indiscriminately or to people whom you do not trust.

3. Find at least one person who is technically competent to understand your idea. Have this person sign and date a statement indicating that he or she has read and understood each page of your idea. Make sure you inform this witness that your ideas are confidential.
4. Obtain a confidential disclosure agreement for valuable protection against the misuse of your idea. Essentially, such a document officially informs someone who is about to receive information about your idea that it is being disclosed in confidence with the clear understanding that the information is confidential, and that the person who receives the idea will keep it confidential.
5. Have the confidential disclosure agreement signed and dated by each party that you share your idea with, at least until the patent application is on file.

Legal advice is warranted at this stage from an experienced, competent patent attorney. You can obtain confidential disclosure agreement forms from your attorney or find them in the *Entrepreneur's Resource Handbook*. Or you can find a credible form in the back of the book *Patent It Yourself*.

A confidential disclosure agreement is a simple contract that any judge can look at to determine if there has been a breach of contract. An inventor has a stronger and more enforceable position if a confidential disclosure agreement has been signed.

The reason to involve a patent attorney at this stage is first to determine if your idea is patentable before you spend additional dollars. An inventor should have a novelty search done before applying for a patent. You can do much of the legwork yourself and work with your attorney to develop a specific business strategy. Even if it is determined that your idea is not patentable, you may be able to license your valuable, confidential trade secrets and know-how.

If you apply for a U.S. patent, it is a good business strategy to continue to keep your business ideas confidential until there is some good financial reason to make them public. Even though legally you do not have any enforceable rights without an issued patent, maintaining your idea as confidential gives you the power to control it until there is a need to make it public or until the patent is issued.

Last, using a confidential disclosure agreement and maintaining the invention as confidential gives you some bargaining power when approaching other parties about your ideas. If a company accepts your idea, you might be able to negotiate to have the company pay some or all of your patent costs.

So-called Poor Man's Patent is No Protection for Invention

Question

I have invented a new machine for manufacturing computer disks. I have documented my invention on paper, dated it, put it in a sealed envelope, and sent it by certified mail to myself. What's the next step to take to protect my invention and then begin to market it?

Answer

Forget the old tale about mailing a dated description of your invention to yourself by certified mail, because it has no value to the Patent Office or to the courts. Your certified document does not provide any credible evidence of the date of your invention.

Instead, contact the U.S. Department of Commerce Patent and Trademark Office, Washington, DC 20231, and ask for information about its disclosure document program. Also ask for material and brochures about the patenting process. Or call the Public Service Center, 703-557-INFO, with questions about the filing process. After receiving this information, send the office a description of your invention, along with a small fee, to establish the date of conception and ownership. The disclosure document is a description of the invention and its uses, which may include photos. The disclosure document will be maintained by the Patent Office for two years.

The person who files the disclosure document first and diligently reduces it to practice has the right to a patent. The document does not give you any patent rights or more time to file, nor does it allow you to use the words "patent pending" on the invention.

You have a two-year period in which to file a patent application that refers to your disclosure document. But you must demonstrate diligence in completing the invention and filing the application in order to prevail over another person who has made the same invention.

The next step is to undertake a novelty search to determine whether your concept or one that is obviously closely related has already been patented or published. The Patent and Trademark Office is located in Alexandria, Virginia; you can locate a patent depository at major public libraries or on the Internet at www.uspto.gov.

You can obtain a patent by yourself or use a professional patent attorney or agent. If you choose to try it on your own, refer to *Patent It Yourself* by David Pressman, which clearly outlines the patenting process. Consider contacting a seasoned patent attorney who is experienced in obtaining patents and can expedite the process.

Acquiring a patent can be an expensive project, so make sure you do it right the first time. Remember to keep good records of your invention, date the documents with a witness, and file the disclosure document early.

Consider applying for a provisional patent application, which allows the inventor to obtain an early filing date with few formalities and at a lower cost than filing a regular (nonprovisional) application. To file a provisional patent application you must fulfill the following five steps:

1. Prepare a clearly written description of the invention that is adequate to allow a person skilled in the art to practice the invention; however, it need not include traditional patent claims.
2. Present any drawings needed for someone to understand the invention; these drawings need not meet the traditional patent-application requirements.
3. Pay the filing fee of $75 for individuals who qualify for small-entity status ($150 for nonsmall entities).
4. Complete a cover sheet identifying the application as a provisional patent application; the invention title; the inventor's and any coinventors' names and residences; a docket number, if applicable; and a correspondence address.
5. If you are claiming small-entity status, present a declaration in support of that claim.

Trademark Protection

When to Consider Obtaining a Trademark

Question

I have started an employment insurance consulting company and was wondering if I should trademark my company logo. Any advice?

Answer

It is a good idea to trademark your company logo at the federal level, especially if you operate in other states besides your own and if you are planning to grow or to franchise your venture. Obtaining a trademark is not a costly, complicated, or lengthy process. It protects your trademark or service mark and distinguishes it from those of your competitors. It not only indicates the origin of the services, but it also can serve as a guarantee of quality.

Your intent to establish a mark can be shown by affixing the letters TM to a trademark or SM to a service mark. These symbols are usually smaller than the actual trademark and most often follow the mark. These marks can be registered with state or federal trademark offices. Service marks are used in the sale or marketing of services rather than products. Since your business provides a service, you would file for a service mark.

A trademark automatically acquires common law legal rights within the geographic area on goods, and nationally if advertised. If it is a word, it should be used as an adjective. It serves as a symbol that a business uses to identify and distinguish its products or services from others. According to U.S. law, a common law trademark is obtained by first use, and it is kept by continuous, proper use. Registering a mark with the U.S. Patent and Trademark Office is optional, but it enhances the odds of avoiding infringement and provides a stronger weapon for contesting infringement. Before a trademark user may file an application for federal registration, the user should place the mark on goods that are shipped or services that are sold in interstate commerce. However, it is now possible to file an intent to use application if there is a bona fide interest in using the mark in the near future.

Filing for a trademark is not the same as filing for a corporate or assumed business name. Registering a federal trademark involves completing a written application form, including a drawing of the work, and providing three specimens showing the actual use of the mark in connection with the goods or services. The filing fee is currently $245. Trademarks have a 10-year life and are renewable for unlimited additional 10-year periods unless abandoned. Proof of continued use and a $100 fee must be filed between the fifth and sixth years or the federal registration will be canceled. Issuance of a U.S. registration takes about 9 to 16 months.

Before applying for a federal trademark, you should perform a search to determine if another person or organization is using the same or a confusingly similar mark in the same channels of trade. If so, you probably cannot qualify for the same trademark. Determine your status before using your mark, since your marketing efforts could be wasted if you must change your mark or logo after you have been using it for some time. Names in use can be found in the *Trade Names Dictionary*, the *Thomas Register of American Manufacturers*, and in the Yellow

Pages. Database searches are also available through most libraries with federal depositories.

Once a trademark is federally registered, the ® symbol, or the words "registered in the U.S. Patent and Trademark Office," may be used. Failure to do so may prevent you from recovering damages for trademark infringement. To register a state trademark, contact your secretary of state.

Trademarks are an important marketing tool in that they help distinguish your goods from those of your competitors. Your business reputation allows you to introduce a new product or service more successfully by simply using your trademark on it. Trademarks add value to your venture as intellectual property and assist in raising capital. For example, the formula for Coca-Cola or the golden arches logo identifying McDonald's is an extremely valuable asset. You can also license the use of your trademark to others. Once you have protected it, you have the exclusive right to use it and seek protection from the courts if someone else infringes on it.

For further information, get a copy of *General Information Concerning Trademarks* from the Superintendent of Documents, U.S. Government Printing Office, Washington, D.C. 20402; telephone 202-783-3238. Or call the Trademark Office's automated telephone service at 703-557-4656 to obtain an application or ask questions. It is also advisable to have an experienced intellectual property attorney review your search and oversee the searching and registration process.

Copyright Protection

How to Obtain a Copyright

Question

I have just invented a board game called "The ABCs of State Capitals" and have obtained a copyright. Now I am looking for funding and someone, perhaps a partner, to promote and sell the game. How do I proceed?

Answer

Obtaining a copyright is the first step to take in marketing a board game. However, what are you copyrighting? Make certain that your copyright covers the layout of the board, the rules, the cards, and the box. This can all be accomplished in one application for a $20 fee. If you have forgotten to include any of these items, file a second application with another $20 application fee to the Registrar of Copyrights in the Library of Congress.

Once you have properly protected your idea, you have accomplished 5% of the work necessary to take a board game to the marketplace. You have only 95% of the additional work left and are entering the entrepreneurial stage. In order to secure funding and a possible partner, you must write a business plan to determine whether your idea is feasible. The business plan will reveal whether there is a market for "The ABCs of State Capitals." Investors will not give you capital if you cannot prove to them that there is a sufficient market for your game to yield a handsome profit.

Who are you going to target as your customers? What is your customer profile? How large is the market? Have you tested the game out with potential customers? Have you acquired any orders? What approach will you use for selling the game? What benefits does your game provide to customers? Is there any direct competition? How is your game board superior or unique to that of the competition? You must answer these and similar questions to prove your market and secure financing.

How much money will you need to undertake the venture, and how much money will be generated? What are potential sales the first year and for the next four years? When will you reach the cash break-even point? When will investors recoup their investment, and what type of return will be generated? What is the risk versus potential return on investment?

Last, what type of management is in place to achieve the goals you have set? What is your expertise in bringing this game to market and managing the business? Who else do you have on your management team?

All these questions should be answered in your business plan. Few investors or potential partners will talk with you until you can show them your plan, prove your market, determine how much money you will need, and project when you will become profitable. If you have not yet written a business plan, consult a book such as *Program for Writing Winning Business Plans*, or take a course specially designed to teach you how to write one.

What Copyrighting Protects

Question

I recently found a game on the market called "The ABC's of State Capitals." I have a copyrighted game that I am selling named "The ABCs of

States and Capitals." How can someone else copyright the name of my game when I have prior copyright? Is this fair?

Answer

Your copyright does not cover the name of your game. It covers the elements of the game itself such as the box, the rules, and the board. If you wanted to protect the name of your game, you should have trademarked it.

Copyrights protect authors of literary works such as art, books, music, motion pictures, videotapes, photographs, articles, software programs, games, and magazines. Registration is a low-cost procedure administered by the U.S. Copyright Office. According to copyright law, a literary work is automatically protected from the time of its creation, but it is best to include a copyright notice on the material.

Keep in mind that a copyright does not protect ideas. It simply gives you the right to prevent others from copying the particular way in which you express your ideas. If you want to protect your ideas, restrict access by making them trade secrets, to be disclosed only under the terms of a written confidential disclosure agreement.

To be protected by copyright, your work must satisfy three requirements. First, it must be original; second, it must be incorporated in something tangible; third, it must fall within one or more of the categories of works provided for in the Copyright Act. Use the copyright symbol, which can be ©, the word "copyright," or the abbreviation "copyr.," or use ℗ for audio works. Also include the year in which the material was first distributed publicly and the copyright owner's name or an abbreviation by which the owner's name can be recognized. You are not required to use a copyright notice on your materials, but it is desirable to do so for protection. Also include a warning statement like "All rights reserved" (which also provides protection in South America) or "No part of this material may be reproduced without permission." Place the notice on your material where it can be seen by an ordinary user under normal conditions (e.g., on the title page).

It is also advisable to officially register your copyright by filing the proper form, which can be obtained from the Registrar of Copyrights, Library of Congress, Washington, D.C. 20559. The cost is $20, and you can do it yourself quite easily.

It takes about three to four months to have your application processed before you receive a certification of registration. A copyright is good for 50 years after the death of the author. If you need additional information, call the U.S. Copyright Office hotline at 202-287-9100. Another excellent resource is *The Complete Copyright Protection Kit,* which contains up-to-date information on how to register, transfer, and legally enforce a copyright and how to avoid violating rights if you use someone else's material. The kit costs $25 and also includes various copyright forms.

Licensing Inventions

How to License a Product to Raise Capital

Question

I have an invention that I would like to sell to a manufacturing company. How do I protect my idea when contacting potential companies about my new invention? How can I obtain a licensing agreement?

Answer

Sometimes, trying to protect your invention before you have applied for a patent can be tricky, and it may be impossible. Many inventors will send a confidential disclosure agreement to a potential licensee thinking that the other party will sign the form, and thereby their idea is protected. A confidential disclosure agreement, in its simplest form, is merely a contract by which the recipient of the information agrees to keep your idea or invention a secret and not to use it.

However, many companies will not sign these agreements unless you have already established a relationship with them. Instead, most send back another agreement for you to sign, stating that the information that you have provided to them is not confidential. They are under no obligation to protect your idea and can use it unless it has been protected by a valid patent, trademark, or copyright. It is recommended that you do not sign such an agreement except as a very last resort, unless you have an allowed patent pending or an issued patent. In the absence of a confidential agreement or a patent, you have no property rights to license. Once you have disclosed your idea or invention without a confidential agreement, anyone who had previously promised to keep it a secret may be released from that duty.

If you have an invention that is innovative and has valuable technology, try to negotiate a patent license agreement. Licensing is an excellent strategy for an inventor to generate revenues without much risk while avoiding costly start-up investments. Licensing gives rights to an entity to make and sell the innovation in return for cash royalties.

Manufacturing companies may sign a licensing agreement with an inventor who has a proven track record and business experience. If you do not have these qualifications, refrain from sending a blind letter about your invention without first establishing a relationship or contact with a potential manufacturer. Once a relationship is established, send a confidential disclosure agreement. Send such letters simultaneously to a number of potentially interested manufacturers. This strategy saves you months of waiting for a possible disappointing response before writing to the next potential licensee. You can get confidential disclosure agreement forms from an attorney or in the books *Patent It Yourself* and *Patents, Copyrights, and Trademarks*.

Keep in mind that negotiating a licensing agreement is a complicated procedure. Seldom does the technology transfer take place in a lump-sum payment. Instead, you will probably have a continuing relationship with your licensee. Such an agreement must be carefully worded and should involve a patent or technology transfer attorney to ensure protection and fairness for both parties. Work with local experts or find a reputable licensing expert or broker who works only on a contingency basis and receives payment from a percentage of the deal. This professional may charge a finder's fee or take an ongoing share of your royalties.

✔ COURTNEY'S SMART TIP
Avoid invention-marketing companies that charge large up-front evaluation fees, prepare a report touting the invention, and then make minimal efforts to commercialize it.

A good place to start looking for a licensee is within your industry. The *Thomas Register of American Manufacturers* is an excellent source for names; your local chamber of commerce and business-support centers can also provide leads. Sometimes, local venture capitalists and bankers might know of potential licensees.

How to Negotiate a Licensing Agreement

Question

Several years ago I started a company to develop sports-related products. I took different ideas, productionized the design, designed and built the prototype and production tooling. I am seeking companies or people to license my products. My problem is locating companies or people interested in entering into a license agreement. How can I find potential licensees?

Answer

You are right on track. The first step in licensing is finding a company or person interested in your product idea. The best place to begin is at your local library. Look through the *Thomas Register of American Manufacturers* for potential names of companies in your industry.

This resource book lists industry manufacturer names and addresses and thousands of different businesses. Also look at Dun & Bradstreet's *Reference Book of Corporate Management* which gives detailed biographical descriptions of many leading companies and their principal officers. All communications with a potential licensee should be directed to top management.

Next, go to the store aisles where your competitors' products are displayed. Most packages give the name and location of a producer. Make a list of these competing companies. They may be interested in expanding their product lines and are a good source for a potential license.

Try to find out as much about licensing arrangements as possible. Organizations that deal with licensing issues include the Licensing Industry Merchandisers Association, the National Association of Small Business Investment Companies, and the National Venture Capital Association. Your local chamber of commerce, small-business development centers, venture capitalists, and banks can also assist with licensing leads.

After you have located businesses in your industry that might be interested in a license agreement, you must determine what you want from such an agreement. Will you ask for any up-front money to pay for out-of-pocket expenses for developing, prototyping, patenting, or other associated costs? Success in negotiating for up-front money will depend largely upon how badly the company wants your idea.

How large a royalty percentage will you ask for? Five% of the wholesale price is generally a good starting point. A fair royalty should give you from about one-quarter to about one-third of the actual profits. What type of exclusivity will you be willing to negotiate for? Be cautious about giving away your exclusivity rights. Consider using exclusivity rights as a bargaining wedge. In most cases, if you can find one licensee, you will probably be able to find more.

How much do you want to be personally involved in marketing the product or overseeing its production? Should you consider hiring a lawyer to represent you during negotiations? If the potential licensing agreement is complicated, it is wise to have legal counsel represent you.

After you have answered these questions and researched licensing arrangements, begin writing query letters to potential licensees.

Incorporate information on the demand for your product, including any marketing research and/or testing results. Identify potential purchasers. Describe the applications and alternatives for the product. List any proprietary rights such as potential or existing patents, trademarks, or copyrights. Explain your qualifications and business background.

Most important, demonstrate how the licensee will benefit from your product. Writing query letters can take considerable time, and you will probably receive your share of "we're not interested" letters. Don't get too excited about receiving a letter of interest. Often, the first interested party will not be your last. Avoid making a hasty decision in signing a contract. A sound licensing agreement will benefit both you and the licensee.

Trade Secrets

How to Keep a Recipe a Trade Secret

Question

I have created a new dog biscuit recipe that has a unique shape, name, ingredients, and appearance. I need to protect my idea before marketing the product and selling it to a major manufacturer in the pet food industry. I have read some books on patents, copyrights, and trademarks but remain confused. Which one of these will protect the recipe, the shape of the biscuit, and the name? I also understand that I cannot get a patent unless I have marketed my product for a time. How do I protect my idea until it gets registered?

Answer

Protecting an entrepreneur's intellectual property can be tricky and complicated. That is why many entrepreneurs seek legal counsel from a patent attorney. You can do much of the legwork yourself and save considerable money.

You could copyright your recipe by contacting the Registrar of Copyrights, U.S. Copyright Office, Library of Congress, Washington, D.C. 20559, by sending in an application with a $20 filing fee. However, copyrighting your recipe will not give you much protection and will make it available to anyone who wants to research the archives. A competitor could change a few minor ingredients, and you probably would not have any recourse against this tactic.

A better approach would be to make your dog biscuit recipe a trade secret. You'll need to exercise a great deal of control to keep your recipe a trade secret and ensure that only a select few have access to it. Take every precaution to keep the recipe a secret. If possible, do not reveal the entire recipe to one person, so that no one except you knows all the ingredients.

There are no filing fees or legal expenses for establishing a trade secret. The law recognizes your trade secret as your intellectual property and protects it as such. You must document that you have made the recipe a trade secret and keep the formula in a safe place. If you allow the recipe to lie around unprotected, the court is apt to tell you that you must not consider the information to be of much value. You must be able to show the efforts you have made to protect your recipe. Use a confidential disclosure agreement that allows you to reveal your ideas in confidence without fear of losing your trade secret status. Then, place specific provisions in employees' agreements so that they will neither disclose to others nor use for their own purposes any trade secrets they acquire while working for you.

✔ COURTNEY'S SMART TIP

Protect a trade secret by stamping all relevant information "confidential."

If the shape of the dog biscuit is unique, you might be able to obtain a design patent on it from the U.S. Department of Commerce, Patent and Trademark Office, Washington, D.C. 20231. The Government Printing Office, Washington, D.C. 20402, publishes *General Information Concerning Patents* for $2. Or consult *Patent It Yourself,* an excellent resource book.

It will be necessary to conduct a patent search. You can conduct the search yourself if your local library has a patent depository for the U.S. Patent and Trademark Office. Or you could contact a professional patent-search firm or patent agent, or have a patent attorney perform the search. Lay as much of the groundwork as you can, and then work with a patent attorney to develop a specific business strategy. To protect your dog biscuit while marketing it, you can use the words "patent pending" on the box once your patent application is on file. This provides a warning until you receive a patent.

Last, if the name for your dog biscuit is truly distinctive, you can trademark it. Federal registration is not needed for a trademark to be protected. However, it is advisable that you obtain one by contacting the U.S. Patent and Trademark Office, cited earlier. Include the trademark symbol ™ or ˢᴹ (if the mark identifies a service) to indicate your claim of ownership, even if no federal trademark application is pending.

Remember, protecting your intellectual property is only 5% of the work necessary to take your dog biscuit to market. But it is an essential ingredient to launching a successful dog biscuit business.

Treat Your Customer Lists as Trade Secrets

Question

Two of my employees recently quit and went to work for one of my competitors. Now I have begun to lose old customers and find that this competitor has changed its pricing structure to pattern mine. What can I do to protect my pricing policies and customer lists?

Answer

It is very likely that your former employees have used pricing and customer information to compete with you. If you have never made this information a trade secret, advised them it was a secret, and had your employees sign a confidential information agreement, then you probably don't have much recourse. Employees who leave your company can easily use such information in their new jobs. Or they could venture out on their own and start a competing company. To avoid this problem in the future, consider designing a comprehensive trade secret protection program for your company.

Trade secrets are any proprietary information used in the course of business to gain an advantage in manufacture or commercialization of products or services. They can be formulas, devices, patterns, techniques, customer lists, sales forecasts, databases, manufacturing processes, or compiled information that has a specific business application. They must have economic value, they must be secret, and you must attempt to protect them. The most significant factors in determining whether your confidential information receives legal protection are (1) the degree to which you take steps to protect the information and (2) the ease of obtaining the information from other sources.

Trade secrets are not covered by any federal statute but are recognized under a governing body of federal and state common laws and statutes. To be classified as a trade secret, the information must not be generally known in the trade.

In order to keep customer and price lists a trade secret, you must keep the information secret and take precautions to keep it secret. First, establish policies on identifying and maintaining trade secret information. Second, require employees to sign a confidential disclosure agreement at the time they are hired that protects against then giving out trade secrets either while they are employed or after they leave the company. Last, mark these documents "confidential" or "secret." Then employees or others coming into contact with the information will immediately be put on notice of its confidential nature and of their duty to avoid disclosure.

Confidential documents should be locked in a vault or other secure location. Trade secret information stored on or accessible by computer must be protected from disclosure to unauthorized parties. Build passwords into your computer system to prevent unauthorized access.

Dispose of trade secrets documents carefully. Don't just throw them in the trash with other, nonsensitive material. Consider purchasing a shredding machine. Also, monitor and limit the duplication of these documents. Use the exit interview to remind departing employees of their confidentiality obligation.

Understanding the details and following these steps are the keys to effectively protecting confidential information. You must be able to demonstrate that you have taken every precaution to maintain such information as a secret, or you could lose legal protection. Also, any visiting sales representatives, vendors, customers, inspectors, or others needing access to such information must be informed of its secrecy and sign a confidential disclosure agreement. One overlooked way trade secrets are lost is through conventions, trades shows, seminars, casual conversations, or similar activities.

Consult *The Complete Guide to Business Agreements*, the *Entrepreneur's Resource Handbook*, or other business form books that contain confidential disclosure agreements. Revise the sample form to fit your situation and then have your attorney review it before implementation. The form should indicate that you consider this information a vital part of your business. These agreements may allow you to stop any signee from using the information. Laws vary from state to state, so check with an intellectual-property attorney.

Last, trade secrets can be sold or licensed and used as a financial strategy for increasing revenues. In today's competitive environment, your continued success may well depend on your ability to protect your valuable trade secrets. Continuous, systematic, and diligent monitoring is essential.

Agreement Keeps Trade Secrets from Competitors

Question

I own a corporate-training company and have developed a copyrighted management-leadership program that I sell and then train others to deliver. Because it has become very successful, I need to protect it against these clients learning my system and then using this know-how to start a competing business. What can I do?

Answer

The best and easiest way to protect your proprietary rights when working with contractors is to have a written contract, known as a nondisclosure agreement (also called a confidentiality disclosure agreement), governing the disclosure. Such agreements prohibit others from using your confidential information or trade secrets for their own benefit or divulging that information to someone else.

Utilize a nondisclosure agreement if you have confidential or proprietary information that your employees have access to, and with third parties if you have to show confidential information to others outside your company.

These agreements are often used to protect technical information but can also be used to protect client lists, methods of doing business, designs, formulations, and similar intangibles that give you a fair advantage over the competition.

Nondisclosure agreements cover situations where valuable information is presented to parties who, in the absence of a promise not to use the information, might use it in a manner that will hurt your business or for their own financial gain. These agreements are legally binding contracts that obligate the person signing it to hold information in confidence.

When the agreement is signed, it becomes a binding contract giving the originator of the idea the right to commence a lawsuit to stop the unauthorized use of the information or to sue for damages for breach of contract if the information disclosed is used without permission.

Nondisclosure agreements should be used whenever proprietary information is shared. It is appropriate when the information is in the idea or concept stage as well as when the originator has a pending patent application.

In the agreement, you must originally define the trade secret in general terms. After the nondisclosure is signed, define specifically what you consider to be the company's trade secrets or proprietary information. It should contain language strong enough to show a court that you consider your proprietary information a vital part of your business and that an injunction or monetary damages for breach of contract should be in order. Once your nondisclosure agreement is signed, you can go to court for a restraining order or an injunction on a simple breach of contract to enforce its terms.

To be entitled to protection for your proprietary information, you must treat it in a protective manner, for example, by stamping all relevant information "confidential," keeping the material secure, and advising all persons who have access to it that it is confidential.

"Work for Hire" Clause Clarifies Role of Employer

Question

I have a computer and software industry consulting company that has developed some unique and valuable inventions as well as software. I now have the opportunity to enter into employment as a technology-development consultant with a service company that provides computer-related solutions for its customers. This position may require developing new software and technology. The president of the service company asked me to sign a technology agreement that states, in effect, that any software (copyrighted material) and inventions that I develop that are related to the company business belong to them. I don't want to give up my past intellectual property or future developments. But if I do not sign the technology agreement, I will not be hired and will miss out on a great opportunity. What should I do?

Answer

It must be very frustrating for you to contemplate the possible loss of your technology and current intellectual property. To start, provide your prospective employer with a detailed list of your inventions and software, in generic terms. Request that they be excluded from that company's ownership rights under the technology agreement. There's a good chance the company will agree to this request.

Next, ask that the terms of your employment agreement limit the company's ownership rights to items related to the company's current and planned future business. With this approach, the ownership in your existing and future nonrelated company developments will remain yours.

Every company has ownership rights in the inventions and copyrightable material that any employee develops within the scope of his or her employment. A company's ownership of such copyrightable material comes into existence as work for hire under the U.S. copyright statute.

The ownership of a copyrighted work does not necessarily vest in the creator of the work. According to the work made for hire definition in the copyright statute, an employer will be considered the author of a work prepared by an employee within the scope of a full-time employment relationship. Similarly, in the case of nonemployees, in nine specific categories of commissioned works defined by the copyright statute, the party who commissions the work will be considered the author if the parties have agreed in writing before the work is initiated that the work is made for hire. In the absence of an employment relationship or an agreement in writing for a work in one of the nine specific categories that the work is made for hire, the party who creates the work will retain copyright ownership.

The ownership of technical inventions and patents made by an employee are automatically transmitted to the employer as a matter of common law established from previous court decisions regardless of whether an employee signs an agreement. The technology agreement the company president is asking you to sign merely clarifies and simplifies the employer's ability to enforce its ownership rights. Many companies want new employees to understand right from the start who owns intellectual property developed during employment to avoid potential misunderstanding during the employment relationship.

You may want to put an appropriate fence around your current and future nonrelated company technology to protect it. Then, you would be safe in signing the company's technology agreement.

Invention Marketing

Beware of Invention-Marketing Companies

Question

I have come up with an invention that I submitted to a company back East. They like it and asked me whether I wanted additional research. I agreed, for $2,000. The research study, 26 pages long, contained only glowing reports. Now, the company wants to sell my invention and is asking for an additional $5,000. However, I am unable to come up with the money. Securing a loan from any financial institution would be doubtful. What do you suggest I do?

Answer

Many companies, most located in the Northeast with local representatives, work with inventors to allegedly help them introduce new products to the marketplace. Beware of such companies, and think twice before sending them any money. The problem is that most of these organizations are long on promises but short on delivery. Here's how they operate:

First, these companies advertise to inventors, offering to research new products to determine potential sales in the marketplace. These initial reports, like the one you received, always paint a rosy picture of potential success. For the most part, they contain demographic information about potential customers, an estimation of the size of the market, and examples of similar successful products, including yearly sales volume. The summary highlights the great potential of your invention and the hundreds of thousands of dollars you could earn.

The charge for a first report ranges from $700 to $800. Unfortunately, this lengthy report you just paid for contains information you could have obtained yourself. The boilerplate language in such studies allows companies to produce them quickly, with little research. These types of reports are always attractively and professionally packaged, and bound in a hard cover with your name embossed in gold or silver.

The next step is enticing you to go for the big plunge and pay between $4,000 and $8,000 for an in-depth marketing and sales plan to bring your invention to the marketplace. The second report is filled with promises of potential success and forecasts of earning much money. However, few of these companies ever deliver on their promises. Instead, they sell you encouragement and potential that are seldom realized.

✔ COURTNEY'S SMART TIP

To determine whether an invention-marketing company is legitimate, ask one of its representatives for at least three references from other inventors in your state whom the company has represented. Contact those sources.

Talk with other inventors who used a particular marketing company to ascertain what kind of services were provided. Was the inventor satisfied? Was the invention brought successfully to the marketplace? How much money did it cost? Is the return on investment worthwhile?

Invention-marketing companies often say they cannot give out names of past clients because of the confidentiality issues surrounding their inventions. But ask yourself how such companies can successfully market a product if it is confidential. If the invention has been patented, confidentiality is not relevant. Any company that refuses to give you references in your state probably has a poor track record. Checking with your local Better Business Bureau is not likely to reveal any meaningful information. The majority of other customers are out of state and seldom send reports of dissatisfaction to the Better Business Bureau. Consequently, the company probably shows a clean record.

A few legitimate companies *do* deliver, but they operate very differently. They provide the up-front money to bring your invention to market. They negotiate with inventors and pay a royalty for products. Usually, they do not invest in unproven inventions or unproven inventors. They are very selective in investing in new inventions. Get references and investigate the company before you invest any more money.

Carefully Check Invention Firms before Signing On

Question

A few years ago, I paid almost $5,000 to a company that was supposed to get me a patent and help me market my idea. It filed for bankruptcy, and I subsequently received three checks totaling $50 from the bankruptcy court as a payment for my claims. I would like to pursue my idea and learn how to go about it without investing a huge sum.

Answer

The problem you experienced is quite typical. Inventors often do not know how to obtain a patent or how to market their products. Instead, they turn to invention-marketing companies. But the invention-marketing industry is saturated with companies that charge high up-front fees and deliver little or nothing, as you experienced. Verify all claims made by invention-marketing companies.

The Federal Trade Commission (FTC) has shown that fewer than 1% of inventors who use invention-marketing firms receive any income from their inventions, even though they pay fees of up to $10,000.

If you are thinking about using an invention-marketing company to take your invention from the idea stage to the market stage, determine if the firm has had experience with ideas in your technology field and what their success rate is.

Ask which patents the firm has secured and request the names and addresses of these clients, including the type of idea patented. Then verify this information with the inventors named on those patents and find out how satisfied they were with the patent work.

Next, determine if the inventions have been marketed successfully. Ask for a list of products that the invention-marketing company has taken from the idea stage to the marketing stage. Obtain the names of the product owners and call them to find out if the marketing efforts of the invention-marketing firm were satisfactory. Ask how much money they have earned from their inventions.

Request the names and locations of the manufacturers producing the inventions, as well as the names of distributors. Determine how successfully these inventions have been marketed and sold.

Finally, check with the FTC, the Better Business Bureau in your area, the consumer fraud division of your local district attorney's office, and the state attorney general's office for complaints against companies you are considering working with.

If the invention-marketing company asks you to sign a contract, ask whether it provides a refund if you are dissatisfied with its services. Check to ensure that any clients you are referred to are not employees of the company.

You may find that the invention-marketing firm will turn you away after asking such questions. Since most have poor track records, they cannot or will not provide answers to your questions.

Also, don't accept the excuse that the information you are requesting is confidential. A reputable company would have no problems answering these types of questions and giving you referrals to satisfied clients.

After your investigation, you will probably decide that it is better to start the patenting process with a patent attorney and market your own invention with local assistance.

How to Get a Technology-Based Product to Market

Question

I have invented a new educational software product that will revolutionize how college courses are taught. I don't have a lot of money to market it. How can I quickly get this product to market?

Answer

First, evaluate the potential of your product idea by addressing the following questions:

- Is the product's technology simple to understand and explain?
- Will potential customers and investors quickly grasp what it does, how it works, and its benefits?
- Does your product have a benefit potential that customers want? If so, what information can you provide to prove that prospects want it?
- Can you build models and prototypes that look like the finished product to prove it works?

If you can't afford to build a low-cost prototype, you will need to find an investor. You can't do proper market research without prototypes. Building a prototype will reveal potential flaws that need correcting. It is a good way to perfect your software.

Once you have a working prototype, it's time to test the market. Research the competition to see if there are any similar offerings. If there are many competitors, you will face great resistance. Also, markets dominated by a few competitors are difficult to enter. Finding market insiders to assist you can help you discover how to best market your software.

Decide what features are unique about your software and why people should buy it. Also, consider how easy it will be to find potential customers.

After evaluating market conditions, determine what it will cost to manufacture your software; if you can find similar software with the same complexity, get quotes from those manufactures. Having a prototype will generate more accurate quotes. If you can't afford to produce it, try to find a manufacturer that is willing to absorb some of the start-up costs.

Now you are ready to estimate what your software can be sold for. Check what competitive products cost. Can you add features that will enhance your software's perceived value? Is the perceived value at least four to five times its manufacture cost, or can it be produced for less than 25% of its perceived value?

The following are some questions you should answer before proceeding any further:

- Do you know how you will distribute your product?
- Is there an existing distribution network through which your product can be sold?
- Does the distribution network have sufficient sales support?
- Is the market size of the distribution network large enough to justify the costs of bringing the product to market?

- Will your sales forecasts yield enough profit to justify your time and effort? Your software should have a large enough profit potential for you to go forward.

If you have answered yes to all these questions, prepare a feasibility plan to explore further whether you should pursue bringing your new software product to market. This is a good way to determine if a new product idea can be successful. There is no quick way to commercialize technology—it takes proper research, testing, forecasting, and planning.

Selling Yourself Puts Teeth into Marketing Idea

Question

I have a new idea for a dental product and have contacted several dental manufacturers about my idea but haven't had any success. What am I doing wrong, and how can I get someone to respond to my product idea?

Answer

Successfully packaging and selling a new product idea is an art that takes careful planning and execution. Before product entrepreneurs can sell a new idea, they must be able to sell themselves to potential manufacturers as competent, knowledgeable, and reliable business professionals.

If you have had previous experience bringing a product to market, highlight this experience, showing that you were able to complete a project successfully. If not, you have to demonstrate your perseverance, which is a difficult intangible quality to prove. You could point to your track record with other career accomplishments.

Making initial contacts during the development phase is critical. Contact key people and establish a working relationship with them before you need their help in manufacturing or marketing your new product. Start a file of key contacts, including a person's name, address, phone number, and capacity for assistance. Summarize your conversations and action steps and follow up on leads.

Potential manufacturers want to see that you have thoroughly researched your idea and can prove there is a market for it. Show that you understand how the industry and market operate. They will want evidence that you have obtained input from potential users of the product. Indicate that you have listened to user feedback and addressed the product's shortcomings.

Find comparative products in your target market and gather critical marketing information. Ask contacts to evaluate your product against others. Record their responses. Decide how your product is superior and pitch its advantages. How is it unique? How will it benefit the user? How does the price compare to the competition? These questions will help you better estimate potential sales volume and profitability.

The components necessary to package an idea before it can be sold are the initial product materials and supporting documentation. Initial product materials should include a product description, its features and benefits, manufacturing requirements, and drawings of both what the product will eventually look like and how it will be used. Try to get both drawings on one sheet of paper.

If possible, develop several different prototypes that illustrate that you devoted time to proving that the product works. Last, prepare an advertising layout, including a drawing or sketch of the product with graphics. You don't have to provide professional drawings or ad layouts.

Supporting documentation contains key marketing information that shows that your new product idea will sell. Develop a marketing plan that includes industry background information, potential market size, market trends, target markets, competitive analysis, and projected retail price.

An excellent resource is *Bringing Your Product to Market* by Don Debelak, published by John Wiley and Sons, Inc.

Pitfalls to Avoid

1. Relying on a U.S. patentability search by itself as an indication that the invention will not infringe on another person's current patent.

2. Overspending on defending a patent or deciding to take an infringer to court.

3. Disclosing your invention to others without first having a signed confidential disclosure agreement or filing for a patent.

4. Contracting with invention-marketing companies that charge a large up-front fee, make minimal efforts to commercialize your invention, and have no satisfied clients that they will identify.

5. Hiring an inexperienced attorney to assist you with protecting your ideas, materials, inventions, and so forth, instead of using an intellectual-property attorney.

6. Not checking for the availability of your company mark or logo before using it, and not including it on all your marketing materials.

7. Sending a blind letter to an unknown person as a potential licensee, asking them to sign a confidential disclosure agreement.

8. Mailing a dated description of your invention to yourself by certified mail, which has no value to the patent office.

9. Making a hasty decision in signing a licensing contract.

The Good News

Protecting intellectual property is not difficult, but it does take time. Doing so can become a great asset to your business if done properly. Always consult an expert intellectual-property attorney to ensure that you are properly protected.

7

Marketing Analysis and Planning

Overview

Marketing mistakes are made because entrepreneurs do not thoroughly research their markets and customers to discover the best ways to penetrate different market segments. If any market-research data is collected, it is mostly demographic information, which is a good start but only one input. Lifestyle, buying habits, and psychographic information is either ignored or only superficially researched, yet it provides some of the richest data. Visiting the library and getting to know your local business librarians is one of the best ways to start. To become more familiar with your industry, contact trade associations for both demographic and psychographic market data. Avoid collecting all your market research information on-line. It is equally important to collect "street-smart" market data by talking to current and/or potential customers, suppliers, and manufacturing representatives and by attending trade shows. Consider using focus group interviews to gain customer insights and perspectives.

Also learn as much as you can about your competition by contacting a competitor or two outside of your geographic area. They will provide a wealth of information. Don't forget to contact your competitors' customers to determine what they are satisfied or dissatisfied with.

After you have collected and analyzed the characteristics of your industry, it's time to prepare a marketing plan that will identify the goals you want to achieve within a certain time frame and list strategies of how you will achieve these goals. At this point, measure the effectiveness of your marketing plan.

Smart Market Analysis and Planning Strategies

1. Become familiar with computer databases and the Internet to collect industry information about your market.
2. Learn as much as you can about your competitors, including their strengths and weaknesses.
3. Turn to the yellow pages to identify your competitors.
4. Use focus groups to gain customer insight and develop innovative marketing techniques.
5. Use mystery shoppers in your store to evaluate your sales staff.
6. Develop an index-card profile on each of your customers, noting demographic information and purchasing habits.
7. Build your own mailing list and use database marketing techniques.
8. Quantify your marketing goals whenever possible.
9. Make your marketing goals specific, measurable, and time specific.
10. If appropriate, introduce your products on home-shopping networks.
11. Use database marketing to track customers and prospects.
12. Ask for referrals from your customers to develop new sales leads and then send a thank-you note for every referral.
13. Ask customers for testimonial letters to use in your marketing materials.
14. Include a response mechanism in your marketing to measure its effectiveness.

Marketing Research

Gathering Information about Competitors

Question

A couple of years ago, I started a monogram shop in a shopping mall. I have found myself struggling to generate profits and expand my market. How can I investigate my competition and learn more about how better to compete with them?

Answer

Learning as much as you can about your competition is an excellent entrepreneurial strategy and a marketing must. Ideally, you should obtain this information before you open and while you are writing your business plan. Some entrepreneurs work for their competition before starting a new business. They try to learn all the ins and outs of the business ahead of time.

One of the best strategies to learn more about your competition is to locate a competitor at a distance. Often, your direct competitors will not divulge much information about their operation. You will be more likely to obtain significant industry and competitive information from a competitor outside your geographic area. Try to find several competitors in other states who operate the same type of business in a similar demographic area.

For example, contact your industry trade association and inquire about the industry leaders with a comparable business in another part of the country. Call or visit those entrepreneurs. Because they will not view you as a direct competitor, they are likely to share a wealth of information with you.

Go to your library and access an information database that contains an industry periodical and journal index. Work with the business librarian to properly search this data source. Look through INFO-TRAC, a database that lists published articles providing both industry and competitive information.

Go to your local city hall to see if any financing statements have been filed on your competitors' pledging collateral. Or check with the secretary of state to see if any liens have been placed on their collateral. Publicly held companies publish annual and interim reports with various governmental bodies. The New York Stock Exchange listing applications and the Securities and Exchange Commission's 10-K and 10-Q forms include offering circulars for new security issues. Some states publish an annual statement of condition about the corporation issuing new securities.

For privately held companies, talk to potential suppliers. Ask them what services your competitor provides. Try to estimate how much volume they can handle. Talk to dealers, reps, and distributors. Find out what they think about competing firms. Sometimes these people enjoy talking about the problems and concerns they have—for example, the problems they have encountered with late deliveries.

Find former employees who have worked for your competitors. Ask them about the problems at your competitor's place of business. Do some comparison shopping. Analyze your competitor's place of business. The more information you obtain, the better prepared you will be to plan your marketing strategy and to launch your new business.

Another strategy is to seek out contact with your competitors' customers. Try to determine what they like about the business and what aspects they are dissatisfied with. If possible, conduct a telephone survey or attend a meeting where competitors' customers will be present. Attend a local or national trade association meeting or convention where you will find a variety of competitors and suppliers. Introduce yourself, ask questions, and listen. Finally, ask your banker, accountant, or attorney for information about your competition or your industry.

✔ COURTNEY'S SMART TIP
Become a detective and learn as much as you can about your competition to differentiate your product and/or service.

Once you launch your venture, continue accumulating competitive information. Projecting market trends and determining your competitors' strengths and weaknesses is an ongoing activity that can give you a competitive edge in the marketplace.

Using Trade Associations

Question

I am planning to open a gourmet chocolate store. I have started to write my business plan, and I am searching for marketing information about my competitors and demographic data on potential customers. What available sources of information are there? Where should I begin?

Answer

There are many different types of organizations and publications to contact to obtain market statistics and demographic information. The U.S. Department of Commerce covers all 50 states and has 47 offices throughout the country. It has tons of data at its disposal, both published and unpublished. Typically, it can provide information by industry, size, and geographic location. Specify whether you are looking for local, domestic, or international data so your call can be directed to the appropriate agency. There may be no charge, or they may charge a nominal fee, depending on the complexity of your request.

Trade associations are also an excellent source for obtaining industry-specific information for marketing statistics and financial data. They provide information on gross industry sales, broken down further into major product categories. In addition, trade associations furnish industry guidelines that can assist you in tracking your business.

Much of the information is reported in percentages, which makes it even more helpful to compare your performance to similar businesses. The percentages are broken down by size of business, sales volume, and geographic area. For example, you can find data on average inventory turn for your type of business, typical gross and net margins for comparable ventures, and average sales and marketing expenditures.

The key is to find the appropriate association for your business. Go to your local library and examine Volume 1 of the *Encyclopedia of Associations*. It contains detailed information on various trade associations, including their addresses, telephone numbers, membership information, and the like.

Write to or call the major trade association(s) relevant to your venture. Ask them what type of data they publish. Inquire as to whether there will be a charge. If you can befriend someone on the association staff, you may be able to obtain meaningful industry information they do not publish. Trade associations are membership based and usually get very excited about new businesses joining their industry. They will try hard to convince you to join up so they can collect a membership fee, which pays for their overhead and operating costs.

Joining appropriate trade associations is money well spent. They have membership lists of like businesses and publish trade journals that contain excellent information on current trends, market surveys, and forecasts in your industry. Such trade journals are a good source to obtain free publicity for your business. Editors write feature stories about entrepreneurs, new products and/or services, and other human-interest stories.

Try to get to know the trade magazine editors who might write about your venture or provide a wealth of additional internal information about the industry. Read the advertisements in trade journals for valuable information about competitors and their products.

Attend the national and regional meetings of trade associations to obtain other types of industry statistics. You can identify major competitors, discover leaders in the industry, meet suppliers and distributors, and learn about the future directions of your industry. You can also talk to experts in your field. Attending some technical sessions will reveal information about future products and new technology. All this information can be yours for the price of a ticket to the annual meeting. Many associations hold trade shows in conjunction with the annual meeting.

Expanding Your Business by Researching the Industry

Question

I have come up with several ideas for selling a new version of backpacks. I am not a designer, craftsperson, or seamstress. But I do want to try to sell these backpacks. I have temporarily named my versions "Brat Packs." What I need are feedback, constructive criticism, and a positive next-step direction. I have not been able to find information from my local Better Business Bureau, chamber of commerce, or other resources. What direction should I pursue as a next step?

Answer

First, you need to nail down both a wholesale and a retail price. How much will it cost you to have these backpacks made? With whom can you subcontract to make the backpacks? How many can they produce? Will you need backup subcontractors?

Begin by finding a reliable and competent subcontractor to produce your backpacks. Ask for recommendations from other entrepreneurs selling similar products. Negotiate with the subcontractor to make several prototypes to take to market. Establish a relationship with the subcontractor to begin making the backpacks for you as soon as you have secured orders.

In the meantime, investigate your competition. Find out what similar-quality backpacks are selling for. Can you be competitive with other backpacks on the marketplace? Will you be able to make the profit margin you want? If you find you have a competitively priced product, you are now ready to go to prospective retailers.

Identify retailers who might be interested in selling your backpacks. Make appointments to see them. These retailers are probably the best source for providing direct feedback about your product. If there are problems or objections to your backpacks, determine whether these objections can be overcome. Go back to your subcontractor and revise your prototype. If you do not encounter any negative comments, ask these retailers to purchase your backpacks.

To obtain additional customer reactions to your backpacks, run a focus group—that is, invite a group of 10 or so potential customers to a conference room to discuss the features of your backpacks. Consider giving each participant a backpack and a $25 check or some other small gift for participating. The quality of responses and amount of participation tend to improve when participants are given some token for their time. Focus groups are valuable, low-cost sources of information on which to try out new ideas before making the financial commitment to sell your backpacks in the marketplace.

Once you have obtained orders from area retailers for your product, you are ready to begin. Before investing a lot of money in your business, determine the creditworthiness of the retailers. Ask for credit references or try to get them to make a deposit on their orders. If you are cash-poor, you might try to obtain an inventory line of credit to produce your product. Usually, lenders will not advance more than 50% of the value of your inventory.

Using Focus Groups

Question

I have a small word-processing business. I'm doing OK but my business is not growing and I've lost a few customers. Could there be something wrong with my services? Maybe my customers have new needs that I don't know about. How can I learn more about their preferences?

Answer

Ask your customers. Keeping your customers means listening to them on a continual basis. Researching customer needs is often the missing ingredient in marketing efforts among business owners. Customers have strong views, undiscovered needs and preferences, good ideas, and a desire to have things improved. They are seldom asked.

Try using focus-group interviews to gain customer insight and help solve your declining sales problem. All business owners can benefit from using this marketing technique with current or potential customers, especially to increase market share. Focus groups help you gain fresh perspectives on customer outlooks as well as obtain new ideas to improve your market position and penetration methods.

In the more sophisticated version of a focus group, marketing experts use one-way mirrors, closed-circuit videotaping, and exhaustive analysis of the recorded sessions. But entrepreneurs are using focus-group interviews in a simpler version that provides a richness of data on a limited budget. Essentially, it is a get-together with 7 to 10 people who are typical of your customer base and who are unfamiliar with one another.

Most people enjoy participating in focus-group sessions and endeavor to give useful feedback. In fact, you will probably find that your customers appreciate being asked their views. They are flattered that you have chosen them and sincerely want to listen to their views. In addition, they realize that you are trying to improve your business. You should pay members a small amount of money or give them a gift for participating.

The moderator plays an important role in the focus group. Consider using a skilled outside moderator to protect against bias. The moderator leads the focus group through in-depth and freewheeling discussions. To find focus-group moderators, look under marketing consultants in the Yellow Pages or call the marketing department at your local college or university. You can also contact your local chamber of commerce for referrals.

A typical focus group takes $1\frac{1}{2}$ to 2 hours. The atmosphere should be relaxed to ensure an informal discussion of participants' opinions and feelings. Serve some light refreshments at the beginning of the discussion. The discussion format and interview questions should be carefully prepared ahead of time. The moderator asks broad questions at the beginning and then focuses the group on the specific information you want to obtain.

The moderator skillfully probes the group, stressing that there are no right or wrong answers and that sharing different points of view is essential. The moderator can take notes during the discussion or have it taped. Findings are then analyzed to interpret feedback from participants and relate it to your business.

Focus groups are rapidly becoming a major entrepreneurial marketing tool for gaining insight into customers' thoughts and feelings. They are an inexpensive way to maintain quality in your business. They help to screen new concepts, generate ideas on how to increase sales, or provide other key information founders want to know. Get in the habit of continually researching your customers' needs and opinions.

Using Mystery Shoppers

Question

I own a small women's dress store in a local mall. Lately, I have received several complaints from customers that my sales associates have been abrupt and discourteous. I have talked to my staff about these complaints. They agree to do a better job and seem to when I am around. Do you have any suggestions as to how I can motivate them to treat customers better?

Answer

Your concerns are well founded. Research shows that the average business never hears from 96% of its unhappy customers. But the average person tells about 10 people about it.

The good news is that about 60% of complaining customers will do business again with a store if their complaint is resolved. Talking with your sales staff and making them more aware of customer complaints is the first step. Karl Albrecht's *Service America* and *The Only Thing That Matters* emphasize the importance of providing excellent service to customers. Ask your staff to read one of these books and then discuss how your business could implement some of the suggested strategies.

✔ COURTNEY'S SMART TIP
Contract with a "mystery shopper" to shop your store and evaluate your sales staff.

Mystery shoppers are being used more frequently in retailing. A mystery shopper pretends that he or she is a customer and evaluates and records how your sales staff interacts with shoppers. The mystery shopper will look for prompt recognition when entering the store. Your sales staff should acknowledge walk-in customers within a minute. Next, the shopper will observe what kind of greeting is given and the way your sales staff builds rapport with new customers:

- Do your salespeople demonstrate product knowledge of your merchandise? Do they discuss and stress merchandise features or benefits? Customers rarely buy product features; instead, they buy because of product benefits.
- Do your salespeople attempt to sell companion items to match the clothing the customer is interested in? How do they assist the customer to the dressing room? Do they attempt to finish the outfit with suggested accessories?
- How do they handle customer objections? What types of comments and suggestions do they offer? Are they honest in their assessment of how various clothing items go together? Do they ask for the sale?
- Do they offer to hold the merchandise or have it put on layaway? How is the customer greeted at the cash register? How is the transaction handled?

Mystery shoppers are an excellent resource to help you understand the type and level of customer service offered at your store. They are also an inexpensive way to evaluate your sales staff. On the average, most mystery shoppers charge about $40 to $60 for spending an hour in your shop and preparing a written report of the sales experience, offering suggestions for improvement.

Look in the Yellow Pages under market research, market analysis, sales training, marketing consultants, or shoppers to find mystery shoppers. Check with your local chamber of commerce or university marketing programs. Check references whenever people are recommended to you. Better yet, ask a friend or business associate to shop your business. Or contact your mall association and suggest that a mystery shopper be hired for all the shops in the mall. Always prepare a list of what you would like to have evaluated before using a mystery shopper.

Another approach to improving customer service is to hold a sales contest offering rewards for outstanding and consistent service. Involve your salespeople in designing both the contest and the evaluation program.

Question

Several years ago I purchased a fast-food franchise that has made a small profit. But lately I have been receiving more customer complaints than usual. Although staff turnover is high in this industry, I continue to provide the same amount of training and supervision. What can I do differently?

Answer

Today, service is king and execution is your most important product. Hire a mystery shopper to determine exactly what kind of service your staff provides. This is an excellent way to monitor employee performance and find innovative ways of improving customer service. Mystery shoppers measure your customers' views of performance, service, and salesmanship.

Mystery shoppers are trained to observe efficiency, honesty, and sales techniques while they pose as regular customers of restaurants, retail stores, or other types of businesses. The normal routine is for mystery shoppers to enter your restaurant and observe staff behavior and the service provided. After gathering enough information, they record and evaluate your restaurant. They will report how long it took before they were waited on, whether the employees came across as friendly and sincere, and whether employees tried to interest them in other products. They observe whether sales are rung up properly and rate the quality of the food as well as the interior of the restaurant.

Mystery shoppers' reports are observational, not judgmental. They quantify customer perceptions and measure individual improvements. The reports can then be used as part of your training and incentive program. It is a way to get your staff focused on the customers, because any one of them might be the mystery guest.

Employees receiving high ratings or perfect scores from mystery shoppers are usually rewarded with some type of special bonus, such as a gift certificate, a parking space, time off, or a small cash award. Sometimes mystery shoppers write notes about deserving employees and give them to the owner. Then you can include $10 or $20 in the note to recognize outstanding performance.

When you recognize excellent performers, other staff members can learn to improve customer service by following their examples. Some owners post shopper reports by the time clock as a way to foster team spirit. The reports can also be used to train new employees, stressing how to become customer-focused and to begin thinking like your customers.

Before hiring mystery shoppers, identify exactly what you want measured. Typical areas for evaluation include the quality of the food; the initial appearance of your store from the parking lot to table; the friendliness, knowledge, ability, and helpfulness of the service and management staff; employee efforts at suggestive selling; and point-of-sale devices.

Never rely on just one rating from a mystery shopper. Instead, have your restaurant shopped several times. Then look for trends and make changes where appropriate. Consult one of the best-selling customer-service books, such as *Service Within* or *Delivering Knock Your Socks Off Service* to get new ideas about improving customer service.

Last, look for other ways to obtain continual customer feedback. Consider giving your customers a short survey card to complete. Offer recognition and rewards to employees who consistently provide exceptional customer service.

Developing Your Marketing Plan and Strategy

Why a Marketing Plan Is Important

Question

Several years ago I opened a fast-service copy business in a small shopette. Although I was the first store offering this service in the area, many competing shops have recently opened, causing my sales to drop. How can I win back customers?

Answer

Successfully marketing a product or service is one of the most complex problems all entrepreneurs face. Every type of entrepreneurial enterprise requires marketing to compete and survive. How does an entrepreneur begin? Before you can decide on which marketing techniques to implement, you must develop a marketing plan.

A marketing plan consists of two primary elements: goals and strategies. Goals will determine the scope of your ambition in a particular time frame and allow you to allocate your resources appropriately. Quantify your goals whenever possible—for example, increasing market share by 10%. Strategies should be specific, measurable, and time specific.

There are many items to take into consideration before developing your marketing plan. Study the growth trends of your industry, evaluate your competition, analyze your key customers, and appraise the realities of the current marketplace. Begin market planning by clearly identifying all the market segments to which you intend to sell. The next step is to arrange the identified markets in order of priority. Target marketing is the fundamental strategy used by successful businesses.

Next, examine the market segments that seem most attractive and target them for penetration. Develop special marketing tactics for each target market—a strategy known as market segmentation. Target your markets and then develop a marketing program for penetrating each one. Your business plan should explicitly identify all markets and then provide the basis for your selection of target markets.

If you have not yet written a business plan, go back to square one and develop it. Each of your identified target markets should be considered almost as a separate marketing program. Unfortunately, many entrepreneurs start their ventures without proper research and without writing a business or marketing plan. Then, when sales stagnate or decrease, they begin to look for solutions. A marketing and business plan can help you devise a strategy to increase sales.

The foundation of your marketing plan will be the marketing mix, which includes such elements as promotion, advertising, publicity, direct mail, sales training, pricing, positioning, and customer service. Many entrepreneurs feel that placing a few ads or using coupon mailers constitutes a marketing plan; then they wonder why they do not achieve better results. When someone mentions marketing, people automatically think of advertising. Instead, new start-up ventures with limited marketing dollars should concentrate on publicity and promotion. There are many inexpensive ways to market products and services.

Deciding how to penetrate each target market is truly an art and takes much planning and experimentation. The difficulties involved in attempting to reach just one market can be overwhelming, especially when there is limited money to spend on marketing products and services. When putting together your marketing plan, consider potential pitfalls and how you will deal with them. If you know ahead of time what to expect, you'll be better able to surmount obstacles as they arise.

✔ **COURTNEY'S SMART TIP**
Start with a modest marketing plan that is short and simple. Allow for flexibility. Reexamine your marketing plan yearly.

It is essential that you be able to track the effectiveness of your marketing plan and measure how well it is working. Then you can allocate your resources to the activities that have the best payoff for your venture.

How you measure the effectiveness of your marketing dollar varies. If you want to find out if an ad brings in new customers, count your current customers and then count the number of new customers after the ad appears. If you want to determine whether a trade show increases customers, track new leads and/or total sales from these leads.

A good technique is to include a response mechanism in your marketing efforts—for example, an invitation to bring an ad in for an extra discount or a free gift. The key is to track the efficiency and return on your marketing investment. Determining which media and what message is working is critical, since this information indicates where to direct your marketing dollars and what to say.

How to Inform Potential Customers about a Product

Question

On camping and fishing trips with my family, I found that I spent most of my time baiting fishhooks for my wife and three daughters. Consequently, I invented a plastic gadget that automatically baits fishhooks. I am a cement finisher and do not have sufficient funds for financing and marketing this product. How can I sell my patent or find someone willing to finance and market an apparatus for baiting fishhooks? I am convinced that the market is out there.

Answer

Developing and patenting a new product for which you strongly believe there is a market is the first step to launching a successful business venture. Figuring out how to sell it is the hard part. Begin by conducting some preliminary research on the number of fishermen and the number of fishing licenses sold annually. Then conduct a beta test with potential customers that will verify and document that your invention truly works and customers would use and recommend it. Try to obtain testimonials from selected experts. You also need to identify what types of fish potential customers could catch with your apparatus and in what types of waters. Contact local fishing stores to find fishermen to test your product.

Next, stop listening to your friends and neighbors who applaud your new invention. Instead, determine if there is a sufficiently large market to justify manufacturing and marketing your product. Take the mystery out of who will purchase your great invention. Check out your competition. If there is none, try to find people who are making a similar product. What has been their track record? Is their product successful? How has it been marketed?

You have two main strategies to pursue for financing and marketing your invention. The first is to bootstrap your venture by producing a small number of baiting gadgets and trying to get one of the local sporting-goods stores to carry them. You can then determine if there is a market and more accurately forecast potential sales volume. In addition, you could ask these stores for a list of their suppliers. Look for suppliers that have accompanying product lines with nationwide distribution. Ask if they would be interested in handling your product.

Try to attend one of the local sporting-goods trade shows. Bring along your baiting apparatus to see if anyone is interested in purchasing it. Or sign up for a booth at the trade show and try to sell the product yourself. Watch some of the fishing shows on television and look for the names and addresses of the producers at the end of the programs. Contact these individuals and ask them about ideas for marketing your product.

Locate some of the primary fishing catalogs, such as *Bass Pro Shops* and *Cabela's*. Contact the catalog companies and ask if they would carry your product. If one of them gives you a large order, you could take the purchase invoice to a lender for additional money to manufacture and ship the product. Catalog companies purchase products at wholesale prices and make their profit by charging the suggested retail price.

Another strategy is to contact a manufacturer involved in producing similar fishing products. The manufacturer might purchase your patent and pay you a royalty on every fishhook baiter sold. Or it might agree to manufacture the product for a percentage of the sales price. Frequently manufacturers have established distribution systems that could carry your product.

Unfortunately, many manufacturers will not do business with you unless you have a proven track record. Likewise, some suppliers or department stores might also require that you have an established customer base. Follow up on these leads by further researching your potential market. Eventually, a fishing manufacturer, supplier, department store, or catalog company should bite your bait.

✔ COURTNEY'S SMART TIP
Marketing is getting someone to start carrying your product.

How to Prepare a Sales Forecast

Question

I'm getting ready to start a new business selling children's toys. I need to make some sales forecasts to determine the size of my market so I can ascertain if my idea is feasible. Can you tell me how to best prepare sales forecasts?

Answer

Forecasting sales volume and testing your market are essential steps to take before deciding whether to launch a new venture.

✔ COURTNEY'S SMART TIP
Use phantom sales to test your toy market by advertising your proposed products, asking for a response, and then gauging the response of your target market to determine if the response is sufficient to justify the venture.

Try selling your proposed products first, and then decide whether to proceed. Your only costs are promotional expenses.

Entrepreneurs may fall into a number of traps when assessing their markets and forecasting sales volume. First, most assume that there is a market and that others are as interested in their product or service as they are. Do not convince yourself that a potential market exists for your idea. Instead, try to prove your market. There are many toy stores around. Why will customers come to yours? What will motivate them to purchase toys from you? You need to obtain some solid evidence that your target market needs your proposed toy store and is willing to purchase from you.

Second, most entrepreneurs tend to underestimate the difficulty of penetrating their intended market. It takes far more time and money to penetrate a target market than most people imagine. Do not assume that everyone who purchases toys will buy from you. Such gross overoptimism not only destroys the credibility of your forecast but can also distort the rest of your projections. Don't overexaggerate your potential market. Most entrepreneurs fall short of their original sales expectations and predictions. Sales forecasts begin with an estimation of the venture's market potential. Then some market penetration factor is applied to it to arrive at the venture's sales potential. The common trap is to grossly overestimate how much of the market the new business will be able to capture.

Third, entrepreneurs regularly pull sales figures out of the air largely on the basis of what they hope for rather than on solid market information. The best way to overcome this trap is to consult with potential suppliers in your industry. They are excellent sources for estimating sales volume. Sometimes they have developed sophisticated statistical models for forecasting your sales.

Also study your competitors' sales experience. What were their first sales? What does your competition now sell? What do new firms in the toy industry usually sell? You can gain valuable insights into sales forecasts by evaluating what others sell now and what they have sold when they first started. Try to find the sales records of some store similar to yours. What were its start-up figures? Remember that sales are the result of marketing and selling efforts. Compare and contrast your selling efforts with those of your competition.

Develop multiple forecasts that will yield different results. Use all of them to gain a better understanding of the range of sales forecasts. You must develop a "must-do" or break-even forecast—that is, the sales volume you must achieve first to break even and then to make a profit. Your sales goals must be directly related to your must-do forecast.

Even the greatest minds in the world cannot accurately forecast economic activity and global events. Astute entrepreneurs set up their ventures in such a way that they can respond quickly to resultant sales volume when market changes occur.

How to Market a Service Business

Question

I have developed a consulting care-giving service for the elderly. I would like to market my services to corporations to help employees on their staffs who are coping with the responsibilities of caring for their elderly relatives. I have been stymied by not really knowing how to market to corporations without personal contact. How can I go about marketing and selling my services? Are there any books you would recommend?

Answer

Marketing services is quite different from marketing products. Our economy is shifting to the service sector. Ninety percent of all new jobs and 67% of the gross national product are generated annually by the service sector. What complicates your problem is that there are many consultants selling similar services.

It is hard to figure out where you are going if you have not given serious thought to and developed a strategy on how to get there. Take the first step by developing a business plan that will help you focus your energies and build a strategy for launching your venture. I suggest that you get a copy of *Program for Writing Winning Business Plans* for a step-by-step method of producing a business plan.

Unfortunately, just having a good idea that you think will sell in the marketplace is not enough. Although you have already developed several brochures for your venture, a detailed marketing plan is needed. *Ideas for Small Service Businesses* covers how to advertise and publicize a service business successfully. It offers practical and innovative suggestions on everything from how to cultivate the right business image to designing and producing effective brochures and ads, to the secrets of generating free publicity.

While preparing these plans and researching your industry, contact both for-profit and nonprofit agencies that are involved in serving the elderly. For instance, contact an association that provides information about elder care services in nursing homes, assisted living facilities, and churches. Be mindful that virtually any service can be duplicated. Therefore, understanding your marketplace, staying on the leading edge, and growing your venture will depend on the soundness of your business plan and marketing tactics.

Home Shopping Can Open Purses for Entrepreneur

Question

I have a new kitchen product that usually sells 2 million units during the holiday season alone. It costs $5 to produce and sells for $19.95 retail. Anyone who has a kitchen is a potential customer. I don't have much money to market my product, although a few retailers have begun carrying it. How can I get it to market quickly?

Answer

One marketing strategy is to consider introducing your product on a television-shopping channel, which gives entrepreneurs like you an opportunity to sell to a nationwide audience. About 80% of these shoppers are female—a primary target for your kitchen product. The Direct Marketing Association reports that shopping channels generated $5 billion in sales in 1996 and projects a growth rate of 10% per year.

Live shopping shows are a sales outlet that never closes, allowing customers to shop at any hour and purchase via telephone or computer. Shopping networks accept new products that have never sold before—if you can prove that your product will sell. It is critical to research your market carefully to determine that potential customers nationwide want your product and will buy it at a specified price. You must be able to convince the network that your product will sell, as they take a risk by purchasing your product and investing time and money producing your sales spot.

Remember to check out the competition. You may find that someone else tried unsuccessfully to sell a product similar to yours via electronic retailing/home shopping malls.

The trick is getting your product accepted by a live shopping show. Highly demonstrable products, which make one's life easier and have mass appeal, are more likely to be selected, especially if you can show a dramatic before-and-after affect.

Television shopping malls select products based on quality, uniqueness, appeal, currency, and demonstration capabilities. Most have in-house quality-assurance programs that inspect each product and representative samples from each shipment. Since they provide a 30-day unconditional return policy, these malls must be certain that you manufacture only top-quality products.

If they are interested in your product, you will begin to negotiate sales terms on each order, including quantities, shipping or pickup dates, payment and credit terms, return policies, and so forth. The level of risk associated with your business and product along with your operating history, size, and other factors all come into play in how terms are negotiated.

Once your product is accepted, you must be ready to do business and have large quantities available for the network's warehouse. Most complete orders ship within 24 hours of purchase, so the merchandise must be in the retailer's warehouse and ready to ship immediately. Also, you must have enough capital to sell to the television network channel and wait for payment. There may be a significant delay after the time you sell your product until you are paid.

Networks bear the expense of preparing the spot for your product. Designers create attractive and eye-catching sets from which merchandise is displayed on the air. Program hosts give demonstrations. Spots typically run from 6 to 10 minutes.

One of the largest leading round-the-clock television shopping channels is QVC. Call 888-NEW-ITEM and ask for a vendor kit to learn how to submit your product for consideration.

Another leading television shopping channel is Home Shopping Network. Its vendor kits contain prequalifying questions regarding what your product does, unique features and benefits, price, market-penetrating strategies, and why the network should purchase your product. For information and to receive a vendor kit, call 800-436-1010.

Television shopping networks are constantly looking for new and innovative products to sell. Product categories generally include electronics, cookware, jewelry, sports and exercise equipment, apparel, health and beauty products, books, videos, and music. Ask each about its vendor fairs and trade shows.

According to Leisure Trends Group Gallup Direct Television Study, 35% of viewers of live shopping shows purchase a product using a toll-free number, while 30% purchase a product seen on a live shopping show later at retail or through a catalog. These buyers are the most price sensitive of electronic retailing, with 17% saying they purchased because of a good price or a good deal, or because they liked the product.

Television shopping channels provide entrepreneurs who'd like to market their new products—immediately and on a limited budget—with an excellent opportunity to sell nationally. For a cohesive marketing strategy, it is important to use direct retailing in conjunction with other marketing efforts.

Continue Drive to Gain Referrals from Customers

Question

I'm trying to increase sales 20% this year but seem to have saturated my market. How can I reach my goal?

Answer

One approach to developing new sales leads is to create a referral program and use your current customers, networks, and new people you meet to generate new business. Start with your current customers by developing a referral form and giving them a variety of ways to respond, such as the following:

- Including the referral form with your bill.
- Faxing it after delivery.
- Mailing it after the sale.
- Posting it on the Internet.
- Distributing it during a focus group.
- Including it with the delivery.
- Asking for it during a follow-up call.

Customize your feedback instruments to meet the needs of your customers. Reward the behavior you want repeated by thanking customers who respond to your request for referrals. Again, personalize your appreciation by writing an individual thank-you note or sending a gift the customer would enjoy, such as a book, a magazine subscription, an audio tape, a gift centerpiece, a bottle of wine, chocolates, flowers, and so on.

Some business owners offer incentives to encourage new sales leads, like a discount on the next order, a free service, or extra products. Others give cash awards, plane tickets, or trips for large orders from a referral equal to 5% to 15% of the sale.

✔ COURTNEY'S SMART TIP

Follow the 80-20 rule—80% of your business comes from 20% of your customers. Concentrate your efforts on that 20%.

Next, examine why some leads have not produced a sale. Contact these leads shortly after they turn you down and ask if there is anything that you can do to win their business.

If not, ask them for a referral to someone they know who might want your product or service. Likewise, contact former customers to determine why they stopped doing business with you to see if it's possible to get them back.

Hold a customer-appreciation event and during the function ask for referrals, explaining how much you value your customers' business and would like to find others like them. Encourage your customers to bring a potential new customer along; conduct a special drawing or giveaway at the event to encourage attendance. Or sponsor a contest and offer a prize for the customer who generates the most referrals.

Contact your network of suppliers for referrals. Remind them that as your business grows, so does theirs. Take them out for lunch or breakfast. Brainstorm about how you can get new leads. Do the same with your banker, accountant, lawyer, insurance agents, or other consultants.

Ask other business owners with complementary products or services for leads, and pass on leads to them. Make it a regular practice to ask for referrals since most people enjoy giving good referrals. Think about offering a commission for leads that turn into sales.

If you cannot fill an order, pass it on to a competitor who can deliver a quality product or service. Ask that competitor to give you an order that they are unable to fill in the future. Your customers will appreciate that you care enough to make sure their needs are taken care of. Last, look for a business with an established distribution system with which you could form a strategic alliance. Negotiate a deal to offer your products or services to its customers.

Always keep networking and expanding your contacts, especially with businesses whose customers need your products and services. Don't be hesitant to ask everyone you know for referrals. Ask your staff to do the same, but lead by example.

Want to Increase Sales? Build a Better Database

Question

I'm thinking about establishing a database to better market to my customers and ultimately increase my sales. How should I go about building a database and what information should I collect?

Answer

It's a good idea to track your current customers as well as qualified prospects by using a marketing database to increase sales. A database sorts meaningful information about customers so you can analyze it and better plan your marketing strategies. It allows you to search and profile customers by different characteristics. A marketing database allows you to store, organize, retrieve, and analyze critical purchasing information. For example, collecting this information enables you to determine how your customers prefer to be contacted. It is the missing link between mass advertising and sales.

The first step is to collect data on your customers and prospects. If you have been keeping customer-profile information on index cards or on your computer, you can start there. Unfortunately, most entrepreneurs do not begin operating their businesses with good customer information. Go back to your sales records and capture the purchasing information on your customers. Pay more attention to retaining good customers, motivating repurchases, and increasing usage rather than winning new customers.

Another approach is to send out a brief customer questionnaire asking for the critical information you need to establish your database. If you think that it will be difficult to collect such customer information, provide an incentive for completing the information you need, such as a coupon, gift certificate, special discount, or eligibility in a drawing for prizes.

If some of your customers still don't respond, call them to obtain critical information such as address, phone, fax, e-mail, income, home ownership, family details, age, occupation, birthday, education, gender, sizes, and so on. If you routinely conduct business over the phone, this is a perfect opportunity to collect this information.

Many business owners call customers after a purchase to check on how they liked the product or service. This is an opportune time to collect any missing customer information for your database. Besides the demographic and lifestyle information you obtain, also collect purchasing information, such as how frequently customers purchase, the amount of each sale, how often they repurchase, and how valuable they are to your business.

If your objective in collecting information is to identify new prospects to be followed up on later with a more intensive sales effort, consider utilizing several different approaches, such as offering free information booklets, audio- or videotapes, a book, a sample, a catalog, or a free coupon in a freestanding insert to those responding to your query for information. Collect enough information to select those most likely to respond to a given promotional idea. Your challenge is to find groups with a high probability of responding to your marketing materials.

When it is justified to enhance your database, new promotions may also generate responses that will add critical information to your prospective-customer lists.

Knowing what to include in your database is only part of the challenge. Collecting high-quality information and correctly entering it into your database are key. Getting it right the first time requires accuracy, constant upkeep, and staff time.

Use database marketing as a tool to achieve increased sales, motivate repeat buyers, build customer loyalty, encourage referrals, and provide growth opportunities to your company. It follows the principle that your current customers are more likely to provide your next sale than new prospects and are one of your most important assets. Database marketing allows you to concentrate your promotional efforts on the best target markets for your products or services.

One small-business database program that I recommend is Target Smart!. Call MainStreet Marketing Software, Inc., for a release date and specific product information at 303-698-2233. To order a copy of Target Smart!, the book by Claudio Marcus and Jay Newberg, call 800-698-2233.

Pitfalls to Avoid

1. Assuming that there is a market for your product or service just because you think it is a wonderful idea.

2. Overexaggerating the size of the market and the number of potential customers who might purchase your product or service.

3. Inflating sales volume.

4. Failing to continually research customer needs.

5. Failing to develop and follow a marketing plan with realistic goals and budgets.

6. Forgetting to ask your customers for referrals for new business.

7. Not researching your market.

8

Market-Penetration Strategies

Overview

Marketing is one of the most difficult tasks for entrepreneurs, who must get it right the first time since they are usually poor. Marketing mistakes are made because entrepreneurs do not thoroughly research their marketplace and customers to discover the best techniques to market their products or services. They do not appreciate the difficulties they face in penetrating target markets and gravely underestimate market-penetration costs. Smart marketing techniques require that you go beyond just knowing your potential customers to understanding the common lifestyle characteristics that they share. Today, astute entrepreneurs recognize the importance of seeing the world through their customers' eyes.

Many marketing dollars are spent foolishly. Most new-business founders think that printing a business card and sending out brochures will bring in customers. Because entrepreneurs fall in love with their products and services, they think people will beat a path to their doorway—that simply having a better product or service will bring in customers. That seldom happens. Instead, people are usually indifferent to the venture.

Smart marketing tools include the following:

- Obtaining free publicity.
- Attending and working trade shows.
- Using focus groups and mystery shoppers.
- Expanding your customer base with existing customers.
- Asking for customer referrals.
- Scheduling follow-up contacts after mailing out marketing materials.
- Using infomercials and home shopping networks.
- Using e-mail and the Internet.
- Using business cards as mini-billboards.

- Buying preemptible television time.
- Developing telemarketing techniques.
- Using sales reps.

Other tools include testimonials, Yellow Pages ads, postcards, faxes, cassettes, coupons, databases, and network marketing.

Smart Market-Penetration Strategies

1. Use phantom sales to test the market with a new product or service.
2. Stay in close contact with your customers by utilizing memorandums, newsletters, faxes, and postcards.
3. Target your market segments and then develop different marketing strategies for penetrating each of them.
4. If you are a new start-up with limited marketing dollars, concentrate on obtaining free publicity through feature stories.
5. When purchasing TV advertising, consider buying preemptible time whenever possible.
6. Use your business cards as a marketing tool by making them memorable and highlighting the unique features of your business.
7. When purchasing a 900 number, shop around for legitimate telephone service bureaus and compare setup and equipment charges.
8. Consider buying an 800 number when 20% of your revenue comes from customers outside your local area.
9. If you are a retailer, consider accepting consignment merchandise that fits your inventory.
10. Try to avoid selling on consignment unless that is the only way to get your product or service to market.
11. Use experienced, reputable sales reps to market your product or service.
12. Enhance your printed brochures by creating an audiocassette.
13. Attractive flyers are cost-effective, give you great flexibility, and complement your marketing materials.
14. Coupons raise the marketing awareness of your goods and help increase sales.
15. To double your current response rates from direct-mail pieces, follow up with postcards, self-mailers, newsletters, or phone calls.
16. E-mail is the fastest and least expensive way to connect with customers.

(Continued)

(Continued)

17. To market successfully on the Internet, you must have customers who shop on-line.
18. Experiment with a home page; track sales and compare the results with those of other marketing methods.
19. Advertise in the telephone books that blanket your target area.
20. When using radio spots, frequency is important.
21. Sales publicity and public relations can greatly increase your response rate from advertising.

Cost-Effective Marketing Techniques

Cassettes Provide Solid Supplement to Sales Brochures

Question

I have been sending my rather expensive sales brochures to prospective customers, but I have not received the response I anticipated. I don't have much money to spend on additional advertising. What else can I do to increase sales?

Answer

Enhance your expensive printed brochure by creating an audiocassette as an alternative selling tool to increase sales. Today, almost all homes and cars have audiocassette players. This may be an excellent way to reach your prospective customers, especially since the majority of people spend an average of 30 minutes commuting to and from work. A built-in advantage of using a cassette is that many times your prospects may pass along your cassette to others. Consider audiocassettes as a marketing tool only if you are certain that your prospects will take the time to listen.

Review copies of other audiocassettes you have received in the mail. Evaluate which techniques were used to motivate the listener to take action and make a purchase. Then design your cassette by incorporating those techniques you found effective.

Costs to produce cassettes vary widely. They can be produced for under $500 and usually are 5 to 12 minutes long. Your audiocassette should include both vocal talent and music. Remember that a single voice heard for a long period is boring. Therefore, consider using a combination of different voices. If you currently advertise on radio, ask the station's personalities to record a few words about your business, and negotiate to have it done free of charge.

If it's important to visually demonstrate your product, another alternative is producing a videocassette. Currently, more than 80% of American homes have access to videocassette players.

Videocassettes are shorter than audiocassettes but cost more to produce. The average cost ranges between $100 and $1,000 per minute. I recommend that your videocassette run between 5 and 7 minutes. It is important to design either an audio- or videocassette that creates excitement. Make sure to have your cassettes professionally produced.

Before deciding to produce either an audiotape or a videotape, hold a focus group with a few of your best customers. Ask them if they would be enticed to purchase your products and services by using either of one of these two electronic marketing tools. Based on their insights, decide which methods of market penetration will produce the best results for your business.

When mailing either audio- or videocassettes, keep in mind that the quality of your mailing list will determine the sales response you receive. Avoid a mass mailing; choose your mailing list well. It may be more effective to mail prospects a cassette as a follow-up to a response from other advertising or from names obtained at a trade show.

When mailing the cassette, include a personal letter. Then follow up within a week or so with a letter or phone calls. Your electronic brochure is one of the first steps in the selling process. It should be used in concert with other promotional tools such as a sales visit, direct-mail pieces, faxes, your home page on the Internet, and personal phone calls.

Offer to send those prospects who indicate interest in your product or service a free audio- or videocassette. You stand a better chance of having your electronic brochure reviewed if prospects have requested one. Your prospects may also show or pass it along to others, increasing the reach of your advertising. Never charge for the cassettes.

Audio- or videocassettes are expensive to produce; make sure you get your message right the first time. Then you may gain a competitive edge by using these proven and effective electronic sales brochures to enhance your expertise and credibility as well as increase sales.

Well-Done Flyers Are Cost-Efficient, Help Business Take Off

Question

I am running out of my rather expensive sales brochures, which have not brought in as many sales as I projected. I'm afraid they are being thrown away without being read. Since I don't have much money to spend on adver-tising, what do you advise?

Answer

Instead of sending out your expensive brochures, try sending flyers, sometimes called circulars. They cost just pennies to produce, can be read quickly, give you more flexibility, and keep your sales message alive. Flyers have many different applications, such as informing, ex-plaining new information, and selling. Use flyers to supplement your other sales literature, catalogs, and so on.

Flyers are most effective when you are announcing a sale or a spe-cial offer or augmenting an existing promotion. Most flyers are $8\frac{1}{2}$ by 11 inches and printed in one color on one side. But there can be many variations, such as printing on both sides and folding the piece in half, making a mini-brochure. Another variation is using a 4- by 9-inch flyer that fits into a standard business envelope. This size is effective when put into standard display racks, placed on counters, or used as a mailing stuffer or insert.

You can add color by printing on color paper with no additional charge. Or you can add color by using colored ink. For a stronger visual impact, include photos, illustrations, or clip art.

The format of a flyer isn't as important as the content and its ap-pearance. Keep your message simple, make your offer timely, and tie in your message with other promotional materials.

Catch the reader's eye with an attention-getting headline that highlights the most important benefit of your special offer. Your mes-sage should be believable and should ignite the impulse to buy.

Make your sales message sound like you are carrying on a one-to-one conversation with the reader. Use the words "you" and "your" fre-quently. Include all information the reader needs to make a buying decision.

You can also personalize your message by handwriting a note to the recipient. Include your full business address, directions for getting there, your telephone and fax numbers (with area code), credit cards accepted, hours of business, and so on.

A good, creative printer can help you design your flyer at no addi-tional charge. Or you can work with your graphic designer.

There are several ways to distribute your flyers, including giving them out at your business or at other business places. Offer to distribute other businesses' flyers at your location. Flyers can also be used as bag stuffers, self-mailers, mail inserts in your or someone else's mailings or as newspaper inserts. You can hand them out in shopping centers, at sporting events, at trade shows, or on street corners as well as slip them under doors, place them on car windshields, or put them in sales racks or on counter displays.

Keep track of which distribution methods bring in the most sales by asking your customers where they heard about your offer. Ask satisfied customers to pass on your flyers to their friends and neighbors.

You can further bootstrap your promotional efforts and keep your costs to a minimum by printing several different versions of your flyers, since they cost as little as three to four cents apiece in quantities of a thousand.

Coupons Effective Low-Cost Marketing If Used Creatively

Question

Besides using newspapers, radio spots, and direct mail, what else can I do with limited dollars to market a new sports-related product?

Answer

Besides using traditional advertising media to market your product, consider using coupons in a variety of ways to reach your target market.

Today, many entrepreneurs are using coupons, and over three billion coupons are distributed annually. Fewer than 3% of these are redeemed, however, indicating that many consumers don't clip or use them.

A 1995 marketing study found that the critical factor in the effectiveness of coupons was not whether they were redeemed, but whether potential customers saw them. People who do not clip or redeem coupons may still make a mental note of the item and later purchase the product or service. Even when a coupon is clipped, the customer often forgets to take it to the store but purchases the item anyway.

Coupons, even after they have expired, raise awareness of your product. Many business owners redeem expired coupons to create goodwill and accommodate their customers. Others honor the terms of the offer without the actual coupon in hand.

Coupons can be distributed in a direct-mail packet, in a card deck, or at retail locations as well as in different print media. You can also print small coupons on the back of a store cash register receipt tape. The main advantage of advertising on store tapes is your ability to hit a specific audience. Contact other storeowners whose products might be complementary to yours to use their tapes. Always offer to trade or barter when using other merchants' store tapes. Don't forget to use the back of your own receipts for coupons. You can also include coupons in your invoices, statements, or other outgoing mail.

Church bulletins are another source for distributing coupons. If your customers live within certain neighborhoods, you are able to reach a defined market at a low price.

Some business owners have tried telephone directory coupons, but the response rate has been uneven. You could also hire someone to distribute your coupons on busy streets or at public events, fairs, and the like.

Team up with a noncompeting business for a special promotion. Giving your coupons to another business can provide an added bonus for their customers. The key is to find a business whose goods appeal to your target market.

Or reward your good customers or those who give you referral business by giving them a one-shot special coupon.

Coupons are also a great way to build your mailing list. On the coupon you can provide space for recipients to fill out their names, addresses, and other specific demographic information. You can segment your markets into specific areas and develop a composite of your best customers. You can also chart how much business comes from repeat sales. Last, always accept competitors' coupons or give an additional discount if your customers bring in a rival's coupon.

It is important to experiment with different ways of using coupons to determine what works best. Always code your coupons so you can track what is most effective. Often, a coupon motivates a prospect to come to a store. This gives you an opportunity to explain other products and services that you offer.

How to Get the Most Out of Mailings to Customers

Question

I have a mail-order business with an attractive brochure that I mail to potential and current customers. However, I am frustrated because these people are not placing orders after receiving my mailings. Fewer than half of 1% place an order, which is down from my earlier 1% response rate. What can I do to improve my sales?

Answer

To double your current responses, send follow-up postcards, self-mailers, or customer newsletters to potential customers one to three months after your initial mailing. Repeat mailings that follow up on initial inquiries should convert into a 10% to 15% increase in sales. You can count on a similar increased response rate every time you re-mail to your list for at least a couple of years.

Postcards are a great and inexpensive way to keep in touch with prospects and current customers. Postcards can not only remind cus-tomers about your products, but also announce special sales and new offerings or serve as coupons. They are inexpensive to print and cost a third less than letters to mail. Another bonus is the extra exposure you receive, since everyone who handles your postcard sees your mes-sage.

To catch people's attention, use big, bold, and catchy headlines. Keep your message short and emphasize your product's benefits. Design the copy so it's readable at a glance. Whether you use postcards or cus-tomer newsletters, create a sense of urgency that motivates people to order now.

If you have a toll-free number use it on your promotional mailings for ordering. If not, consider getting one since that will also increase your response rate.

Order extra postcards and use them as handouts at business meet-ings and other promotional events. Postcards can also be effective as customer thank-you notes and for other customer correspondence.

One-page customer newsletters can describe new products and their benefits. You can personalize them by including a personal note or helpful business resource. Customer newsletters are an important extension of your mail-order business. Remember that constant con-tact builds strong bonds with customers.

An added benefit to repeat mailings is that your mailing list gets updated when undeliverable pieces are returned. If after updating your mailing list you find it does not generate enough sales, consider swap-ping your mailing list with another mail-order owner in a complemen-tary noncompetitive business.

Usually no money is involved when mailing lists are swapped, and you can mail to the list as frequently as you want. I recommend that you and the other business owner sign a simple list-swapping agreement stating that all names on your lists can be rented to other mailers in the future. The agreement should state that there will be no charge or any money exchanged for swapping your mailing lists now or in the future. Both of you should sign and date the agree-ment.

New Business Requires Access to a Mailing List

Question

I am interested in obtaining lists of people who might buy wildlife art pieces so I can start a new business. Could you give me advice on how I can rent mailing lists?

Answer

Today, direct mail is the world's largest advertising medium, and mailing lists are key to success in this industry. First, learn as much as you can about the direct-mail industry and how it works. Contact the Direct Marketing Association, 6 East 43rd St., New York, NY 10017, 212-768-7277. This organization provides information on trends and statistics and will refer list companies.

Before selecting mailing lists to rent, define your best target market and then decide how to find people or organizations in these markets that would be most interested in purchasing wildlife art.

There are several different types of mailing lists, including response lists, compiled lists, business lists, and house lists. Since your business is new and you don't have an existing house list, consider using response lists that consist of consumers who have previously responded to a direct-marketing offer.

The advantage of using a response list is that people on this list have identified themselves (by their own choice) as people with a specific interest and have demonstrated that they are willing to respond to a direct-marketing offer.

On the other hand, compiled lists contain names and addresses drawn from various sources such as registrations, memberships, directories, and so on. List compilers provide lists of market areas that include specific psychographic and demographic characteristics. However, compiled lists don't indicate a person's previous willingness to respond by mail. Business lists involve business-to-business selling and are used to sell general business products and services.

Many list compilers publish directories of lists for rent. An excellent reference guide is published by Standard Rate and Data Service (SRDS) in Wilmette Illinois. Its *Direct Market List Sources* contains over 1,700 pages of detailed information about every mailing list available.

Prices for names typically range from about $50 to $90 per thousand labels with a minimum order number of names required. There are surcharges for segmentation on various characteristics selected and a minimum number of names for test quantities. Segmentation usually costs an additional $10 per thousand. You can order names and addresses on pressure-sensitive labels so you can stick them on envelopes and mail your promotional material. Even though you'll spend 10 to 20 times more for direct mail than for advertising in the mass media you can select prospects more efficiently.

To rent mailing lists, I recommend you contact established list brokers, which are companies specializing in direct marketing. They are excellent marketing resources and can become an important part of your marketing team.

List brokers provide thousands of names and addresses of people in specific professions—businesses and organizations as well as coordinate list rentals. They have a wealth of industry experience on how various lists have worked for their clients and can recommend lists that will produce the best results. Ask about the accuracy guarantee various list companies offer.

Contact your industry association or local chamber of commerce for recommendations of mail list brokers or look in the Yellow Pages of the phone book.

Overall, you will receive valuable marketing advice without paying more than the cost of directly renting mailing lists. Once you start your business, immediately begin compiling your own house mailing list, which will become the most profitable source of future resales and a valuable asset to your business.

Using Business Cards as Marketing Brochures

Question

I am starting a new pet store in an area shopping center. I am in the process of designing a logo to use on my stationery and business cards. My printer advised me to keep the card simple while another friend advised me to include more information about my business. What do you suggest?

Answer

This is a difficult question to answer since the design of your card depends on your industry and target market. Most entrepreneurs regard their stationery and business cards as just props needed when launching a new venture. Your business card, letterhead, and stationery should reflect the image you are trying to project.

Most often, business cards are simple, plain, and unimaginative printed paper rectangles that are handed out without much thought. Business owners fail to realize that they can use their business cards as an effective, inexpensive marketing tool.

Business-card design trends are becoming more creative. Why not design yours to sell your particular products and services rather than just providing your contact information? Distinctive business cards range from those made with unusual materials and imprinting methods to those that convey a solid message and establish their own identity.

To determine how effective your business card is, observe what others do when you hand it to them. Do they look at it and comment or put it directly in their pockets? If it goes in the pocket, you have failed to catch their attention and may want to redesign your card. Next, look at other business cards and notice what catches your eye. To attract attention and create an impact, use a variety of sizing, type, and spacing.

Design a card that is memorable and highlights the uniqueness of your venture. Your business card should have the same typeface as your letterhead and stationery. Present a consistent image. Make sure that your business card directly communicates to your target market. It may be necessary to design several different business cards that appeal to different segments of your market.

Think of your card as a mini-billboard. Some experts suggest including the services and benefits you offer. Many times business cards give only the basics—name, address, and phone number. They fail to indicate what kind of business it is and what special services and products it offers. When glancing through cards, people frequently forget where they received the card and what business the company is in. Don't let this happen to you.

Be creative and use design alternatives. Instead of using an average-size business card, consider using a card that fits into a Rolodex or one that folds in half. A folding card can feature your services and serve as a brochure, a wallet-size advertisement for your business. The outside of the card contains standard business information, while the inside contains a headline followed by a list of features and benefits.

Add color to your card if possible, either as background or to make the type stand out. Adding another color may raise your printing bill about $20 but is well worth the cost. Also, various textures might enhance your card, such as a high gloss or matte finish or the rag content of the paper you select.

Make the most of your business card to help with your referral business. Never be without one. A good business card can be as effective as a TV commercial. Ask for business cards of other contacts you meet to follow up with later. Mail out your card with letters and other brochures.

✔ COURTNEY'S SMART TIP
Revise your business cards every four to five years to keep up with new trends and changing tastes.

For more information, contact Avery N. Pitzak, president of the American Business Card Club, at 303-690-6496. This association is a worldwide network for exchanging business card designs and ideas. It costs $10 to join the club and to receive its newsletters and other mailings.

Marketing on the Information Highway

E-mail Effective Way to Reach Your Customers

Question

I have never used e-mail to correspond with my customers, although several of my friends insist I should start using it. I feel it's impersonal and I'm afraid they won't read my message. What do you advise?

Answer

I recommend that you begin using e-mail to communicate with your customers, suppliers, employees, colleagues, and others when this tool is most appropriate.

Many entrepreneurs use e-mail as a communication tool because of its speed, lower costs, efficiency, and increased ability to help you network. Not only does it save money, it also provides an extra benefit to your customers. The U.S. Postal Service estimates that since 1990, about 30% of what had previously been first-class mail is now sent by either fax or e-mail.

Using e-mail has several advantages. First, delivery is faster than with most other alternatives. It takes only seconds or minutes for e-mail to travel across long distances. Postal mail is now being called "snail mail."

One of the main features of e-mail is its low cost. E-mail is the least expensive way to connect electronically with customers, suppliers, lenders, and others. You don't pay extra for each message you send, unlike with phone calls or mail. No long-distance charges are incurred as with sending by fax. It takes only a little extra work to send your e-mail message to thousands of customers. And you don't need a fancy computer to use e-mail.

Another advantage is that e-mail is efficient and easy to use, increasing your productivity. You can quickly transfer documents into a word processing or database program rather than retyping them. You can also answer five e-mail messages in the same amount of time it takes to answer one phone call. People usually read their e-mail messages soon after they arrive rather than letting correspondence stack up for days.

More important, e-mail allows you to think about what, how, and when you want to answer instead of responding with the first thought that comes to mind. Also, you can rapidly return quotes when submitting bids.

Some companies put their e-mail addresses on their hangtags or other types of advertising. Customer newsletters can show up within minutes of being sent electronically. E-mail increases customer interaction as well as frequency of contact.

However, there are also important disadvantages to consider. Security can be a serious problem. E-mail is truly a public network compared to confidential correspondence. Other people have access to and can read your mail. Caution—avoid putting any confidential information on the Internet or e-mail.

Second, if a computer or network link goes down, it could take several days for a message to reach the intended address.

In some situations e-mail can be a poor medium, such as when discussing problems or sensitive information with staff. Sometimes face-to-face contact and the opportunity to read body language is important. Don't use e-mail in these instances.

Selling Products on the Internet Has Its Benefits

Question

Many of my colleagues have been talking about selling their products and developing new markets on the Internet. Should I market my products on the Internet?

Answer

Many business owners are marketing their products and services on-line and using the Internet to communicate customer benefits and increase sales. Marketing on-line can create closer customer relationships as well as identify new market niches and ways to customize your goods.

Although the most common use of the Internet, also called the Net, is to distribute marketing materials to current customers, it also allows you to save on printing, postage, long-distance, and travel costs. Using e-mail might also be able to reduce your 800 number costs. It's also an excellent way to communicate with customers in remote locations or to expand internationally. Since you can customize each message, it makes your marketing more personal.

Entrepreneurs are discovering that the Net is an effective tool to improve customer service, customer retention, and product development. It is an excellent marketing-research tool for you to identify new markets and prospects as well as monitor your competition. You can keep tabs on your industry, identify new trends, and search for articles and abstracts that would take days in the library to find. In addition, you can retrieve competitive information on prospects and be more prepared for sales calls.

The Net is also ideal for conducting marketing surveys. There are more than 800 computer-related discussion groups on the Net where users ask each other various questions.

Many entrepreneurs communicate with their customers by using "listserv" or "mailbot." Listserv is a way to send a single e-mail message to many people. A person who signs up to participate in a listserv gives his or her permission for you to send product information. Listserv can stand alone or can complement a home page.

Mailbot is similar to a listserv; however, it distributes information to individuals who send inquires rather than you sending a message to large groups of people. It distributes information only on request, automatically sending out what's requested. It can be programmed to send prices, general information, or specialized marketing materials. Your Internet provider can set up both listserv and mailbot.

To be successful on the Net, you must have customers who shop on-line. Or, if you have customers who purchase by mail, you might try marketing on-line. The hardest part is attracting people to your site since they come to it by choice.

In addition, you must be able to update your home page regularly, offering new information and giving people a reason to return to your site. Keep it fresh by continually changing the content and flagging it on the home page with a "new" sign. Make sure the information on your home page is attractive and concise. Use short sentences and paragraphs.

Some companies offer incentives, such as high-tech coupons, on-line discounts, entry into a sweepstakes contest, or a gift, to get a potential customer's name, address, and other demographic information for their databases. Since online marketing is relatively new, some companies find instant success while others' success is minimal. It depends on how many of your customers use the Net and how innovative, current, and entertaining your site is. Give users a reason to come back often and add your site to their browser bookmarks.

To get more mileage from a Web site, some companies connect their Web page to a shopping mall or industrial park where many products and services are already being sold. This is a form of cooperative advertising where companies cross-market their goods.

Think about including a hyperlinks, also called hotlinks, which are highlighted text or buttons that take a user to another page of information or to another site. Hotlinks are an especially effective means to take the browser directly to your order form.

Last, don't forget to market your Web site off-line in all your advertising and on your marketing materials, business cards, stationery, or clothing items. The Net offers some exciting opportunities to improve your marketing, communication, and service to your customers. Knowing what is on-line and observing your competitors' home pages will go a long way toward saving you time and money marketing on-line to increase sales and grow your company.

Advertising

Will Advertising in Yellow Pages Pay Off for Firm?

Question

Recently a person from the telephone company called to sell me Yellow Pages advertising. Should I get a listing or an ad in the Yellow Pages?

Answer

The attractiveness of using Yellow Page advertising is that most homes have a copy of the Yellow Pages book, and people who look there are usually in a buying mood. Yellow Pages are an arena for attracting prospects, since statistics show that about 50% of the users purchase products or services.

Some businesses get many local customers from the Yellow Pages, especially when the business provides emergency services, such as plumbers or a locksmiths, or if it is a retail business. Other businesses attract few new customers from the Yellow Pages, especially if their market is narrow with a limited number of customers. Determine if your prospects look in the Yellow Pages and if they are appropriate for your product or service.

First, look to see if there is a clear-cut heading under which to place your ad. If there isn't, you might not get many customers from a listing. You might find that more than one Yellow Page category classifies what you do, such as word processing services that are listed under both "Secretarial Services" and "Typing." In this case, look to see which category contains most of the large display ads or boldface listings. It is reasonable to assume that this is where customers look most often. In some instances, you might want to advertise under more than one category.

Next, check to see if your competition advertises in the Yellow Pages. If lots of similar businesses use listings, it may be worth a try. If you find only a few listings, try to determine if it is because this advertising attracted few new customers. Determine what percentage of these companies' business comes from people who have located them through the Yellow Pages.

If you decide to advertise in the Yellow Pages, make sure they are part of your local telephone company, part of the local phone book. Anyone can publish Yellow Pages that may or may not be distributed widely.

Advertise in telephone books that blanket your target area. If you market nationally, then use Yellow Pages in all appropriate cities, including those where you don't have offices. There are also specialized Yellow Pages, such as silver pages for seniors and ethnic Yellow Pages.

Also consider business-to-business Yellow Pages. Today, many large metropolitan areas have these editions. Make sure your ads are in all the books your target customers regularly use.

Don't direct your customers in other advertising you use to get your telephone number from the Yellow Pages. You'll send them straight to your competition. Instead, refer them to the white pages.

Two good references are *Yellow Pages Advertising, How to Get the Greatest Return on Your Investment* by Jeffrey Price, and *Getting the Most from Your Yellow Pages Advertising* by Barry Maher. These books list the headings looked up most often for residences as well as other invaluable information such as cleaners, physicians and surgeons, department stores, television dealers and services, taxicabs, beauty shops, and air-conditioning contractors.

Magazine Ads Help You Target Your Audience

Question

Is advertising in a magazine effective? What kind of a response rate can I expect, and what are the best months to schedule ads?

Answer

Advertising in magazines can be effective and tends to yield a better response for businesses that have a line of different products or services to sell. Magazines have a broad reach but do not necessarily generate a high response rate. Although response rates vary greatly, a rule of thumb is that a well-written ad placed in carefully chosen magazines will get a response rate of about one-tenth of 1% or less of a magazine's audience. If you do not choose the right magazine, the response rate could be much lower. If your business can make a profit on this type of response, then you should consider magazine advertising.

Some of the benefits of using magazine ads include the ability to measure response rate with coupons or special offers. They can also pinpoint target audiences and are ideal for projecting a quality image because they have a high reproduction quality and a longer life span than newspapers. And because many readers identify with their favorite magazines, you can gain credibility simply by association.

However, magazine salespeople will provide pass-along counts of their readers—claiming that every month readers route their magazines to others—thus increasing the size of the magazine's readership. You can't rely on getting pass-along readership, so therefore, don't count these estimates.

Magazine circulation figures are not extremely helpful either, since they represent only how many magazines publishers mail, not how many are read. In addition, if the magazine sends out many free copies, the actual readership may be lower than stated. Also, circulation figures tend to stay flat all year and are only an indication of circulation—not readership.

If your products are used as gifts, October, November, and December are good months to run magazine ads. However, you could get lost in a myriad of holiday ads. If your products or services are not gift oriented, response rates increase when it's cold in most parts of the United States (during the winter months of January, February, and March), because people tend stay home and read more. Likewise, response rates go down during summer months when people spend more time outside and less time reading magazines. Remember, however, that special trade issues or seasonal specialties differ from regular monthlies. Ask the ad salesperson about special issues.

Keep in mind that you must be able to experiment. If your ad is not right or you choose the wrong magazine, you may be very disappointed in the response. Although a few magazines reach a broad spectrum of people, most are published for special-interest groups. Although subject areas are highly specialized, the geographic area in which each magazine is circulated can be quite broad. For impact in your hometown, advertise in major local or regional editions. To locate magazines in your prospects' target markets, consult a copy of Bacon's *Publicity Checker/Magazines*.

Some entrepreneurs use classified ads in magazines to attract new customers, as the cost tends to be much less than for display ads. Most often, classified magazine ads are used to obtain inquiries rather than sell products. Since they are much smaller than display ads, they cannot present a lot of information to close a sale. You could get fewer inquiries from a classified magazine ad than a display ad and then have to follow up by sending sales materials—an added expense that raises your total marketing cost per order.

Remember, technology is changing the way we communicate, and some larger magazines are going on the Web and offering interactive versions of certain portions of their magazines. The smaller, industry-specific vertical magazines, which most entrepreneurs use, are also beginning to experiment by going interactive on the Web. I recommend that you watch and experiment with this new area.

Radio Advertising Can Be Effective If Tailored to a Particular Market

Question

I have a rental business. Should I advertise on radio?

Answer

Some entrepreneurs have found that radio ads have increased sales if their customers listen to the radio, if they advertise on the right stations, and if their goods lend themselves to radio.

There are more than 400 million radios in homes, cars, offices, and so forth, and spots may cost less than you think. Radio allows you to reach a small geographic area at an affordable price. Unlike TV, most stations don't charge for their production costs.

In recent years, radio stations have better defined their market segments so you can better match your customers with the stations' audiences. Therefore, it's important to research and evaluate the audiences of the radio stations in your market area. Match your customers and prospects with appropriate radio stations. Radio time sales staff can give you this demographic information so you can find that important customer match.

Advantages of radio include its speed, ease of personalization, and flexibility (it allows you to make last-minute changes and to alter your message easily), and it is relatively inexpensive. You can also tie your message to news or special events.

When using radio spots, frequency is important. Most studies show that ads need to be repeated four to six times before a customer will be motivated to purchase. Rule of thumb—try to hit your target audience with at least 10 spots a day. Also, concentrate your spots during a few days of the week. Usually, the best time to run radio ads is during the afternoon drive time when people are returning home. For some products, early drive time works well, while for others, midday programs may be effective.

Radio spots can be bought as run of the station (ROS) or at specified times. ROS is cheaper because a station can air your spot during its open times, which are usually less desirable.

Consider using air personalities to deliver your spots live. You can give them a fact sheet instead of a fixed script. Your ad will tend to be more sincere—it'll be slightly different each time it is delivered, but it won't become monotonous. This works well when you have given your goods to the announcer. Ideally, he or she will talk about it on the air longer than the time allotted for your spot, giving your ad more credibility. This succeeds when the announcer is dynamic and articulate. If not, you may be better off having a produced commercial to ensure quality control.

One of the main disadvantages of using radio spots is that the spot goes by quickly and may not be absorbed by the listener. Some listeners change stations when commercials are aired. That's one reason that you may have to run radio spots on more than one station.

Rates are always negotiable. Always negotiate for the number of spots, not the dollar amount of your buy. Then compare the price for a certain number of spots with that charged by other stations. Barter for spots by giving the radio station your product.

It is usually better to use 30-second spots versus 60-second ones unless you have a complex product or service, which requires more time.

If your budget allows it, use music, sound effects, or both. Radio stations and production facilities have libraries of sounds that can be rented at nominal cost.

Some entrepreneurs have found that the most effective radio programs are interview shows and news features. You can try to get free publicity through interesting stories about your company or its goods. You may qualify for free event listings or public-service announcements on local or public radio. Offer to be on a talk show. Contact your local radio stations and ask for a free media kit. This will give you an indication of what information they require and how to prepare your own kit.

Last, remember to track audience response so you can discover which station brings in the most business. This is an excellent opportunity to coupon-test your response rate. You can air a different offer on each station and then track which offer produces the most sales. Experiment and track results to determine if this is the right medium for your business.

Testimonials Are Method to Boost Business

Question

I started a computer consulting business over a year ago. Most of my business comes from referrals. To increase my client base, I sent out direct-mail pieces that have not given me the response I anticipated. What can I do to get a better response rate?

Answer

Selling intangible consulting services is much harder than selling a product. It requires immediate trust from potential buyers. To quickly establish the credibility of your consulting company, use testimonials. When prospective customers see testimonials from people they identify with, they gain confidence in your new company. It's a great way of proving that others love and stand by your services.

Properly used, testimonials are an excellent way to expedite sales. It's surprising how few entrepreneurs effectively use testimonials in any of their promotional materials. Usually, they don't cost a penny.

There is nothing quite like an honest face and the signature of someone to give credibility to your consulting services. Every time you make a major claim about your service, provide a satisfied-buyer testimonial.

A good testimonial assures the precise benefits a satisfied customer has received from your service. The person giving the testimonial should be someone your potential customers relate to and admire.

Don't be bashful about asking your customers for testimonials. Most will be happy to tell you how they feel about your services. Their comments are more influential than your advertisements.

Follow these suggestions to obtain testimonials. First, send out a questionnaire or customer satisfaction survey to your customers soliciting their opinions and comments. Include a section with prewritten statements about your product, such as "Which of the following statements would describe how you feel about this product?"

Also, ask what your customers like about your service. Inquire how you could improve upon the service they received. Ask if they would recommend your service to a business associate. Last, ask if you can share their statements with other potential customers. Most people will say yes.

Respondents who check appropriate statements or add desirable statements of their own can then be contacted by telephone. Ask them to sign a written release and give you permission to quote them by name in your marketing materials. If the respondent agrees, commission a local photographer to take a photo and secure the signed release.

Another way to obtain testimonials is to call customers after they have purchased your service and question them about their satisfaction. Write down their verbal comments and edit their statements to reflect their opinions in the most positive way. Send them a copy to review for accuracy and permission to quote.

If you are lucky, you could receive an unsolicited letter in the mail. Immediately write back thanking this customer. Request his or her permission to use the letter in your promotional materials.

Do not use people's names without first obtaining written permission to quote their statements in your marketing materials. Ask your attorney to check your permission statement to ensure it's appropriate for the situation.

Testimonials must be based on actual use of your product. If the testimonial is a statement of opinion, identify it as such to avoid the impression that the person has a professional or authoritative basis.

The more testimonials you have, the better. Collect several testimonials and use those that are most appropriate for each marketing piece. It usually doesn't matter how old they are. They are more believable than ads and give you clout in the marketplace.

One of the key problems in using testimonials is that they take time to obtain. Another problem is that you might not be able to get a release to use the testimonial in advertising.

Once you have the testimonials you need, incorporate them in every promotional piece you develop. You can add key phrases in direct-mail pieces, advertisements, brochures, newsletters, flyers, and so on. Or you can feature the entire testimonial letter in your reception area. Frame the letter and hang it on a wall in your office. You could also put testimonial letters in an attractive scrapbook that you leave on the table in your waiting room for customers to read.

Don't forget to ask those who give testimonials if they would like several copies to give to their business associates or friends. Offer them an incentive such as a discount or coupon for spreading the word about your products. Or you could offer to give them an incentive every time someone they have talked to purchases from you and mentions their name.

Testimonials are powerful sales tools and can build immediate trust and credibility in your services.

Public Relations

You Need a "Hook" When Seeking Free Media Coverage

Question

My local newspaper just wrote an article on my business. How can I get more press coverage from this article? Should I send it to another editor?

Answer

Most likely, other editors from the major media will not write a new article on the same story you pitched before. Your angle is no longer fresh. You need to find a new "hook" to secure more publicity.

However, you could contact editors from trade or professional journals, special-interest periodicals, or other newsletters or magazines published from organizations you belong to. Make a list of these editors and see if they might be interested in writing about your angle.

✔ COURTNEY'S SMART TIP
The best way to increase the chances of getting publicity is to develop an angle or a newsworthy hook.

Your news story helps you only once—unless you reprint it and use it in your marketing materials. There are many other things you can do with publicity you receive to market your business. Reprints of stories enhance your image and give you more credibility. These stories are more believable than your own advertising and promotional material.

Reprints also make excellent sales aids. Obtain permission from the media, then copy your story on glossy white paper stock for a more elegant look. Some national magazines or journals offer their own reprint services.

Add reprints to your media kit, or create a kit and use it in publicity efforts for prospective customers. Use reprints to get on an interview show or booked as a guest speaker.

✔ COURTNEY'S SMART TIP

Establish a relationship with the media instead of blindly sending out press releases. After sending your story for press release, follow up and ask if and when the story will be used.

Develop a letter or flyer offering your services as a speaker. Attach your biographical sketch and include the publicity you have received. Write your own speaker introduction and mention these stories to build your credentials. Then include reprints as part of your handouts at your speeches or presentations.

Excerpt parts of the story and include that material in your company brochures or newsletters. Or insert the entire reprint in your brochures. Attach reprints to your business card and give them to prospective clients.

Think about creating a flyer and turn your reprint into ads, posters, or direct-mail pieces. Begin by putting a headline at the top of the page and use the story as a graphic. Add the name of your business, your address, business hours, and other critical information at the bottom.

Include reprints of your stories and articles in your business plan to strengthen your image. Send reprints to your banker to keep on building your credibility and integrity. Create a testimonial sheet and include the publicity you receive.

Laminate or frame the printed pieces and hang them on your office walls or in merchandise displays. Exhibit these reprints at trade shows, community fairs, or business-to-business expos.

You have everything to gain and little to lose by trying to seek additional publicity to advance your business. Remember, publicity breeds publicity. As Oscar Wilde said, "There's only one thing in the world worse than being talked about, and that is not being talked about."

Pitching Product to the Press Helps Get the Word Out

Question

I'm introducing a unique food product in the marketplace. How can I get a feature story about it in a newspaper or magazine?

Answer

Develop a public-relations program and use it to supplement your advertising and promotional campaign. Publicity is an excellent vehicle for entrepreneurs to use when introducing a new product or building a fast-growing company. It's a cost-effective and creative way to market.

The first step is to target specific media that reach the audience you want. Choose the media most advantageous for your product.

Knowing who to reach, how to communicate with them, and how to entice them to write about your product is an art, and it takes time. If you do it yourself, identify editors who might be interested in your story.

Read stories published by your target media so you can learn what they write about and determine what they might need. Editors are constantly under pressure to deliver news and feature stories that appeal to their audiences.

Next, develop an angle or newsworthy hook. Think about what is different or unique about your product and how it might interest a large number of people. If you can't think of one, it's critical to learn how to make news. Look for seasonal trends or news issue tie-ins. To increase your chances for publicity, include a free offer or inexpensive special discount. To establish and build credibility, make sure that your product does what you say it does and that your information is accurate.

Have your story written before you contact the media. You never know when media people need to fill space and will use your story because it is convenient. Consider writing both a short piece and a longer story since space availability varies.

Identify the editors who are responsible for the type of story you are pitching. Start by establishing a working relationship with these sources. Call to schedule an appointment. Take editors out to breakfast, lunch, or coffee. If the editor seems busy, ask if there is a better time to call. Make it a point to know the best time to reach them. Since media people are exceptionally busy, they may just ask you to send the story.

Secure a referral if possible. If not, you can make a cold call if you are knowledgeable about the publication and type of stories.

Before sending out a promotional piece, consider contacting an editor to see if he or she is truly interested in your story. Be prepared to discuss several different angles to your story. This ensures that your materials will be put in the requested material pile and not the unsolicited materials pile.

Make your pitch in 30 seconds or less. Be professional, polite, warm, and concise. The editor is deciding on you as well as your story. Treat the media person as a peer and make yourself a valuable resource person able to provide industry information and answer the editor's questions.

Add a brief, personal handwritten cover note to the material, you send. After sending materials and giving people an opportunity to review them, follow up. Ask if you called at a good time and make sure the person is not working under a deadline. Ask if and when the story will be used.

If the editor says he or she is not interested, ask how the story might be adapted to meet the publication's needs. You might be able to reconstruct your angle to make the story suitable. Or ask if another editor might be interested in your story. Then inquire what types of stories the editor is interested in. Thank the editor for his or her time and leave the door open for another try.

If you reach voice mail, leave a clear, concise message. If the editor doesn't return your call within two days, call back in the morning before 9:00 A.M. or leave another message with an editorial assistant.

Remember, when you provide the media with the information about your product, editors decide whether to cover your story and what to write about it. You have no control. That's the difference between advertising and publicity. With advertising, you control the message.

Telemarketing

Using 800 Telephone Numbers to Expand Market Share

Question

I have just self-published a book and plan to sell it from my office at home by advertising in trade magazines and appearing on both radio and television talk shows. Would it be a good idea to set up an 800 telephone number for orders, or would an 800 number be cost-prohibitive?

Answer

If more than 20% of your projected revenue will come from clients outside of your local calling area, installing a toll-free 800 number is an excellent marketing strategy. Many marketing surveys reveal that customers first call businesses that advertise a toll-free 800 number. And for every long-distance customer who would normally call you, you can expect to gain two more customers if you have an 800 number. Your average revenue per transaction should indicate whether the cost of installing an 800 line is cost-effective for your business.

Today, telephone and communications systems provide many timesaving and cost-effective features to entrepreneurs. Obtaining an 800 number is not as complicated and expensive as it used to be. It is as easy as setting up a business telephone line. You do not need a separate telephone line installed for your 800 number, as was required in the past. Many of these new 800 features are offered as a result of the growth of entrepreneurship and small businesses.

One variety of toll-free telephone service allows callers within the United States to place orders or make inquiries by calling 800 lines that are answered by commercial communications organizations. These companies provide a complete range of services, from telemarketing fulfillment to database development.

The costs of 800 services vary widely. Start your research by contacting the major telephone companies and comparing their prices and services. Ask if there is an installation charge and, if so, how much it is. Look for special promotions. Sometimes the companies will offer installation or a month's service for free.

Monthly fees for an 800 line vary from $6 to $20, plus per-minute use charges. Ask if the company offers a volume discount. If you average a certain dollar amount per month, you may be eligible for such a discount. The cost for inbound toll-free telephone reception and order-taking services is usually a monthly minimum fee for a certain amount of orders.

Check to see if the company offers any special discounts for heavy usage from certain areas. For example, if your business receives many calls from a particular city, the company may reduce the charges with a favorite city discount. Such discounts are available both nationally and internationally. Also ask if the company gives credit for wrong numbers. To avoid potential problems with wrong numbers, request an 800 number that has not been assigned for some time.

Telephone billing policies are critical to business owners. Look for a company that bills in six-second increments rather than by the minute. Then, if a customer calls and you talk for one minute and 10 seconds, you will not be charged for the full two minutes. This will save you some money.

An 800 number adds credibility and is cost-effective for home-based businesses. It will give your customers the impression that you have a solid and reputable company even if you work out of your garage or basement. It adds credibility and prestige to your image regardless of whether you operate a small or large venture.

Using 900 Telephone Numbers to Sell Products and Services

Question

I have a small financial-management consulting company and recently read an article about 900 numbers. How can I go about setting up one of these numbers for my business?

Answer

It's the immediacy that entices callers to initially dial 900 numbers for either information or service. What keeps them calling is the currency, professionalism, and uniqueness of the information being offered. If you can provide quick, convenient, and accurate information, a 900 line may be a good supplement to your business. However, it is important for you to thoroughly research 900 lines to see if you can be successful using them. Your credibility and reputation in the industry will determine whether potential customers call your line.

Essentially, customers pay a per-minute fee to receive the information the business is selling on the 900 line. This pay-per-call service has experienced tremendous growth over the years and currently generates nearly $1 billion a year in sales. Telephone companies act as carriers of the lines and handle all the billing of 900 calls on the consumer's regular phone bill. Calls are charged at a predetermined rate, and the carrier is paid a percentage of each call, or sale. The balance is sent to the information provider within 30 to 90 days of billing.

Three phone companies that provide 900 numbers are Sprint, MCI, and AT&T. They offer similar services but charge and bill somewhat differently, and each has different policies on processing collectibles. All three companies offer discounts for volume usage. At this writing, standard charges for businesses using a 900 number are about $3 for the first minute and $1.50 for each additional minute. The average 900 call lasts 10 minutes. Of course, the length of calls varies with the type of service or product being sold.

Start-up costs vary tremendously, depending on the type of information being provided. For many entrepreneurs, these costs may seem extremely high. That's why it is important to contact a telephone service bureau that has a good reputation and reliable references from both the carrier and customers. Typically, a service bureau has a fully equipped and staffed facility that services a number of different information providers.

Several reputable service companies help owners start and operate 900 lines. Call-Interactive, 402-498-7000, works out of Omaha, Nebraska; and WTS, 214-920-1900, is in Dallas, Texas. Look for other service bureaus that do business in your industry. Ask your industry association for referrals. *Always get referrals*.

The Information Industry Association in Washington, DC, is involved with the creation and distribution of information services. In exchange for a stamped self-addressed envelope, you will receive a free two-page brochure entitled "Customer Service Guide for 900 Programs." The booklet explains how 900 lines work and provides a mini-directory of 900 numbers along with other valuable information. You might also look into *Entrepreneur* magazine's business guide, "Operating a 900 Number for Profit." Or consult Robert Mestin's book *How to Succeed with Your Own 900 Business*.

Remember, there are ongoing marketing costs associated with a 900 line. Experts suggest that entrepreneurs allocate enough dollars to market their 900 numbers for at least six months without relying on incoming revenues. Like any other marketing technique, 900 numbers do not automatically make customers beat a path to your doorway. How you market and advertise a 900 line will significantly affect your sales.

Expanding Your Market through Consignment

Accepting Consignment Goods to Expand Inventory

Question

I am trying to market wood-laminated canoe and kayak paddles but I am having trouble getting my product in sporting goods stores. Several managers of these stores have offered to take my products on consignment. Should I accept their offers?

Answer

Generally, consignment is not a recommended route for an entrepreneur, unless the product is new and untested in the market, and it's one of the only ways you can get your product into retail stores. One of the key problems is that middlemen or distributors may not give your consigned merchandise as much attention as the goods in which they have their own money invested. The profit margin for retailers is less on consigned merchandise, so their motivation to sell your product may be lower. They are usually more concerned with selling products that cost them money if not sold. If you choose consignment, you might consider offering incentives to retailers to motivate them to sell your goods more quickly.

Another major problem with consignment is that you cannot count any delivered merchandise as a sale. Consignments should not be recorded in your ledgers. You do not know whether the transaction is a sale until it is either paid for or returned. All that has occurred is that some of your goods are being stored on someone else's shelf or in a warehouse. For these reasons, consignment merchandise causes numerous accounting problems. Since consigned goods are not sold, they cannot be counted as income. If the goods are shown as accounts receivable, you are falsely inflating your income statements, and your financial statement becomes distorted. Consigned merchandise should be tracked separately to avoid such problems.

Further, once the goods are sold, it may be difficult to receive payment for them. Record keeping and sales reporting must be kept current and verified regularly, and periodic inventory counts must be made to ascertain sales in order to receive payment for goods sold. How will returns be handled? Auditing consigned merchandise is an administrative headache.

Other obstacles abound. What happens to your merchandise when the retailer is cash-poor and is unable to pay for sold merchandise or declares bankruptcy? Damaged merchandise can also be an ordeal. Some employees are not as careful with consigned stock. If any of your merchandise is damaged, you must take it back and absorb the damage costs.

✔ COURTNEY'S SMART TIP
If you decide to put your merchandise on consignment, buy insurance coverage.

Consigned goods remain your merchandise and not the property of the retailer. What would happen if your merchandise was damaged by flood, hurricane, or fire? Insurance is essential and can represent a significant added expense, depending on the value of your goods and the conditions under which they are sold and warehoused.

Bankers, venture capitalists, and other lenders will look at consignment merchandise with a jaundiced eye. They much prefer to see solid sales in which money comes back, not your goods. You may be painting a weak image of your company if many of your goods are on consignment.

On the positive side, placing your goods on consignment may allow you to gain wider distribution. Distributors do not have to pay to carry your goods and might be willing to add them to their product lines at no cost. This could be an avenue of additional sales. Also, you can control the pricing of consigned merchandise and thus avoid price-cutting in the marketplace. If your goods sell, you should be able to convince the retailer to purchase them outright on a regular basis. This might enable you to establish a solid market position.

In certain situations, you may have no choice but to place your goods on consignment. If your merchandise is going to sell at the retail level, a consignment deal must be accepted. This is especially true if you have new, untested products or if you want retailers to stock a large inventory in anticipation of forthcoming demand. Astute entrepreneurs should carefully consider all the pros and cons before placing their goods on consignment. Consignment is great for the retailer but could be a disaster for you.

✔ COURTNEY'S SMART TIP

Instead of consignment, consider giving the retailer delayed-payment terms with generous return privileges.

Using Sales Representatives

Using Sales Reps to Market Products and Services

Question

I have just developed a new software product, and I am considering using sales representatives to market my software. Is it a good idea to use reps, and how do I go about finding good ones?

Answer

Contracting with independent sales representatives can be an excellent way for you to market your product, especially if your venture is underfinanced. Many entrepreneurs use outside reps as their initial sales staff and marketing department.

Sales representatives are granted the exclusive right to sell your product in a certain territory. Sometimes, they participate in setting the price, terms of sale, and/or other marketing decisions. An important advantage is that you do not add sales reps to your payroll. Reps get paid only when the customer pays for the goods sold. No sales, no collection, no pay. Commission checks are not written until you receive payment for the goods. This approach enhances your cash flow and minimizes the capital requirements for your business.

Good sales reps have knowledge of a specific territory and prospective customers. Generally, they carry several products in the same line. Thus, their frequency of contact per customer may be higher than with a hired sales force. Their customer lists are extremely valuable and can give your product or service instant credibility. Last, you can build a rep team much more quickly than a direct sales force of your own.

On the other side, reps may have more productive lines than yours and therefore devote much of their energies to promoting their bread-and-butter lines with the highest sales. Commissions may be high. Depending on the industry, reps may want between 5% and 25% as commission. Also, reps may need a great amount of time and support from others in your company to close a sale. They are sometimes difficult to monitor, train, and motivate. Reps may lack the time to successfully promote a new line and build up your markets. Overall, you lose some control over your market and customers by using reps.

One good method of finding competent reps is to search in the trade directories. These directories identify what reps are in a given area, what types of lines they handle, and what types of customers they service. Or find out what reps your competition uses. Look up a manufacturer of complementary products and call the sales manager to inquire about what reps are used.

You can also contact various local or national associations of reps and dealers. Some organizations employ a variety of sales reps who cover large territories. Search them out at your industry trade shows along with independent reps. Chambers of commerce often maintain lists of reps and agents as well.

After identifying several reputable reps, ask for references from current clients. Make a thorough check. Many reps have convincing sales pitches but mediocre performance. Ask the rep to schedule a few sales calls to some of his or her prospective customers, and accompany the rep on these calls. Observe the rep's sales techniques and ability to close the sale. Clarify the sales volume you expect from the rep's territory. Draw up a performance contract based on a guaranteed amount of sales. If the rep does not perform, then you can cancel the contract. Be careful of escape clauses that allow reps to bail out when it seems advantageous to them.

If the sales rep is your only means of penetrating the marketplace, any rift in your relationship can place you at risk. Use several reps or rep organizations to market your product or service.

How to Introduce a New Product at a Trade Show

Question

What are the advantages of marketing at trade shows to introduce a new product or service or to expand existing markets?

Answer

For a relatively low cost, you can reach a large number of high-quality prospects by spending a few days attending or exhibiting at the right trade show. Thousands of trade shows are held all over the world but finding the *right* one can be tricky. The question to consider is this: What trade shows should you attend to intercept your target customers?

Studies indicate that 50% of the people attending trade shows do so for the purpose of seeing new products and services. Thus, they are ideal marketing opportunities for entrepreneurs. Many founders claim that the success of their ventures is largely attributable to the effectiveness of using trade shows.

What are the benefits of attending trade shows? First, the prospects, many whom you probably do not know, come directly to you. It is an excellent chance to encounter people in the industry whom you would otherwise never have an opportunity to meet. Second, you can display and demonstrate product quality or superiority. You can answer any questions from prospects about your product or service. In addition, you can use this meeting to establish a successful business relationship by inviting them to a follow-up breakfast, lunch, or dinner meeting.

Here are some entrepreneurial dos and don'ts when it comes to attending trade shows:

- Do select a trade show at which the right prospects will be attending, and visit as many exhibits as possible. Preplan your marketing strategy and set some specific objectives to achieve while attending the show.

- Develop some quick screening questions to ask, so you can quickly identify solid prospects. Follow up on all leads and contacts as soon as you return to the office.
- Don't wait until the last minute to sign up for booth space. Instead, try to secure prime exhibit space. Don't run out of product to sell and/or samples to give away. Don't use giveaways that have nothing to do with your product or service. Don't run out of business cards.
- Don't allow anyone representing you to wear inappropriate clothing. Ensure that people are properly trained to answer all questions from prospects.
- If you plan to exhibit, promote your product or service in advance by sending out invitations to visit your booth. Talk to exhibitors before the show to determine possible tie-ins.
- Hold a meeting with everyone on your team who will be covering the booth. Assign specific responsibilities to those involved in your exhibit. Reward the high achievers who get the most orders.
- Have news releases to give to reporters and editors who visit. Some seasoned entrepreneurs prepare press kits to disseminate at the show.
- Evaluate your performance while the experience of participating in the trade show is fresh. Determine what worked best, and continue using the most productive approaches.

Successful entrepreneurs learn to work trade shows for all they're worth. Nowhere will you have a better chance to meet the key players in your industry and learn what is happening. The contacts you make can ultimately provide you with significantly increased business that will firmly establish and increase your market share.

Pitfalls to Avoid

1. Underestimating people's inertia and the difficulty of penetrating your target market.

2. Miscalculating the amount of time and money it takes to successfully penetrate your market.

(Continued)

(Continued)

3. Paying too little attention to developing a current customer base to expand sales.

4. Purchasing untested mailing lists and sending marketing materials without an immediate follow-up call or additional mailings.

5. Sending out brochures and thinking that many people will respond.

6. Putting your goods on consignment without purchasing insurance to cover loss or damage.

7. Failing to use performance contracts when hiring sales representatives.

8. Failing to pay earned commissions to your sales reps in a timely manner.

9. Designing and using standard, unimaginative, plain-white business cards.

10. Attending a trade show without researching who will be attending and identifying your target customers.

11. Sending out press releases without first contacting the media, determining their interest, and then following up about possible publication.

12. Failing to give away samples or gifts while exhibiting at a trade show.

13. Wasting time on bad customers.

9

Financing Your Venture

Overview

Looking for start-up and expansion capital is an ongoing and increasingly difficult task for entrepreneurs who are always short of cash. Most entrepreneurs fail to realize that personal savings and/or friendly money finance most start-up ventures in the early stages of development.

Your success depends on the type of business, its age, your industry, financial contacts, referrals, how much money you have already invested in the venture, how much money you are looking for, and matching the outside money sources to your business and expansion strategies.

Choosing the right source to contact is key to your future growth and development. A few money sources are interested in initial market research and development, but look to later stages of growth when the venture has an operating history. Some finance only small amounts of money while others have no maximum limit. Some finance only debt, some prefer equity, and some look for a combination of the two. Some investors want to be a part of the management team, while others don't want to be involved.

There is a wide range of financing sources, terms, and conditions, which makes raising capital even more difficult. For example, banks are structuring loans with less leverage, requiring heavy collateralization from homes and personal or business assets.

Most commercial banks are not interested in making loans to start-up ventures. If a bank turns you down, ask if the institution is an SBA lender. Many financial institutions are using SBA lending to offset their risk on loans to young companies. If the bank still turns you down, ask an investor to guarantee your loan.

Some entrepreneurs turn to venture-capital firms or angel-capital (private-investor) networks for seed money to launch their businesses. Here, too, the young start-up business can hit a wall. Most venture capitalists prefer to invest in older, more developed companies that offer opportunities for high growth—up to 60% to 70% annually.

The result is that most entrepreneurs fund their ventures with personal savings or money from friends and family. The most common funding sources at the early start-up stage involve M&Ds (moms and dads). Other sources of financing include professional acquaintances, past business colleagues, potential customers and suppliers, government programs, other entrepreneurs, private investors (commonly called angels), and corporate strategic alliances. One of my venture-capitalist friends labels many of these sources DDFFs (doctors, dentists, friends, and other fools).

One of the more contemporary financing approaches involves credit cards. Some entrepreneurs who cannot secure a bank loan or a line of credit finance their ventures by getting cash from different credit card companies. Sometimes, founders select members of their management team on the basis of how many different credit cards they possess and the lending limits on each card.

Another contemporary source of funding involves various types of factoring and financing companies. A factoring company purchases your accounts receivable and then advances you cash. Instead of looking to the borrower's credit, factors look at the credit of the borrower's customers and usually do their own collecting. Finance companies are secured lenders that provide funds that are backed by the borrower's assets. This collateral includes accounts receivable, inventories, plant, and equipment. Or founders use suppliers, leasing, private placements, or small-business public offerings as funding alternatives.

You can't know too many people or funding sources in the money market. The name of the game is contacts and referrals—made *before* you need money. Network with all money sources because many of the old deal makers are out of the picture or are now applying different criteria to their financing decisions. The rules are constantly changing in the money-raising game.

Smart Strategies for Financing New and Existing Ventures

1. Learn as much as possible about the money market and how to raise capital from different funding sources.

2. If you are raising money from friends and family, structure the deal professionally by signing a note or other type of agreement concerning the terms of the loan.

3. If your friends or family do not have any cash to lend you, consider asking them to guarantee the loan.

4. Contact the economic-development agency in your city or state to find out about government seed-capital funds.

5. Avoid looking for a banker for a financing relationship. Instead, look for a lender that is interested in you and your venture.

6. Get referrals to money sources you are considering contacting for capital.

7. Always have an updated business plan and current financial statements when meeting with potential lenders or investors.

8. Use lines of credit to accommodate cash flow crunches and seasonal credit demands of your business.

9. To create your own line of credit, submit credit card applications simultaneously to obtain several cards with cash-advance privileges.

10. Consider using factoring to solve short-term cash flow problems when you experience long delays between making and selling your product or service.

11. Consider establishing a strategic alliance with a corporation to secure funds to develop and/or expand your product or services.

12. Sell stock through the Small Corporate Offering Registration (SCOR).

13. Who has control is a critical factor in any capital structure.

14. Try to avoid personal responsibility for corporate debts; don't sign personally for a company obligation.

15. The equity control of a company's voting stock is the key to control.

16. Reinforce or establish a good relationship with your banker. A banker who has an understanding of your business and how it is run may be more inclined to lend credit.

Developing a Financial Strategy

Seed Capital for New Ventures

Question

Where can I find money for my new lawn care and sprinkler business?

Answer

Finding capital is a standard problem for most entrepreneurs. Raising money is an art. Fortunately, it is one you can learn. It is critical to gain knowledge of the money market, the people in it, and how to interact with them. The fact is that alternative (nonbanking) sources provide the best avenue for aspiring entrepreneurs. Each of these sources is discussed here.

Self-Financing

There are many virtues to financing your new venture yourself. These range from being able to maintain total control of your business to being able to use the cheapest source of money. You can furnish your own capital through savings, income from a second job, or internal financing of an existing business. If you start your business on a shoestring, you can expand when you have generated enough capital. For entrepreneurs who love freedom and independence, this is one of the easiest and best approaches to take.

Relatives and Friends

Parents can also be a good, quick, and excellent source of financing. Even if they do not have large savings in the bank, they may have other assets that can be converted into cash. They may own a house free and clear of any mortgage payments and could possibly obtain a second mortgage. Alternatively, mom and dad could cosign a loan for your business. Uncle Clyde, Aunt Tillie, or your old school buddy could also loan you money for your new business. There are times when this is the wisest action to take; however, there may be problems later on. Be careful with money from extended family or friends. First, approach the deal professionally, as you would with an outside or traditional money source. Cut your deal, commit the terms to writing, and honor it as you would a deal with outside investors.

Verbal agreements can be disastrous and people's memory will fail over time. Family and friends can nag you to death and be tougher than outside creditors. If you lose this money, you'll pay for the rest of your life both in respect and in relationships.

Professional Advisers and Business Associates

Outside investors such as lawyers, business advisers, board members, successful entrepreneurs, and other professionals may invest seed capital in your venture. Informal investors often have noneconomic reasons as well as capital gains in mind when they invest. Sometimes members of the infrastructure will contribute their professional fees in exchange for stock in your company. To find such investors, ask for referrals.

Credit Cards

One of the more novel approaches to financing new ventures is obtaining cash through plastic (i.e., credit cards). Some entrepreneurs have recruited members of their management team on the basis of the number of credit cards they held and their credit limit on these cards. When additional capital was needed, the management team just applied for additional credit cards. This is a costly way to finance a business, but when people are desperate, they become very creative.

Customers in Hand

Look to your potential or current customers as plausible sources of financing. There may be instances when customers want your product or service so badly that they will either put a deposit up front with their order or supply the money you need to process and deliver the order. Existing customers can be an extremely cheap source of money. Ask for an installment or prepayment when they place an order. Even if you give customers a discount for paying COD, you may be money ahead.

Question

I would really like to start a new business and be my own boss. How can I get seed money to start such a business? Any information you have would be helpful.

Answer

There are no easy answers for locating money to start a new business. Seed money, sometimes called venture capital, is the money that goes into a business before it starts operating. Don't confuse seed money with seed capital from venture capitalists.

Sources of financing and penetrating a market are the two major problems most start-up businesses face. It is easier to attract financing if you have a track record and a proven market. But most start-ups do not have either.

The most common source of financing a start-up business is yourself. The second most common source is "friendly money" you obtain by contacting people you know and asking them to invest. There are many advantages to using your money to start the venture. You maintain control of the business while utilizing the cheapest form of financing available.

Once you have exhausted your own financial resources, think about contacting relatives, friends, business associates, and other private sources. If they do not have much money in savings, they may have other assets that can be converted into cash. They may own a home on which they could obtain a second mortgage. Or they may have stocks, bonds, or other assets that could be pledged.

Unfortunately, most entrepreneurs think of the bank as the most likely place to find financing. Although banks are often the quickest and cheapest source of money, they are probably the worst place to go unless you have sufficient collateral to guarantee the loan. Banks require assets that can be used as collateral along with a visible means of paying off the loan at a reasonable time in the future. Businesses usually need several years of operating history before they are considered creditworthy; most cannot get financing unless someone agrees to guarantee the loan.

Typically, a bank will ask for historical as well as pro forma balance sheets, income statements, cash flow projections, year-end financial statements, tax returns, and a business plan. The bank will also request a current personal financial statement and your personal tax returns for the past three years. Founders of new ventures do not have this type of information. Banks seldom furnish start-up money. Any money you are able to borrow from banks at the beginning of your venture will probably be loaned to you personally or on some basis other than your business.

✔ COURTNEY'S SMART TIP

Pursue friendly money sources. Network with everyone you know. Ask people if they can refer you to others who may be interested in investing in your type of venture. Keep widening your circle of funding contacts with successive referrals.

Studies done over the past 25 years indicate that most seed money for start-ups comes directly from the entrepreneur, partners associated with the business, and wealthy individuals. You can locate potential investors through the SBA; your banker, lawyer, or realtor; or other professionals. A limited amount of seed money may be available in your local community from regional development agencies. Contact the economic development office in your area to find out about such programs. Other sources of seed money are mortgage brokers (using your house equity as security) and credit unions.

Your ability to raise money depends on the soundness of your venture, your sales skills, how exciting you make the deal, your sources of friendly money, and the prospect's appetite. Use the following checklist as a guide to developing a financial strategy and securing funds for growth.

Smart Money Sources at a Glance

1. *Friendly money.* Friendly money sources include yourself, mom and dad, relatives, and friends. This is one of the quickest, cheapest, and easiest financing methods, especially for new start-ups.

2. *Commercial banks.* If your venture has no collateral, few assets, and/or little operating history, banks may not be a good source of funding. You must be willing to pledge your personal assets to secure a bank loan. Banks look for both primary and secondary sources of repayment.

3. *Finance companies.* Finance companies are primarily asset-based lenders, extending financing against receivables, inventory, equipment, and other hard forms of collateral.

4. *The SBA.* The SBA grants two types of loans. The most common type is a bank loan for which the SBA guarantees a large portion, typically 70% to 90%. The SBA in turn will require that the loan be collateralized with personal commitments from the principals.

5. *Leasing companies.* Leasing companies loan to businesses for the purchase of automobiles, trucks, computers, office furniture, and other equipment to help offset the initial outlay of cash for major purchases. Entrepreneurs usually are required to provide a personal guarantee to secure the lease.

6. *SBICs.* State financial aid is provided through SBICs (small business investment centers) licensed by the SBA. Typically, an SBIC makes loans for equipment purchases, facility improvements, new buildings, and sometimes working capital.

(Continued)

(Continued)

7. *Venture capitalists.* Venture-capital firms specialize in investing money in return for an equity position. They look for ventures that offer extremely high growth potential in a short time—for example, ones in which they can quintuple their investment in five years. Venture capitalists fund only about 1% of the deals that come across their desks.

8. *Investment bankers.* Investment-banking firms specialize in taking companies public through an initial public offering (IPO). They look for businesses that will achieve maximum growth with the right infusion of capital.

9. *Private placement.* A private placement is an investor-based securities issue that is exempt from the registration requirements of public offerings. Private placements involve offering stock, subordinated debt, convertible debt, or some other option to friendly sources, wealthy individuals, or venture-capital firms via a private-placement document.

10. *Small Corporate Offering Registrations (SCOR).* This gives owners a simplified process to raise money by selling their own stock to the public. It is a shortened prospectus offering up to $1 million in stock.

Tapping Traditional Money Sources

Borrowing from a Bank

Choosing the Right Bank

Question

I have been operating a small landscape business for eight years. It does well in the summer but dries up during the winter months, forcing me to deplete my savings. I have tried snowplowing as a second business, but it rarely brings in enough additional income. I would like to open a sandwich shop and have been seeking a small-business loan for $25,000. I have not been able to find a bank that is willing to loan the funds. Where can I go?

Answer

Before approaching a bank for a commercial loan, you must write a business plan that proves to the loan officer that you have thoroughly investigated your venture idea and can demonstrate that the business will earn a profit, that it has growth potential, and, most important, that you will be able to repay the loan. Even then, the bank may decide not to make the loan.

Why? Many banks prefer not to fund new ventures. They like to see a track record of a couple of years. "But," you say, "I have run another small business for eight years. Isn't that enough?" Because you have operated a landscape business does not mean that you can manage a sandwich shop. Management skills are not necessarily transferable from one industry to another. Besides, you have chosen a high-risk industry—the restaurant business.

Do you have any experience in the restaurant business? If not, does anyone on your proposed management team have such experience? You must be able to show that you or someone associated with your new venture has related industry experience. A well-written business plan will confirm that there is a need for a sandwich shop in the location you have chosen, that there are enough potential customers in the surrounding area to support your business, and that you can generate a profit.

If you are able to prove all these facts, seek out banks that specialize in working with entrepreneurs and making loans to start-ups. Try to find banks that loan to restaurateurs. Talk with friends, accountants, attorneys, insurance agents, and other business consultants. Try to secure referrals to loan officers representing at least three different banks.

✔ COURTNEY'S SMART TIP

Avoid cold calling on a banker. Whenever possible, ask someone to call the banker and extend a personal recommendation before your first meeting.

Developing and writing a business plan, establishing a banking relationship, and securing a loan could be a lengthy process. Start early. If possible, establish a banking relationship with a potential lender long before you need a loan. A bank's willingness to fund a start-up venture depends on its policies, current loan requests, and existing loan portfolio. If you do not have enough collateral to borrow against, or do not have enough assets in the business, you probably won't get a bank loan.

Try to secure a government-backed loan through the Small Business Administration or through state and local government revolving-loan funds. The SBA loan program provides a guarantee to banks of up to 90% of loans to small businesses, with maximal exposure of up to $750,000, or in special situations up to $1,000,000. Since not all banks are SBA lenders, ask the loan officer which government-backed loan programs the bank participates in. You might also contact your state's office of economic development to find out about local and state loan programs.

Question

I am getting ready to start a small data-processing business and need to find a bank that will work with me, set up my accounts, and perhaps loan my business funds to expand at some future date. Do you have any suggestions on how to establish a satisfying banking relationship?

Answer

Finding the right bank and loan officer is an art—and a difficult one at best, since bankers usually have a different perspective on businesses than do entrepreneurs. Discovering the right loan officer who understands your business and supports your strategic plans takes time and effort.

Successful banking relationships are built on the personal ties you develop with your banker. Search for several different banks that target businesses like yours for clients. Begin by contacting the bank at which you have your personal accounts, if the bank can meet your business needs.

Smart Guidelines for Establishing a Banking Relationship

1. *Get referrals.* Speak to colleagues, accountants, lawyers, insurance agents, or other business consultants. Knowing the right person to talk to through an introduction from a business associate is a good start in building a banking relationship.

   - Always act professionally. Set up an appointment. Don't just walk into a bank and introduce yourself. Dress for success. First impressions are critical. Demonstrate that you run a professional business.

2. *Be prepared.* Always bring in an updated business plan and current financials, such as cash flows, income statements, and balance sheets. Bankers need to know that you have thoroughly investigated the venture, proved that the business can earn a profit, and shown that the venture has growth potential. Offer to drop off the business plan before the meeting so the banker can have an opportunity to review your venture.

3. *Look for compatibility.* Determine how accessible the banker will be to meet with you regularly, return phone calls, and discuss your business problems. If possible, find a banker who has lending experience in your industry. A banker can be one of the most important professionals on your team.

4. *Ask about lending limits.* Determine if your financial requests can be accommodated. Make sure you give your banker a specific loan amount. Bankers become frustrated when discussing loans with entrepreneurs who are not sure of how much money they want or need.

5. *Shop around for services and rates.* Know what you want from the banking relationship and determine whether a bank can provide all the services you require. Banks have different objectives, charge different fees, and set varying interest rates. Refrain from negotiating the terms and rates of your loan until after the bank has approved your request.

> **✔ COURTNEY'S SMART TIP**
> Establish a banking relationship with a potential lender *before* you need a loan.

Developing a banking relationship and securing a loan take time. Start early. A bank's ability to lend to a start-up business varies and depends on the number of current loan requests and the bank's existing loan portfolio. If you do not have enough collateral or do not have enough assets in the business, obtaining a business loan will be difficult.

How to Obtain a Line of Credit

Question

I periodically need temporary injections of money to help me with my cash flow peaks and valleys. Is establishing a line of credit a possible solution to this problem? How do entrepreneurs access and use bank lines of credit? Are they difficult to obtain, or are banks fairly willing to grant them?

Answer

As a result of seasonal credit demands, entrepreneurs frequently encounter difficulties managing their cash flow. This is especially true of business start-ups during their early stages of development when they have not diversified enough to generate a constant positive cash flow. Once inventory has been purchased, it is necessary to ride out the cycle until accounts receivable have been collected. Without sufficient working capital, a serious cash flow problem could develop. These types of cash flow problems have forced many entrepreneurs to close down businesses that were making money on paper, but just ran out of cash.

Lines of credit accommodate the seasonal credit demands of your business along with ups and downs in your cash flow. They also enable you to purchase inventory in anticipation of future sales. Discuss establishing a line of credit with your bank at the beginning of your relationship. If you are just starting your business, the bank will probably not grant a credit line immediately.

A line of credit is a standard service provided by many banks that serve small businesses. Getting the loan approved depends on the business's ability to repay and/or the personal assets of the owner—for example, a second mortgage on a home, assignment of stocks and bonds, or assignment of the cash value of life insurance policies.

Banks extend a secured line of credit to most start-up ventures. The line may be unsecured if the business can demonstrate consistent earnings, an excellent capital position, and multiple sources of repayment. Traditionally, banks will commit a specified maximum amount of funds from which you are permitted to draw on as needed. You have the right to repay and reborrow during the agreed-on time, which usually will not exceed a year. You pay interest only on the outstanding principal.

In addition, the bank needs to know how you will repay the line when your first source of repayment does not come through. Bankers look for enough elasticity in your operations to accommodate temporary reversals in adverse situations. What happens when you discover that your inventory is not selling as projected? What secondary sources of repayment are available?

Banks may also require you to pay down your line of credit when you have not followed your payment schedule, even though the total amount of money that you borrowed is not due for several more months. Banks do not like to approve lines of credit for use in managing cash flow. Instead, lines of credit are intended for cyclical borrowing needs at identified paydown intervals. A failure to pay back the money on schedule indicates a potential problem in your ability to manage cash.

Smart Tips for Establishing a Line of Credit

1. Most likely a bank will not issue a line of credit to a new venture without the owner's personal guarantee of repayment.

2. If your business is relatively new and the bank is not satisfied with the primary and secondary sources of repayment, it may ask for personal collateral from you to secure the loan.

3. If the venture is a partnership or corporation with more than one principal, the bank will most likely collateralize the loan from all the principals involved to obtain a line of credit.

4. You must present reasonable financial documents that follow standard accounting practices to obtain a line of credit.

5. Unless you are a well-established business, you must provide pro forma cash flow documents that demonstrate your ability to pay back the money. Pro forma balance sheets and income statements will also be required.

Examine Revolving Loan Options Carefully

Question

I'm interested in obtaining a revolving loan from my bank so I can purchase more inventory for the Christmas season. My business is only a year old, it does not have many assets, and I'm cash-poor. I have not been able to get dating from my suppliers and have to pay them 30 days after my order is delivered. Is this the best type of loan to obtain because of my seasonal inventory situation?

Answer

Not necessarily. If you need cash to purchase inventory to prepare for the Christmas season, most likely you will not receive the cash from Christmas sales for six to seven months. If the bank calls the loan during the interim period and you are short of cash with no other lending alternatives to pursue, you might be forced to close down your business.

You are right that a revolving loan agreement is where the bank lends money up to a certain amount for a specific time. The borrower can repay and borrow again as long as the maximum amount of the loan is not exceeded. Each time the borrower needs more money, a new loan is signed. Old loans are destroyed and reissued in the new loan amount as the borrower's cash needs change.

Sometimes this process is simplified when the bank uses a master note or loan that records each advance and repayment. Or an account may be established that similarly records each transaction and provides a monthly statement that shows the activity and the current balance. In essence, a revolving loan is an agreement that provides for a full repayment of the amount borrowed at some time in the future. The banker can continue to roll over the loan amount indefinitely.

But problems can occur when the bank suddenly notifies you that it does not have sufficient funds to use as working capital and is calling the loan. The bank's regulators could have demanded such an action and they have no alternative. This frequently occurs when the revolving loan is not paid down at least once during a 12-month period. If this situation occurs, you are responsible for repaying the note on the date specified by your banker.

Unfortunately, you have all your cash tied up in inventory waiting for Christmas sales. Your inventory cannot be immediately liquidated to pay off the loan. Sometimes entrepreneurs find themselves in this situation and have nowhere to turn for cash.

Securing a revolving loan is ideal in this situation only if you can negotiate a substantial grace period before you are required to repay the note. Or negotiate for the right to convert your revolving loan to a fixed-term loan, which in essence is the same as obtaining a grace period with a definite expiration date. Don't sign the revolving-loan agreement without getting either of these options.

It is critical for entrepreneurs to know about all the special loan options available and understand all the conditions outlined in the loan agreement. In addition, it is important to examine the true interest rate for the loan. Carefully review it to determine if a compensating balance and a commitment fee are included in the loan agreement.

For example, the interest on the loan agreement may appear to be uncomplicated. But if the interest rate is floating, you have no control or way to accurately measure the interest cost of the loan.

Likewise, the bank may require that you keep a compensating balance in your checking account as long as the loan is outstanding. In effect, you are paying interest on the money borrowed while being required to keep a certain amount of money that is earning little or no interest. You need a good accountant and/or a computer to track how much you are truly paying for the loan.

Last, the bank may demand that you pay a commitment fee for the amount of the loan not drawn down at any time. Therefore, you are paying for the privilege of being able to increase the amount borrowed up to the loan limit. If this situation arises, ask the banker to adjust your interest rate downward to account for the commitment fee.

Read all the provisions in the loan agreement. Negotiate for protections of a grace period or for converting your revolving loan into a fixed loan. Last, calculate the true interest rate and negotiate any commitment fee. If the real costs of the loan are higher than the interest rate of your credit card, use that card, or seek a line of credit. If this financing option does not work for you, explore using your purchase-orderers to obtain financing or contract financing. Contact a local financing or factoring company.

Some Loans Call for a Guaranty

Question

I recently went to get a loan from my banker, who told me that I would need to sign a personal guaranty. One of the reasons I incorporated my business was to protect my assets and not sign personally for anything related to my business. Is this standard, and do I have to sign a guaranty?

Answer

Typically, bankers require a personal guaranty when you're securing a commercial loan, especially if you cannot offer collateral owned by your business. The personal guaranty provides that if your corporation defaults on the note signed by the business, you are personally responsible for the debt. You are right that one of the main advantages of incorporating is to protect your personal assets from the debts of your business. But the personal guaranty could impact this advantage.

Lenders are reluctant and take great caution when lending money. They typically require both a primary and a secondary source of repayment to ensure they can collect on a loan. The primary source could be the firm's revenue flow and the secondary source the sale of collateral. Seldom will they lend money in the hopes of collecting on the collateral if you default. They want their money back with interest, not your property or business.

Also, most bankers insist on your signing a personal guaranty to make certain that you and your management team have maximum motivation to pay off the loan. They explain that they are testing management's faith in the business and ensuring that you and your managers devote all your efforts to operating the business profitably.

If you fail to pay, lenders want to ensure that the borrower can repay the debt with secured collateral. If your business doesn't have any, the banker will look to the owners. They don't want the borrower to be able to walk away from the scene unscathed with the lender left holding the bag.

If there are multiple owners, the bank will ask that all of them guaranty the loan, and each will be jointly and severally liable. This means that the owners will be liable for the entire amount. If your co-owners are not as solvent as you, then you will be liable for the entire amount.

How to Secure Merchant's Credit Card Status

Question

I am contemplating starting a small direct-mail business. I am considering setting up a merchant's credit with Visa/MasterCard as a convenience for those ordering merchandise from me. How can a new mail-order enterprise obtain merchant's credit card status? I found one book on the subject that costs $135. Do you have any suggestions?

Answer

It is difficult for a new business owner to establish credit and receive immediate approval from a bank for merchant's credit card status. But it can be done. It hinges on the relationship you have established with your banker. Developing a good, sound relationship and proving your creditworthiness can ensure that you receive approval to use Visa, MasterCard, or other types of credit cards in your business.

Bankers are reluctant to approve credit card usage for a new mail-order business because of numerous credit card scams—especially when there are no signatures accompanying customer orders. An owner could set up a bogus mail-order business, advertise nationally, receive thousands of dollars in orders, close up the business, and skip town with a big wad of cash before customers even expected to receive their orders. A few bad apples have spoiled it for many new mail-order business owners.

Who is liable when such a scam occurs? The bank. Therefore, bankers view mail-order businesses as extremely risky, unless the business owner is well known in the community, has a proven product or service, and has an established business and operating history of chargebacks. Most bankers also realize that new products and/or services could be defective. There may be a high rate of customer dissatisfaction and, consequently, chargebacks. What type of warranty do you offer? What are your return policies? How quickly do you deliver new orders? If the chance to dispute charges in your business is great, bankers will shy away from approving credit cards for your business.

Some industries are riskier than others for credit card charges and typically have higher rates of chargebacks. For example, businesses selling services by telephone and offering mail-order vitamins and water purifiers have poor credit card histories. Also, telemarketing companies and businesses that use fulfillment houses to fill orders have higher-than-average chargebacks.

If the bank is skeptical about approving credit cards for your business, suggest that it hold a certain amount of funds for 90 days or so before you can collect your credit card charges. Such an arrangement could be written into the merchant agreement you sign with the bank. Or propose that the bank set up a reserve account or certificate of deposit that will guarantee a certain amount of funds if your chargebacks are higher than anticipated.

✔ COURTNEY'S SMART TIP
Shop around for the best credit card rates available. These rates are always negotiable.

Individual banks have varying rates, depending on how much they mark up credit card services, how good a customer you are, how many accounts you have with the bank, and the volume of business you do. These rates are always negotiable. The longer you have been in business, the more negotiating power you have. Regardless of the terms, bankers will perform due diligence to ensure that you are a reputable business owner, have a reliable product, and are creditworthy.

Credit card processors will also monitor your chargeback status. Once chargebacks have reached 5% or greater, they will start to worry. If your chargebacks reach 7% or 8%, they will most likely cancel your credit. Instead, they like to see 1% to 2% chargebacks. Their customer-service area regularly observes how many complaints are received on your products or services. Either the bank or the processor can cancel your credit at any time. Once you receive approval, guard your credit.

How to Calculate Goodwill on a Balance Sheet

Question

I am a sole proprietor and have been in business for over three years, operating from my home in retail sales. I am pursuing an SBA-backed loan through a local bank. The loan officer advised me to include goodwill on my balance sheet. I don't know how to calculate this figure. I called many different sources but none could help. Can you tell me how to compute goodwill for my balance sheet?

Answer

Determining a reasonable goodwill figure for your balance sheet is most difficult. There is no universal rule on how to figure goodwill, which adds value to your venture. Essentially goodwill is based on future earning expectations. However, the difficulty lies in deciding the best way to measure and value future earnings. Goodwill is essentially the amount of the asking price for a company over and above the company's tangible net worth. In other words, if your asking price is higher than the venture's tangible net worth, you are selling goodwill. Sellers try to build in as much goodwill as possible, whereas buyers hope to minimize it. Sellers attempt to convince buyers that purchasing their company's name, reputation, and contacts is worth the higher price.

In most instances, goodwill is considered only when a company is being sold. Even though a strategic location, an impeccable reputation, or a superior product may create goodwill, it is usually not recorded by a company on its financial statements. Complicating the issue, lenders view goodwill very differently and focus on separate issues. Some look at it in terms of what presence the venture currently has in the marketplace, considering such factors as prestige and renown of the venture, record of successful operations over a long period, favorable customer relations, and ownership of a trade or brand name. Other lenders look at goodwill as an amount that indicates the venture's future profitability.

Overall, most bankers consider goodwill "blue sky"—that is, only the owner's assumption of what the venture is worth over and above its tangible net worth. It is possible to add goodwill to your balance sheet as a noncurrent asset in the intangible column, which includes such items as leasehold interests, patents, trade names, trademarks, and organizational expenses (i.e., fees).

However, be prepared for lenders to discount this entry or eliminate it completely. Goodwill is not looked at as a major cash driver of the business. Instead, the strengths of the owner and the management team are evaluated, as well as the strengths of your industry and the community you serve. On the balance sheet, lenders evaluate the net profits of the business and calculate the percentage of net profit in relation to total sales. They look for how much of your earned net profit is put back into the business in the form of retained earnings.

It is almost impossible to value the goodwill of your sole proprietorship, since you and the business are one and the same. If you sell your venture for more than its tangible net worth, then goodwill becomes an asset on your balance sheet. If you feel that a concrete valuation is important, you might contact a valuation expert or professional appraiser for assistance. Establish detailed and creative documentation to support the valuation you use.

If you are purchasing a business, remember that goodwill is not everlasting. A business with goodwill at the time of acquisition may lose some or all of its goodwill a short time later.

Venture Capitalists

Finding the Right Venture-Capital Company

Question

I am considering the possibility of starting a bus/shuttle service to transport bar and restaurant patrons. How can I attract and contact venture-capital firms?

Answer

Venture capital is probably one of the least understood areas of financing. Many entrepreneurs think that these investors do the early-stage financing of relatively small, rapidly growing enterprises. Venture capital is better defined as a professionally managed pool of participation through stocks, warrants, or convertible securities. If you think you have a venture that might qualify for venture-capital financing, here is how you go about locating and contacting venture-capital firms.

The first step is identifying venture-capital firms that might be interested in your company. You can consult *Pratt's Guide to Venture Capital Sources*, which lists more than 700 venture-capital companies and the types of companies they invest in. *Raising Venture Capital and the Entrepreneur* is a comprehensive guide to discovering money sources available through venture capitalists. You could also contact the National Venture Capital Association, which publishes an up-to-date list of its members and will send out free copies when requested. Contact one of the venture-capital clubs in your area. The Association of Venture Clubs in Salt Lake City, 801-364-1100, can provide a list of clubs. (See the "Contacts" section in the resource checklist at the end of this book.)

✔ **COURTNEY'S SMART TIP**
Always secure an introduction before contacting a venture-capital firm.

The more you can network with the infrastructure and other entrepreneurs to obtain referrals to venture capitalists, the better chance you have of securing financing from these investors. The referral may involve only a telephone call alerting the venture capitalists that your business is deserving of their consideration. Be sure to expose your deal to more than one potential venture capitalist.

Avoid mailing your business plan arbitrarily to many different venture capitalists. Safety in numbers is not the case when obtaining venture-capital financing. The best way to proceed is to contact 5 to 10 venture capital firms that, according to your referrals, have a reasonable probability of being interested in your company.

During the first contact, describe the venture, its products, the experience of your management team, the amount of capital sought, and the expected performance of the venture two to three years down the road. At this point, you must persuade the investor to find out more about your venture.

After this initial call, the venture capitalist will quickly evaluate whether the venture is worth having you submit a business plan or perhaps make a presentation. Experts estimate that 60% to 80% of all ventures presented to venture capitalists are rejected during the first contact. Venture capitalists will agree to review your business plan only if they believe that your idea has significant growth potential in an expanding market, that your management team is well qualified to operate the venture, and that their investment will earn an appropriate return in terms of capital appreciation.

Studies suggest that venture capitalists focus on five areas in their investment screening:

1. The caliber of your management team, including a successful track record and relevant experience.
2. The industry and technology of the venture.
3. The distinctive characteristics and uniqueness of the venture.
4. Your financial data, including pro formas of cash flow documents, balance sheets, and profit-and-loss statements.
5. The overall terms of the deal.

The management team is of key importance. Most venture capitalists would rather invest in a first-rate management team and a second-rate product than the reverse.

If the venture capitalist discovers no major flaws in the preceding areas, you will be asked to make an oral presentation to the investment group. At this stage, only 10% to 20% of all entrepreneurs who originally contacted the venture capitalist are still being considered. Don't be discouraged about being turned down at this point. Your venture must fit the investment objectives and philosophy of the firm. The firm must decide on the number and portfolio mix of businesses, buyout opportunities, types of industries, and geographic regions. The intuition or gut feeling of the venture capitalist toward your deal also plays a significant role.

Private Placement Offers Alternative Source of Funding

Question

I own an private company and need financing to expand the business, fund an acquisition, buy out a partner, or sell to my management team. I don't wish to take my company public. What suggestions do you have?

Answer

A private placement may provide the optimal source of financing for your company. A private placement is a capital-formation transaction that is privately negotiated with individuals or institutional sources to meet a company's financing or shareholders' liquidity needs.

Private placement may take the form of senior debt, subordinated debt, convertible debt, preferred stock, common stock, or some hybrid form of these instruments. Key transaction determinants include the stage of the company's development, historical and projected financial performance, current capital structure, anticipated use of funds, investment time horizon, and desired exit strategy.

The private-placement market is clearly growing. According to the Wellesley, Massachusetts–based newsletter *Private Equity Analyst*, financing commitments to private equity limited partnerships totaled $27.2 billion in 1995 and $33.6 billion in 1996. Companies that pursue this funding route are also typically exempt from filing registration statements with the Securities and Exchange Commission. This reduces the paperwork, time, and money associated with the financing. Private placements are typically completed under exemption from Section 5 of the Securities Act of 1933. They fall under alternative rules depending on the size of funding and the nature and number of investors.

Transactions of less than $500,000 are frequently directed toward groups of private investors and small venture-capital firms. Private equity funds and institutions are primarily interested in funding transactions beyond this level. Larger institutional credit sources include insurance companies, public and private pension funds, and banks. Private equity limited partnerships, Small Business Investment Companies, and mezzanine funds, which is a layer of subordinated debt between senior term debt and equity, serve as the principal sources of equity or quasi-equity funding for small- to middle-market companies.

A company should prepare well for the private-placement process to increase the likelihood of a successful transaction outcome. Although significant capital is currently available, investors remain quite discriminating with respect to the opportunities they will pursue. As a result, the company should differentiate itself as a high-quality financing opportunity.

In preparing for the private-placement process, several factors should be considered. First, prepare a concise financing memorandum that accurately presents the company's historical results, management strengths, marketing plan, and anticipated financial performance. This presentation should also specify a logical use for the requested funds and establish financial strategy alternatives for investors with respect to their return on investment capital.

Second, identify investors who are favorably disposed to your industry and comfortable with the size of your proposed transaction. Also ensure that the company's current shareholders maintain a consistent time horizon with the proposed investors regarding value realization or exit strategy. Shareholders must also possess realistic expectations with respect to the company's valuation and the transaction's potential ownership dilution.

Last, a company should select an experienced financial adviser to structure the transaction and manage the private-placement process. The firm's attorney and accountant may also play important roles in the process.

Private Placement Takes Time, Money, and Expert Advisers

Question

I'm interested in raising expansion capital for my privately held company. How does the private-placement process work, and what are the costs involved with completing the financing?

Answer

The general phases of the private-placement process include organization, socialization, negotiation, and closing.

The initial organizational phase includes the determination of current and prospective funding requirements, structuring of the financing, and preparation of the financing memorandum and associate solicitation materials.

In addition to providing background on the company's products or services, markets, historical performance, and management, the financing memorandum should clearly and logically specify the uses for the requested funds, the company's targeted financial strategy, anticipated financial performance, and prospective return on investment for investors.

A successful solicitation phase begins by the establishment of appropriate quantitative and qualitative criteria for investor selection. The size and structure of the financing stage of the company's development, the nature of the product or service, and industry and geographical location, among other considerations, will help guide the solicitation effort.

A successful effort usually identifies a substantial number of prospects. Those prospects responding favorably to the overture will then sign a nondisclosure agreement before receiving the complete financing memorandum.

The negotiation process usually begins shortly after the investor's initial site visit. Typically, investors propose financing structures that have proved successful in their prior transactions. An oral or written deal outline usually precedes a formal letter of intent or agreement in principle. The negotiation process may deal with a wide range of issues such as business valuation and ownership, corporate governance, reporting, and management compensation. This phase of the process provides the owner a useful litmus test regarding the potential relationship with the prospective investor.

Depending on the complexity of the transaction, the private-placement process may take from six to nine months to complete. Given the potential impact on business operations, ownership, and financial outcomes, it is critical to secure experienced financial and legal advisers for the private placement.

The direct costs associated with the private placement usually include monthly advisory or process-management fees. Legal expenses are also incurred as the documentation phases of the project ensue.

Financial advisers also typically earn success fees upon the consummation of the transaction. Success fees may range from 1% to 5% or more, depending on the size, structure, and complexity of the transaction.

The private placement takes time, money, and expert advisers. It does allow for great financing flexibility around the capital needs of your company so you can achieve your expansion goals.

Taking a Company Public

Pros and Cons of Going Public

Question

I own a medical-supply company and have a great opportunity to triple the size of my business during the next year. To do so, however, I need capital— about $6 million. I have met with several venture capitalists but have no deal yet. I am thinking about taking my company public. Should I pursue this strategy?

Answer

Taking a company public (called an IPO if it is an initial public offering) raises capital through federally registered and underwritten sales of the company's shares. It may take you more time and cost you more money than it is worth. Another consideration is that required disclosures to stockholders and others about company products, performance, and financial condition may be better kept secret, especially from your competitors.

The legal, accounting, and administrative costs of a public offering are higher and riskier than with other ways of raising money. Legal fees alone can easily cost $75,000 or more. Filing fees with the SEC and in the state in which the company does business can add another $50,000 to $100,000. Audited financial statements, pro forma statements, and summary financial statistics could range from $20,000 to $150,000, depending on the size of the company and the complexities of the audit. Financial printing fees for the prospectus, SEC registration statement, and official notices could run $40,000 to $100,000. It is not uncommon for a small IPO of $6 million to cost up to $500,000 before any proceeds are realized—assuming the offering is successful. There is always the risk that the public will not purchase the entire issue or even a major portion of it. However, the company must still pay for these expenses.

Numerous federal and state securities laws and regulations govern these offerings. Taking a company public requires not only significant up-front expenses but the ongoing expense of complying with SEC regulations and reporting requirements. The time required to maintain the status of a public company can often be better devoted to operating the company, and the diversion of management attention could adversely affect performance and future growth opportunities. Management time has a real cost to the company and must be considered along with other standard expenses.

Once the company goes public, the management team may focus more on maintaining the stock price and computing capital gains than on effectively operating the company. Short-term goals of trying to maintain or increase a current year's earnings could be counterproductive and take precedence over longer-term goals of slowly strengthening the business. Trying to consistently increase earnings when the best strategy is to temporarily retrench can seriously damage the company in the long run.

Last, the value of the company's stock achieved through the public offering may be sketchy. If there is no real market for the stock, there will be no active trading and the value of the shares could decline to practically nothing. This is an inherent risk in taking a company public.

Only a small number of new or young ventures go public on one of the stock exchanges. New ventures suffer from lower stock evaluations and usually have to give up more equity. Because your stock is listed does not mean that you will realize a liquid gain. The SEC has strong restrictions on the timing and the amount of stock that officers, directors, and insiders can sell in the public market. It may take a number of years after the initial public offering before you realize a liquid gain.

Going public might be a terrific way to raise substantial sums of capital, but it is also a costly gamble. This strategy could backfire and your company could be worse off financially. The stage of your growth, the goals of the underwriter, and economic conditions must be right for the issue to be successful.

How to Find an Investment Banker for an IPO

Question

I need to raise about $10 million to expand my software company and I am considering taking my company public. Is this a good idea, and how do I go about finding an investment banker?

Answer

Taking a company public may be one of the best and most lucrative ways to raise major amounts of capital, assuming the company has approximately $5 million in sales. It is possible to raise long-term capital to initiate major expansions, acquisitions, and recapitalizations or to increase the value of management-held shares. As a rule of thumb, money raised from selling equity shares is considered long-term capital and should be used only to acquire or develop long-term assets.

One of the advantages of going public is that the company can obtain a higher stock price from an initial public offering (IPO) than from venture capitalization, debt financing, or private placement. An IPO also establishes a public price for the stock and gives a company a sense of wealth. Going public adds financial stability and increased borrowing capability. It also gives the owners an exit. No interest payments are required and the company can decide what, if any, dividends to pay.

Assuming the cost and SEC compliance procedures can be managed, there are other considerations about whether to go public. First, the company must be incorporated and large enough to hire a complete management team. The composition, expertise, and strength of the management team are key factors, as is the ability of the owner to promote the quality of team members. The products or services offered by the company should have high growth potential over the next five years. The more glamorous the products or services, the better the chances of selling the company's stock. It is also recommended that the company have one or two new products or services on the drawing board, ready to be introduced over the next two years.

Investor appeal and public imaging are of key importance in taking a company public. Trade show participation, advertising campaigns, and other market-promotion strategies are all good ways to bring attention to the company's products or services. The potential market and industry trade statistics should be growing. The company should have two to three years of progressively improving profitability, and pro forma projections should show continued profitability. It will also be necessary to clear up any lawsuits, insurance claims, IRS discrepancies, bank disagreements, or other potential problems that could tarnish the company's reputation.

Once you have decided to proceed with an IPO, find a competent underwriter to handle and sell the issue. An underwriter will probably charge an initial fee of 1% to 2% of the issue's value, plus commissions of 7% to 10% of the value of the actual stock issued. The best way to locate a qualified underwriter is to get references from a national accounting firm or from legal counsel. Usually, accountants and lawyers with experience in SEC regulations provide the best referrals for underwriters. Most underwriters are located in major cities, particularly in New York.

It is paramount that the underwriter be interested in your industry, in your company, and in you. Some underwriters focus only on firms that are looking for over $10 million in going public. Some specialize in new ventures, while others prefer to deal with firms that have several years of seasoning.

The decision of whether to take your company public requires serious consideration, careful planning, and the right economic and market conditions. Most entrepreneurs who are successful with IPOs spend several years planning their strategies and revamping their companies. Overall, IPOs are not a good financial strategy for most entrepreneurs, since investment bankers focus on financial deals of over $5 million—a figure that leaves out about 95% of new business ventures.

Tapping Alternative Money Sources

SCOR Another Source for Financing New Software Product

Question

I need to raise about $800,000 to produce a new software product that further expands my company's product line. My company is too new and lacks sufficient assets to obtain a bank loan. I've looked into doing a private placement but don't have the money to finance this offering. And I'm skeptical as to whether I could attract enough qualified investors to commit large amounts of capital. Do you have any other suggestions?

Answer

An alternative to consider is utilizing Small Corporate Offering Registration (SCOR), which offers a quicker and less expensive way to obtain equity financing and go public. Your company can issue its own publicly traded stock to investors with a minimum of cost and regulation.

Created by the SEC, SCOR is a shortened process for registering stock offerings up to $1 million each year, and shares can be sold for no less than $5 per share. It was designed for small-business owners to raise capital by selling publicly traded stock. Today, all states except Alabama, Delaware, Florida (pending), and Hawaii accept SCOR offerings. SCOR registrations must be registered on a state-by-state basis.

SCOR costs less than doing a private placement or an initial public offering, both of which have many restrictions. Although cost varies significantly depending on the size and structure of the transaction, professional fees, and the marketing savvy of the entrepreneur, owner, and management team, the average expense to take a company public through SCOR ranges from $8,000 to $15,000, which includes filing fees, legal work, and accounting documents. However, your time and energy should be factored into the costs.

One reason that it costs less to use SCOR is that the SEC exempts it from most of the SEC registration and reporting rules that apply to larger stock sales. This translates into lower legal and accounting fees. Investors don't have to be qualified, which means that your friends, family, or business contacts can purchase stock. It's an attractive investment alternative for them since their stock provides liquidity and is not restricted to resale.

Although the process is quicker, easier, and less expensive than other types of stock offerings, it is labor-intensive and is not for everyone. In addition, your company must meet the SCOR requirements, which you can obtain by contacting a security analyst in your state.

To begin the process, complete a 30-page SCOR form (Form U-7), which contains 50 detailed questions and serves as the prospectus for the stock sale. To reduce legal fees, complete as much of the U-7 form as you can yourself before having an expert review it.

To be successful with a SCOR offering, you need a sound business plan that identifies the company's long-term goals. You must also be willing to spend the time and energy to complete the prospectus and to market and sell the stock. You need to identify prospectus investors and prepare marketing materials. Last, you need enough money to fund the expense of this offering.

Although SCOR looks like an attractive alternative, only about one in five companies that seek SCOR financing succeed. Stock is hard to sell because there is no formal place to sell it. SCOR stock can be sold on NASDAQ's electronic bulletin board, but it's still difficult to attract investors. It's expensive and time consuming to sell SCOR shares. SCOR allows stock to be sold through advertising, seminars, direct mail, or other approved means of mass solicitation. If you have a built-in audience, it's easier to be successful with a SCOR offering.

Another reason that companies are not successful with SCOR is because a company has only 12 months to raise the money after the filing is approved by state regulators. If you cannot raise the money during the 12-month period, you must start the process all over again. Recently, the SCOR marketplace established a centralized market for the public trading of SCOR shares that should make it easier to sell shares. All investment money from a SCOR offering is placed in an escrow account until both the company's minimum investment amount is raised and the money is released to the company.

If you are interested in pursuing a SCOR offering, I recommend you work with a local brokerage firm or financial specialists who are experienced with SCOR offerings. They have established contacts in different states and can help you establish a trading market for your stock by creating and building public awareness. Many have Web sites for advertising and promoting SCOR stock. An alternative is to hire a marketing or public relations firm to create market awareness.

SCOR offerings are easier than some of the other alternatives but are not necessarily a sure thing. Therefore, you should have a contingency plan in place if you are unsuccessful in a SCOR offering.

Financing a New Venture without Personal Assets or Collateral

Question

I would like to start a computer consulting and word-processing business but need some start-up capital. I do not have any personal assets or collateral. Where can I find alternative sources of financing?

Answer

Nontraditional sources of financing include suppliers, sales of distribution rights, hard-assets lenders, and commercial finance companies.

Suppliers

When you are able to delay paying for the materials you receive, your vendors can help finance your venture. The more you can delay paying them, the longer you can use their money and save your own to cover operating expenses. Sometimes you may be able to receive payment from your customers before having to pay your suppliers. This tactic is called extended-term financing, or trade credit. There may be times when you are able to take 30, 60, or 90 days to pay for supplies. This means you have obtained a loan of 30 to 90 days. Suppliers offer such trade credit as a way of getting new customers and will often build the bad debt risk into their prices.

However, the cost of money may be expensive. You may have to forgo attractive discounts for paying early. Missing a "2/10, net 30 days" discount costs you 36% on an annual rate. You lose 2% for using the money an extra 20 days. But this may be the only alternative you have to exercise.

Other forms of trade credit include special or seasonal datings (a supplier ships goods in advance of the purchaser's peak selling season and accepts payment 90 to 120 days later) or consignment (a supplier ships inventory on consignment and does not require payment until an item has been sold).

Sale of Distribution Rights

There is money to be made in distributing the output of your new venture. Often, people will pay money to obtain the distribution rights for goods. Franchises do just that in franchising systems. To get a lot of money from a distributor, you must be prepared to give a lot in return. The person may ask for the distribution rights for a large area, such as everything west of the Mississippi. Before selling any rights, put the distributor on a performance-guarantee contract.

Hard-Asset Lenders

Certain firms are in business to lend money against hard assets, such as equipment and machinery or tangible assets with a recognizable liquidating value. Most firms that use hard-asset lenders have exhausted other avenues of borrowing, largely because of poor credit ratings. Prime plus 10 is a good interest rate in this segment of the money market. While hard-asset firms are best known for their activities in consumer credit, they still do a large business with commercial institutions.

Commercial Finance Companies

Frequently, commercial finance firms lend money to businesses that do not have a positive cash flow. They tend to be more aggressive than commercial banks in lending. Essentially, they are asset-based lenders, extending credit against receivables, inventory, or equipment that they are familiar with.

Using Fund-Raisers for Obtaining Seed Capital

Question

I would like to own a business but don't have a lot of money in savings. I don't own a house, and my car is several years old, which means I can't borrow much money on it. I need about $350,000 for a down payment on a new business. I am thinking about using a fund-raiser to raise the capital that I need. I understand that a fund-raiser will charge a fee. Do you recommend this approach? What are the pitfalls? Is the fee negotiable?

Answer

Fund-raisers can be an excellent source for raising money if they are reputable and if your venture fits that source of money. Investors want to see evidence of the planning you have done to launch and operate your new venture.

✔ **COURTNEY'S SMART TIP**
Have a well-written, attractive, and professional business plan to bring to any source of capital.

To develop a list of contacts and fund-raisers, look in the Yellow Pages under business brokers or financial consultants. Talk to your banker, attorney, accountant, or other entrepreneurs for leads and referrals to fund-raisers who are known in the community and work in your industry. Once you have received the names of potential fund-raisers, check the types of deals they have recently completed. Are they similar to yours? Is the amount of money raised in the same range as what you need?

Some fund-raisers work only with business owners who need $1 million or more. Others specialize in deals over $5 million. Most fund-raisers will not handle deals of less than $500,000. It takes too much time and effort to try to raise money for smaller ventures. Some will not work with start-up businesses at all. Like lenders, fund-raisers prefer to see that the entrepreneur has invested money in the venture. Make sure that the money source fits your business. Carefully check credentials.

✔ COURTNEY'S SMART TIP
Check the credentials of money finders. Ask for and call all references. Find people who are interested in and understand your business as well as have a good reputation.

Many of these deals are cloaked in clever scams involving loans from foreign countries at low interest rates. Just keep in mind that there is no *Santa Claus* in the money market. When you deal in the money market, be prepared for an unusual cast of characters. Money attracts all sorts of motives, some good and many bad.

First, money often attracts people who cannot be trusted. They look upon the money market as the direct way to riches. Be careful who you deal with. Don't think it's easy to spot these types of people. They often have the best addresses and the best-looking offices, and they can be very persuasive.

Second, the financial world is loaded with incompetents who will promise you money but not be able to deliver. They don't have the contacts they profess to have.

Third, there are dreamers who really think they can do something for you, take you public or whatever, but they are wrong. Many of these people are simply unrealistic. They are easy to spot, but unfortunately you may not want to spot them. You want what they tell you to be true. You like their dreams.

Finally, there are people working around the fringes of the money market who just don't know what is going on.

Realize that fund-raisers do not raise money for nothing. All charge some type of fee. Fees charged vary depending on individual rates and the amount of money raised. Some fund-raisers require up-front money to cover expenses incurred researching the information contained in the business plan. Often, they charge up to 3% of the amount of money you want just to conduct a due diligence check on your business. On top of that, most charge 10%, up to $1 million, and a sliding scale over that amount. To know exactly what these services and requirements of people might be, write up and sign a letter of intent.

Fees may be somewhat negotiable, depending on the deal and its terms. Some fund-raisers will not negotiate on fees. Their policy is take it or leave it. Essentially, you are paying for their contacts and expertise. Also, it takes time to research your business plan and to negotiate and structure the deal.

An alternative approach is to contact local financial consultants or registered brokerage firms that work with private placements—investor-based securities offerings that are exempt from SEC registration and are limited in distribution. Although most of these firms specialize in selling stocks and bonds, some of the smaller ones also handle private placements. However, most larger firms do not handle smaller private placements.

You could also identify local opportunities for joint venturing with manufacturers and other companies that have been successful with similar types of ventures. Many local newspapers print an annual list of the top 100 companies in their area. Scan this list of potential corporate partners that might be interested in your product or service.

Most of these sources are interested in deals of more than $500,000. For amounts less than this, you will need to find other types of private investors or use friendly money.

Private individuals are often the ones who will invest seed money in a start-up venture. They may have differing motives for venture investment and are often willing to accept higher risks than institutional sources. Sometimes these investors act independently, having strong confidence in their ability to evaluate deals and business owners. Your friends and contacts may play a key role in locating private investors. Create a circle of acquaintances that can act as money sources for your venture.

Finding Business Angels to Fund and Grow Ventures

Question

I've just finished writing my business plan to open a trendy restaurant but need $300,000 investment capital. I have 12 years of experience managing a restaurant, but I don't have that kind of money and lack sufficient collateral to obtain a bank loan. None of my family or the people I know have that much cash. How can I find an investor?

Answer

Finding a private investor willing to invest $300,000 will not be easy. However, you have taken the first step to raise capital, which is completing a business plan outlining how the business will run, who will operate it, the amount of capital needed, how it will be spent, and the return for the investor.

Private investors, sometimes known as business angels, may be one of your only sources of risk capital. Angels are wealthy individuals or a group of individuals who provide money, usually in the form of a loan, to seed and/or grow ventures. They are successful self-made businesspeople who put their experience and money into new entrepreneurial ventures. Usually their goal is to earn a 20% to 40% return after their initial investment has been paid back.

It is estimated that the angel community invests upward of $25 billion annually in U.S. ventures to get equity and/or a percentage of revenues. Recent studies show that there are more than one million angels in the United States. Typically, they invest small amounts of their own money, ranging from $20,000 to $500,000, in businesses with which they are familiar and that are located within a 50-mile radius of their homes.

The good news is that they love start-ups, but the bad news is that angels are very difficult to find. Your accountant, lawyer, banker, trade association, or professional groups should be able to recommend angels. Another good source into your local angel community is the venture-capital clubs in your area. Or call the Association of Venture Capital Clubs in Salt Lake City, Utah, at 801-584-5443; this organization can provide a list of clubs.

You might also think about using intermediaries, who are advisers to angels, such as merchant bankers (a UK bank providing, among other services, long-term venture capital or risk capital rather than short-term loans normally handled by commercial banks), financial consultants, and planners who specialize in raising smaller amounts of investment capital. Look in *The Wall Street Journal,* where you can find ads for services that specialize in matching entrepreneurs with angels. Also check the Yellow Pages under "investment management," "financing consultants," or "financial planners." Financial consultants and planners usually work through a brokerage firm and are involved in managing angels' investments. When working with intermediaries, remember to be cautious. Check out their references and their track records. Get referrals from lawyers, bankers, accountants, and insurance brokers.

✔ COURTNEY'S SMART TIP

To find angels, use intermediaries who are advisers to angels, such as merchant bankers, boutique bankers, financial consultants, and planners.

Accessing angel networks is another way to find private investors. More and more private investors have discovered they can be more successful finding good deals and sharing due diligence by pooling their resources in an angel network. Universities, government agencies, and nonbank lenders have established angel networks that match entrepreneurs with investors. They work like a dating service, providing initial contact between you and the investor.

Go on-line—look at angel networks' Web sites and explore ACE-Net service (www.ace-net.sr.unh.edu), sponsored by the U.S. Small Business Administration's Office on Advocacy. It's an on-line listing service that seeks to connect entrepreneurs with potential investors. Angel networks vary in size, sophistication, orientation, and location. The most successful networks have an experienced staff who aggressively market their services. Many of these networks specialize in certain industries, like high-tech or biotech companies. A good resource to consult is *Finding Your Wings: How to Locate Private Investors to Fund Your Venture* by Gerald A. Benjamin, published by John Wiley & Sons. This book includes valuable information on angel financing.

Remember, there are all different types of angels. Some just want to grant loans and collect interest, whereas others want to invest their money and make a good return. Some don't want voting rights in the business, whereas others demand it. They may want to take on an advisory role, become a board member or chairman of the board. It all depends on the angels' goals, the industry, and the size of their investment.

Establishing Corporate Strategic Alliances

Question

I have been looking for money to finance the growth of my two-year-old computer company. I have approached many different sources, but none has been willing to loan me money. Where can I look for funding beyond banks and venture capitalists?

Answer

Many new ventures make ideal candidates for corporate joint ventures. Today, as traditional lenders continue to tighten up their borrowing practices to entrepreneurs, corporate partners are becoming a major new avenue for financing. A joint venture or partnership agreement with a major domestic or foreign corporation can provide badly needed funds for research and development as well as growth opportunities. There has been a significant increase in the number of direct investments by large corporations in new ventures during the past 10 years.

A corporate strategic alliance offers several advantages to entrepreneurs. First, corporate partners are usually willing to wait longer to receive a return on their investments than are bankers or venture capitalists. Often, corporate partners are interested in taking an equity position in a business and do not seek as high a percentage of ownership as do venture capitalists.

Second, they can contribute more than just money to the new business. They may be able to offer good business advice, extend moral support, and provide state-of-the-art technology. Finally, a corporate strategic alliance can furnish valuable contacts in the business and financial community.

The chief disadvantage of a corporate strategic alliance is the loss of control. A corporate partner might demand that certain things be done when the entrepreneur is opposed to taking such action. Changing the corporate mission and goals could cause the corporate partnership to sour.

Elements in structuring a strategic alliance with a large corporation include finding a well-capitalized partner who has or is considering financing new venture proposals. Look for corporations that are interested in early-stage ventures like yours and have already invested in your industry. Work with your local business librarian to find various listings of potential corporate investors. The key is finding corporations with the resources but not the time, commitment, or creativity to get involved themselves.

✔ COURTNEY'S SMART TIP

Ensure that corporate allies have a strategic fit with your company. Try to ascertain whether they are familiar with your market, product, technology, and service area.

Another option is to contact a corporation that might be interested in the right to license your product in certain areas. Go to the store aisles where your competitors' products are displayed. Nearly every package gives the name and location of its producer. Many corporations are eager to expand their product lines into new areas, or to sell improved versions of currently available products. With a licensing arrangement, you receive royalties and a ready-made marketing system without giving up equity.

Several good books are available for investigating licensing and finding corporate partners. *Dun & Bradstreet's Reference Book of Corporation Management* gives a detailed biographical description of more than 75,000 principal officers of more than 12,000 leading companies. *Standard & Poor's Register of Corporations, Directors, and Executives* lists 45,000 corporations and detailed information on some 450,000 potential licensee contacts. The *Million Dollar Directory* and the *Middle Market Directory*, both from Dun & Bradstreet, list thousands of companies with assets exceeding $500,000. Another excellent book, *Winning Combinations* by James W. Botkin and Jana B. Mathews, focuses on the coming wave of entrepreneurial partnerships between large and small companies.

Using Credit Cards to Finance a Venture

Question

I have been trying to find additional financing for my new venture but have not been successful. I have gone to several banks for a line of credit but have been turned down. A friend suggested that I use my credit cards for the cash I need. What do you think?

Answer

A number of struggling entrepreneurs—especially those who are not yet considered creditworthy by traditional lenders—have used credit cards in the early start-up phases of their ventures for working or expansion capital. Used judiciously, credit card financing can act as a bridge to get new ventures over initial financial cash binds.

However, consider this source *only* when there is no other way to secure operating capital. When you run into a cash crunch, credit cards may be the only available option. You should be able to acquire an unsecured line of credit of $1,000 to $5,000 from each credit card source. This type of cash advance is very similar to obtaining a line of credit from a bank. You can get cash when you need it by taking your credit card to your bank to receive cash or have it deposited in your account.

The major pitfall is that most credit card bills require payment in 30 days and carry high interest rates. You must consider whether paying higher interest rates is worth having the extra money immediately. In addition, you are personally liable for the debt. Keep in mind, too, that many credit card companies charge an additional fee or a higher-than-normal interest rate for cash advances.

The best way to use this method of financing is to submit credit card applications simultaneously so you can obtain several cards with a cash advance privilege. By applying for credit to a number of different sources at once, you can truthfully disclose that you have no other outstanding loans. Shop for the lowest rates possible. Credit card interest rates are extremely competitive, and newer companies may offer lower interest rates and more services.

Avoid using credit card financing to start a new venture or to pay for fixed expenses, such as equipment. Entrepreneurs should have enough cash from their own resources to launch their businesses. But if you are not yet bankable, credit cards can provide needed capital very quickly, only when sales will help pay off the debt quickly.

✔ COURTNEY'S SMART TIP
Use credit cards only as the last resort as a cushion for cash crunches. Replace credit card financing with conventional loans as soon as possible.

From a tax standpoint, the same tax deductions are available with a credit card loan as with any other business loan. The right to deduct interest rates is determined by the purpose for which the money is used. Regardless of how high the interest rate is, interest is deductible at the time it is incurred, not when it is paid.

If you have other ways of financing your working capital, use them. If not, credit cards are a costly option for short-term or seasonal cash needs. Truly creative entrepreneurs using credit cards for operating capital have given a new meaning to our credit card economy.

The Small Business Administration (SBA)

Obtaining an SBA-Backed Loan

Question

I have come up with an idea for a new business, but I am at the starting point and desperately need to know how to obtain financing. I am interested in securing funding from the Small Business Administration, but I do not know how to contact this agency or how to proceed. Can you help?

Answer

The SBA is a significant source of financing for small businesses. Typically, SBA loans are used to finance plant construction or expansion, to purchase equipment, and to provide working capital. Under the SBA's Guaranty Loan Program, loans to entrepreneurs from private lenders, usually banks, are guaranteed for 80% of loans up to $100,000 and 75% for loans over $100,000. Working-capital loans generally have maturities of five to seven years. Longer maturities are used to finance fixed assets, such as land and buildings. Lenders apply directly for SBA loans for their customers. Essentially, you are a customer of the bank, and the bank is a customer of the SBA. You will not deal directly with the SBA but will work through your lending officer.

Smart Tips for Obtaining an SBA-Backed Loan

1. Develop a business plan that contains proper financial projections, including cash flow, profit-and-loss statements, and balance sheets. Make your projections month by month for the first year of operation and then annually for the next three to four years.

2. Prepare a current personal financial statement for any principals involved in the venture.

3. List the collateral to be offered as security, including an estimate of the present market value of each item.

4. State the amount of the loan request and the purpose for which the funds will be used.

5. Establish a business relationship with a full-service bank that participates in government lending programs.

6. Make an appointment with your loan officer and ask him or her to finance your loan.

7. If the loan is turned down, ask about the possibility of using the SBA's Guaranty Loan Program.

If the bank feels that you are a creditworthy customer and is willing to apply for the SBA loan, which greatly minimizes its risk, it will prepare a loan package to submit to the SBA. This loan package will contain the bank's credit analysis of your venture and the loan request.

The SBA will perform an independent review of the loan package. It will determine whether the business is eligible under its guidelines and whether the entrepreneur meets its credit requirements. The agency closely evaluates whether your sales and financial projections are realistic. In addition, it scrutinizes your repayment ability.

Many banks have signed participation agreements with the SBA. However, only 50% of these banks are active lenders and send in applications for SBA loans. Further, only about 25% of these lenders aggressively pursue SBA loans. Therefore, it is important to determine whether a potential lender regularly participates in the SBA's loan programs.

The interest rate the bank charges you will vary. A bank can charge up to 2.25% above the New York prime rate for loans with maturity dates of less than seven years. On maturities over seven years, the bank may charge up to 2.75%. An interest rate can be fixed or variable, depending on your negotiation and relationship with the lender.

The SBA does offer a direct loan program, but currently the funds are available only to Vietnam-era veterans and other disabled veterans who have a 30% or more compensable disability. To obtain additional information about the SBA's business loan programs, call its business-development division. Ask for the brochure "Business Loans from the SBA."

You could also contact a local small-business investment company (SBIC), a privately owned company, licensed by the SBA, to provide equity capital and long-term loans to entrepreneurs. Your local SBA office can provide you with a list of SBICs.

Financing Production through the SBA Contract Finance Program

Question

I own a growing manufacturing company that is running out of equity capital just as business is expanding and sales are increasing. My banker said he could not loan me any more money. How would I finance the expansion of my production plant and equipment?

Answer

Go back to your banker and ask him if it would be possible to obtain a loan through the SBA Contract Finance Program. This is a special financing program designed to lend a business money on the basis of a specific contract or purchase order from a customer. If your bank does not work with the SBA, or if you have already borrowed the maximum amount of SBA-supported financing that your business can qualify for, you may have to look to other sources.

Local certified development companies (CDCs) are interested in fostering business in their communities. The major criterion for obtaining a CDC loan is that for each $15,000 lent, the business must create one new job or prove the retention of an existing job that might otherwise have been eliminated. Minimum loans are $50,000, but the average loan is between $1 million and $2 million. Borrowers usually pay 10% of the loan value collateralized by property, machinery, equipment, or fixtures.

Creative loan packages may also be available through your state's department of commerce. Remember, these types of loans are made for specific transactions to existing companies, not for market development.

Commercializing New Technology through SBIR Programs

Question

I am the founder and president of a small electronics firm that needs capital for research and development. My banker told me that some of my new products may closely coincide with some research currently being conducted under a federal grant at our local university. Can I obtain research funding as well?

Answer

There is a good possibility that you can obtain funding through the SBA's small-business innovation research (SBIR) programs. SBIRs allow small businesses to commercialize technology that they own or wish to develop through federally funded R&D grants. This program provides first-round grants (feasibility studies) of up to $50,000 and second-round grants (commercialization of technology) of up to $500,000 for R&D projects of interest to various government agencies. Ask the SBA to place you on its SBIR mailing list. You will receive periodic listings of areas of research that the government is interested in pursuing.

Next, ask the SBA about the Cooperative Research and Development Agreement (CRADA) program, established to help businesses acquire technology from the federal government for the purposes of developing a technology of interest to both parties. A substantial portion of the R&D funding and/or facilities can be provided by the government for this purpose.

In addition to these programs, there are opportunities for acquiring licenses for federally developed technology through the National Technical Information Services (NITS) and the Federal Laboratory Consortium (FLC). (See the "Contacts" listing in the resources section for this chapter at the end of this book.) In addition, most universities have set up licensing organizations or foundations to implement the transfer of their technology to qualified licensees.

The SBA or any university that sponsors technical research, research parks, or incubators can assist you in identifying the many opportunities that you might be interested in for your electronics firm. Even though you may have to cut through some red tape, the outcome can be rewarding. Once your technology has been acquired, you will have to pay royalties to the government or university. However, such royalties are usually far less costly than conducting your own R&D.

Small Business Has Another Capital Source

Question

I am looking for money to expand my software company. Four different venture-capital firms I contacted have turned me down. The last firm suggested that I contact an SBIC. How do they work, and where are they located?

Answer

Most likely you were turned down by several venture-capital firms because they do not consider your company a high-growth prospect or do not think you plan to go public or be acquired. Venture-capital firms always expect a high return on their investment and a method of exit.

Small business investment corporations (SBICs) exist to supply equity capital, long-term loans, and management assistance to qualifying small businesses.

The privately owned and operated SBICs use their own capital and funds borrowed from the U.S. Small Business Administration (SBA) to provide financing to small businesses in the form of equity securities and long-term loans. SBICs are profit-seeking organizations that select small businesses to be financed within rules and regulations set by the SBA. There are specialized SBICs that are known as SSBICs. These are a particular type of SBIC that provide assistance solely to small businesses owned by socially or economically disadvantaged persons.

Only firms defined by the SBA as small are eligible for SBIC financing. The SBA defines a company as small when its net worth is $18.0 million or less, and its average net (after tax) income for the preceding two years does not exceed $6.0 million. For businesses in industries for which the preceding standards are too low, alternative size standards are available. In determining whether a business qualifies, all of the business's parents, subsidiaries, and affiliates are considered.

Currently there are about 180 SBICs in the United States, with financial resources totaling over $2.6 billion. They make investments ranging from $100,000 to more than $1 million and are a good source of long-term capital for small businesses that lack the potential to become major businesses.

Under a new program, $345 million in government-backed equity financing will be made available to small businesses during 1995, stimulating small-business growth. Participating SBICs are raising new funds to invest in small firms by issuing securities backed by the SBA and sold on the bond market. The proceeds from the sale of the bonds go to the SBICs, who will buy stock in small firms in exchange for ownership. When the companies are sold or go public, the SBICs and the SBA will receive a return on the initial investment. Each SBIC establishes its own investment criteria.

The Small Business Equity Enhancement Act of 1992 established the new program. Approximately 24 of the SBICs nationwide are licensed to participate in the program.

To be eligible for SBIC financing, you must qualify as a small business, defined as a business that is independently owned and operated, has a net worth no greater than $6 million, and has an average after-tax net income of less than $2 million for the prior two years. In addition, you must be able to meet the business loan guidelines under the traditional SBA guaranty loan program.

For the most current SBIC or SSBIC list, contact your local SBA office or the National Association of SBICs (NASBIC), 1199 Fairfax Street, Suite 200, Alexandria, VA 22314, 703-683-1601, or contact the district SBA office located in the blue pages of the telephone book.

Factoring

Using a Commercial Factoring Company to Finance a Business

Question

How can I use a commercial factoring company to finance my small business?

Answer

Factoring is designed to increase cash flow when funds are limited and accounts receivable are high. It is short-term financing to solve short-term cash flow bottlenecks. The cash-poor company sells its accounts receivable at a discount to a commercial finance company known as a factor. Cash is made available to the entrepreneur as soon as proof of shipment is provided or on the average due date of the invoice. Most factoring arrangements are made for one year.

Factors make their money by acquiring a company's invoices and collecting on them, charging the business a fee. Unlike banks, factors buy, pay for, and own the receivables outright. If your creditors don't pay, the factor may incur a loss. Some factors require that the entrepreneur establish a reserve for bad debt of approximately 5% of the account. If the account is not collected within 120 days, the factor will draw against the reserve. If the receivables eventually are collected, the factor's return on investment exceeds that of conventional lenders.

Many business owners use factoring when their banker turns down a loan request that they had tried to guarantee with their accounts receivable as collateral. Under factoring, accounts receivable are not used as collateral against a loan but instead are sold directly, at a discounted value, to a factoring company. For example, if the factoring company uses a one-time charge and discounts 6%, then for every $1,000 in receivables, the seller receives $940.

Some factors discount according to a schedule, paying a smaller percentage up front and then paying an additional percentage depending on whether the receivables are collected within 30, 60, or 90 days.

The factor takes over the entire collection procedure, including mailing the invoices and doing the bookkeeping. Each of your customers is notified that the account is owned by and payable to the factor.

If you are a new business and your accounts receivable are evaluated as marginal credit risks, you may not be able to find a factor that will accept your accounts receivable. Let's face it: although they take greater risks and are more liberal lenders than commercial banks, factors need to be assured that your customers will pay their bills. They will execute substantial credit checks on each debtor and carefully analyze the quality and value of the invoice before buying it; they look to the strength of the receivables and creditworthiness of the invoices that you are selling them. Factors will also establish credit limits for each customer.

Factoring is not the cheapest way to obtain money, but it does quickly turn receivables into cash. The advantages of factoring are receiving a cash injection quickly, paying bills in a more timely manner, obtaining more credit, and fostering better growth than traditional borrowing. Also, the fee is an expense and offsets taxable income. Essentially, the entrepreneur is buying insurance against bad debt.

The chief disadvantage of factoring is the high cost of money relative to traditional borrowing. Also, to many entrepreneurs, factors receive outrageously high returns. A business concerned with cash flow but not with collection might want to pursue the less costly route of using accounts receivable as collateral for a commercial bank loan.

Overall, factoring can be compared with using a credit card for your business. Factors work best with businesses that have cash flow problems because of long delays between making and selling goods and then collecting cash. Start-up ventures, emerging businesses, and service companies are prime candidates for factoring. For recommendations and references about which factoring companies to use, talk to your trade associations, to members of the infrastructure, and to other entrepreneurs in your industry.

How to Use a Factoring Company to Fund Growth

Question

About a year ago I started a small advertising and public relations firm that is doing well but at times experiences cash shortages, especially when the payroll must be met. A friend suggested that I look into factoring companies as a source of financing. Do you recommend using them?

Answer

In the past, factoring was used as a last resort and was concentrated in the manufacturing and clothing industries. Today, all types of ventures—temporary office services, janitorial services, computer companies, pet shop suppliers, and many others—readily use this type of financing. Factoring has become the fashionable way for cash-poor start-up ventures to acquire working capital.

Typically, entrepreneurs use factoring as short-term financing to solve their short-term cash flow problems, especially when they are unable to borrow funds from traditional lenders. Many banks steer away from such asset-based lending because of the unpredictable nature of the underlying collateral and the difficulties in liquidating it.

In factoring, you sell your designated accounts receivable to the factor and draw against this line of credit as cash is needed. Typically, factoring companies secure their interest with your accounts receivable. As a rule, factoring companies accept the loss if your customer goes broke and cannot pay the bill that has been factored.

Factoring companies are accounts receivable managers that give business owners more time to concentrate on marketing and growing their ventures. Factoring enables a business to take advantage of discounts for large orders or advance payments for raw materials. It allows the entrepreneur to use the venture's tangible assets for securing other types of financing. Factoring can also finance growth by providing quick funds to take advantage of business opportunities.

In factoring, you deposit your accounts receivable with the factoring firm. These accounts are processed and reside there until cash is needed. If you run short of cash on payday, you can call the factoring company and cash out a portion of your accounts receivable immediately—provided that proof of shipment has been secured or the average due date on the invoice has been reached.

The services provided by factoring companies range from evaluating customer credit to mailing invoices to pursuing collections. Regardless of how long you have been in business, factoring companies will evaluate the creditworthiness of your clients. They carefully analyze the quality and value of your invoices and look closely at each customer's credit to determine risk, since they need to be assured of receiving payment. Their collection services are designed to try to preserve your relationship with your customers. By contrast, a collection agency may use techniques that result in a loss of goodwill between you and your customers.

For more information, call National Factoring Services, Inc. at 303-592-1919 or 800-253-6700, or other national factoring companies.

Funding for Nonprofit Organizations

Question

I began a nonprofit organization, the Colorado Horse Rescue, to help horses that were impounded by the state and counties of Colorado. We are the only approved horse shelter in the state. We adopt horses out for a fee, match children and horses for 4H programs and hold horses for owners until they are able to "bail" them out. We are desperately in need of additional funding, management assistance (since we are growing so rapidly), and a sound growth plan. Where should we turn for help?

Answer

Nonprofit companies face particularly severe challenges, both as start-up ventures and as ongoing businesses. There never seems to be enough funding, and raising capital through revenue generation is difficult at best. The situation worsens in tight economic times when corporate, foundation, and individual donations tend to shrink.

To address the need for additional funding, the Colorado Horse Rescue group should research foundations that have a specific interest in funding animal-oriented nonprofits and then submit a grant proposal to them. Thousands of private foundations promote specialized projects, regions, minorities, and special-interest groups. Some offer technical assistance or counseling to nonprofits and small businesses. All offer grants or low-cost loans. The challenge is to find the foundation that fits your organization.

For information about foundations, contact the Foundation Center in New York at 212-620-4230 or the Council on Foundations in Washington, DC at 202-466-6512. *The Chronicle of Philanthropy* is a newspaper directed to issues in the nonprofit sector including fund-raising and grant distribution. For information, call 800-347-6969. A comprehensive resource, including names and addresses of large and small foundations, is *Free Money for Small Businesses and Entrepreneurs*. In addition, many states publish foundation directories that contain local grant sources.

Another avenue open to your group is fund-raising. Consider developing diverse funding sources from special fund-raising events, membership dues, individual donations, earned incomes, and so on.

A key player in such fund-raising efforts is your board of directors, which you must have if your business is incorporated. One of the major responsibilities of a nonprofit board is to generate the funds necessary to support the programs of the agency. An excellent resource book on building nonprofit boards is James Hardy's *Developing Dynamic Boards*.

To get the board involved and to generate a financial-development strategy, you might hold a strategic planning session facilitated by an outside nonprofit expert. During the session, the consultant will provide information on board roles and responsibilities, including the skills and expertise needed to direct an effective nonprofit organization. Then the consultant will facilitate a discussion of mission, goals, objectives, and strategies. The result will be a strategic plan that outlines where the nonprofit wants to go in the next three to five years and how it plans to get there.

Another excellent source is the National Executive Service Corps (NESC), headquartered in New York at 212-529-6660. This nationwide network of organizations provides management assistance and coaching to nonprofits through retired executives who have extensive experience in marketing, finance, and other functional areas.

Pitfalls to Avoid

1. Cold calling on a lender or investor. Always try to get a referral.

2. Calling on a lender or investor without bringing along a complete business plan for the lender to review and evaluate.

3. Mass mailing your business plan to potential investors.

4. Contacting the SBA directly about obtaining a bank loan. The SBA is not a lender. Instead, find out if your bank is an approved SBA lender and will consider doing an SBA-backed loan.

5. Putting a monetary value on business goodwill. Most lenders will consider goodwill "blue sky" and will discount or delete any balance sheet amount in excess of the venture's tangible net worth.

6. Responding to advertisements that ask you to send upward of $100 for lists of venture capitalists. You can obtain these lists from your local library.

7. Using credit card financing to start a new venture or to pay for fixed expenses such as equipment.

(Continued)

(Continued)

8. Contacting venture capitalists for start-up funding. Very few ventures, start-up or otherwise, will qualify for or ever receive venture-capital funding.

9. Paying a high price to use other people's money will usually handicap you until you repay the debt.

10. Thinking that using your collateral will release you from all liability on the debt.

11. Paying high up-front fees to fund-raisers.

12. A company must pay costly up-front IPO expenses out of earnings even if it is unsuccessful.

13. Undertaking a private placement without the advice of a competent attorney skilled in these offerings.

The Good News

Entrepreneurs who carefully plan their financial strategies and correctly forecast their cash needs at the onset will be more successful at raising capital. Being able to match the right money source to your venture, considering its stage of development and growth potential, will most likely produce the funds you need when you need them.

10

Selecting the Best Business Advisers

Overview

Hiring outside advisers and utilizing members of the entrepreneurial infrastructure are key strategies for operating a successful venture. Too many times such personnel are chosen because they are friends or relatives of the owner. This is one of the biggest mistakes an entrepreneur can make. Those selected should balance out the management team, bringing in expertise that the owner lacks and the business strongly needs.

Entrepreneurs give equally little thought to selecting members of the infrastructure—lawyers, accountants, and other management professionals. Again, they usually choose people they know, regardless of their expertise and reputation. Because most start-up ventures cannot afford to take on additional employees to handle various management functions, infrastructure contacts become especially critical. They must be seasoned professionals, chosen solely on the basis of their expertise. This is the only way to build a strong management team besides hiring one. On an informal level, friends, associates, suppliers, and vendors can be good sources of outside advice.

Establishing a board of directors and an outside board or council is one of the best investments entrepreneurs can make to strengthen the stability and growth potential of their ventures. An outside board gives a fresh perspective and objective feedback about the operation and its strategic direction. Unfortunately, few founders seek enough of such advice. Often they neglect to establish a board of directors or advisory council because they think no one would want to serve on a board or that setting one up is too much work.

Smart Strategies for Using the Infrastructure and Business Professionals

1. Find a lawyer experienced in small business and establish a working relationship before you ever need to hire counsel.

2. To save on legal fees, complete as much up-front work and information gathering as possible before meeting with your attorney.

3. Never talk to another party's attorney without having your own attorney present.

4. To reduce legal costs, use standardized forms of conducting routine business, but always have your attorney review them before implementation.

5. To avoid surprises with legal bills, estimate the number of billable hours for your legal project and then negotiate a cap or ceiling on the total fee.

6. Select an accountant who is also a good business adviser—one who is familiar with your industry, knowledgeable about tax planning, and committed to building and managing a sound cash flow.

7. If you are considering raising venture capital or going public, contact an accounting firm that has a track record working with promising smaller businesses.

8. Before you begin a small to mid-size venture, obtain a business-owner's policy to cover all your major property and business liability exposures.

9. Ask your local or national professional and/or trade association if it has a group insurance arrangement with specialty brokers or insurers.

10. Avoid "I can do it all" consultants.

11. Use a written consulting agreement that specifies work assignments, responsibilities, and compensation.

12. Assemble a board of directors to add credibility to your venture, enhance your corporation's assets, and obtain management expertise and advice.

13. Establish an advisory board to serve as your in-house management consulting team.

14. Look for advisory board members or board directors who have the specialized knowledge and skills you lack.

How to Find a Lawyer for Your Business

Guidelines for Hiring a Lawyer

Question

I am in the process of selecting an attorney to assist me with some legal matters in starting my new business. How do I find a good attorney who is reasonably priced and specializes in small business?

Answer

In this highly complex legal society, entrepreneurs need competent legal advice. Ironically, this can be the most difficult assistance to find. Simply contacting your local legal society is not the solution. In most cases, it will not recommend an attorney. Instead, pay attention to the lawyers used in your industry. Who represents local entrepreneurs in your field? Who seems to win the court cases? Ask your fellow entrepreneurs to describe their experiences in working with local lawyers.

Accessibility should be a key factor in your decision. Remember that the demand for legal services is unpredictable. Rarely will you know in advance that you are going to need legal advice. For example, you have an opportunity to purchase a business on particularly advantageous terms, but a memorandum of agreement needs to be drawn up immediately. You cannot begin your search for a lawyer now and then wait several days or weeks to meet at his or her convenience. Evaluate how quickly an attorney can or will respond to your requests.

The size of the firm is another important consideration. The legal profession is dominated by several very large firms with dozens of partners. Many of these firms have substantial political power and many contacts. A large legal firm offers certain advantages to the entrepreneur. First, it can call upon expertise in many different fields. If you have a tax problem, it has tax experts. If you have a problem with the Securities and Exchange Commission, it has specialists in the field. If you are taking your company public, having a large, prestigious law firm behind you can add significant credibility to your venture. Thus, with one legal connection, you have rented yourself expertise in just about every area in which you will be operating.

However, the big firm presents disadvantages as well. If you operate a small business, you may not be an important enough client. Your concerns may be ignored or else assigned to a rookie, just out of law school, who has little experience in small-business concerns. Second, the legal fees may be prohibitive. A large firm might easily charge you $3,000 to $5,000 for incorporating your business, whereas a smaller firm might charge $300 to $500. For these reasons, some entrepreneurs use smaller firms that are more eager for their business.

Start by asking your friends and business contacts for their recommendations. Perhaps your banker or accountant knows a competent attorney with considerable and practical experience in small-business affairs. After you establish a list of potential business lawyers, set up a series of interviews. Ask for referrals of other entrepreneurs they currently represent. Find out how many years of experience they have had working with entrepreneurial companies. Determine what their particular small-business expertise is. Describe a routine legal matter to take care of and evaluate how they would handle it.

Last, determine how well you relate to each lawyer you interview. Is there some chemistry between the two of you? In the end, selecting a business lawyer is a personal decision.

✔ COURTNEY'S SMART TIP

It is paramount that you and your business attorney get along and have a similar business philosophy.

Remember, this is an age of specialization and there is far too much for any legal consultant to know. There are legal specialists in taxes, patents, securities, and so on. You will most likely select an all-around business attorney and then use specialists when the need arises.

Guidelines for Controlling Legal Expenses

Question

I am starting a bakery business. Several friends have recommended different lawyers for me to use as legal counsel. Do you have any advice on how to choose the best lawyer for my bakery?

Answer

Before deciding on the right lawyer for your business, evaluate the scope of services you are likely to need in your new venture. Decide whether you are looking for a one-time legal service or seeking a long-term relationship to handle various legal problems. Find a lawyer who is familiar with your business—you will get better and more appropriate legal advice. Make sure the candidates you are considering have extensive experience in small-business affairs.

Next, consider what size law firm would be the best for you and whether it would be beneficial for you to retain more than one firm for specialized needs. For example, if you want to obtain a trademark logo or a patent, you'll need to find lawyers with special expertise. Remember that whatever the size and reputation of a law firm, your ultimate success depends on the lawyer with whom you are working.

Check the references of lawyers recommended by your colleagues. Contact their firms and ask for résumés or brochures that describe their practices. If this material is not available, ask for some representative clients to contact. Find out if those clients have legal concerns similar to yours and if they have been satisfied with the services provided.

Then go to your public library and consult various directories on lawyers and their credentials. The most comprehensive is the *Martindale-Hubbell Law Directory*, which lists law firms nationwide and provides detailed information on the background of the firm, its areas of specialization, and in some cases its major clients. The directory also gives ratings for legal ability, ethical standards, professional reliability, and diligence. These ratings are based on confidential recommendations solicited from other lawyers.

Other directories include *The Lawyer's Register by Specialties and Fields of Law*, the *Attorney's Register*, the *U.S. Lawyer's Referral Directory*, the *Directory of the Legal Profession*, and state-by-state blue books of lawyers. In addition, most local bar associations publish lists of local lawyers with some basic information about credentials and expertise.

A useful checklist of interview questions for lawyers is found in *100 Ways to Cut Legal Fees and Manage Your Lawyer*. This excellent publication runs the gamut from how to choose a lawyer to how to act as your own attorney. The book costs about $12 and can be ordered by calling 800-638-6582 or by writing to the National Chamber Litigation Center, 1615 H Street NW, Washington, DC 20062.

Schedule interviews with the lawyers you are most interested in retaining. Many lawyers offer an exploratory session free, so ask if there will be a charge. If so, find out how much. Will the fee be credited toward initial services? Try to get a sense of how you relate to the lawyer during the interview. The right chemistry is extremely important.

✔ COURTNEY'S SMART TIP
Credentials are important, but the lawyer-client relationship is critical.

Choosing a lawyer is a time-consuming process, but it is well worth the effort you spend.

Question

I am in the process of negotiating a licensing agreement for my product. How can I control my legal costs and best utilize a lawyer?

Answer

There is an art to using a small-business lawyer advantageously. Legal advice is another form of outside expertise that must be managed effectively. Below are some guidelines to follow when contacting a small-business attorney.

1. *Assist your attorney by conducting a preliminary investigation and obtaining all necessary information in advance.* The more legwork, investigation, and information gathering you accomplish on your own, the more money you will save. Give your attorney all the important documentation required to aid in the decision-making process. Use your lawyer's expertise to review the issues surrounding the legal matter and to bring up potential risk factors.

2. *Use standardized forms for conducting routine business.* Entrepreneurs use many different forms in operating their business—legal forms for organization and incorporation, lease forms, tax forms, intellectual property forms, and so on. Using standardized forms can save you expensive legal fees as well as time. Be sure to have your attorney review the forms you will prepare so they can be tailored to fit your particular needs. Reliable form books include *The Complete Book of Corporate Forms*, published by NOVA.

3. *Decide when to involve your business attorney in negotiations.* When you are trying to buy or sell something, do not involve a business attorney until you have established some common ground of agreement. Both the buyer and the seller must have an initial contact— in order to discover whether an agreement is possible. Use your business attorney to review the situation, point out risk factors, and then draw up the legal documents to finalize the deal. The ultimate business decision has to be yours.

4. *Listen to your attorney's recommendations.* There may be some instances when tax or technical problems in the deal require resolution. You may not be able to judge the true impact of the deal you are considering entering into. Good counsel should clearly tell you what you are about to agree to and its implications. Lawyers are

experts at pointing out the risk factors associated with a business deal.

5. *Beware of lawyers who are in court all the time.* Although litigation is a cost of doing business, it is also expensive. Many entrepreneurs have discovered that the only winners in a court case are the lawyers. A competent lawyer should do everything possible to keep you out of court. Litigation is time-consuming, frustrating, costly, and hazardous to your health, both mentally and physically.

6. *Beware of lawyers who refuse to go to court.* On the other side of the coin are the attorneys who lack the necessary skills or motivation to represent you in court and who will do everything possible to avoid it. They will suggest settlements and compromises, sometimes giving away your position to the adversary to avoid litigation. At times, you will have to draw the line: "Okay, this is the way it is going to be, or we'll sue." Your posture has to be that you are perfectly willing to go to court to secure your justice.

7. *Never talk to another person's attorney by yourself.* Always have your lawyer present when the other side brings counsel. Lawyers have superior knowledge about the law and may try to bluff you. An ethical attorney would never speak with you directly without your attorney present. Never let the adversary's lawyer talk with you alone. Once you have retained legal counsel, all correspondence should be handled through your attorney.

8. *Discuss fee arrangements with your attorney up front.* Determine the costs associated with representation in all legal matters at the beginning of the lawyer-client relationship. Many entrepreneurs negotiate a written fee arrangement with their attorneys before any services are rendered.

In summary, select a lawyer with the experience and expertise that fits your needs. Do all the legwork first and collect all necessary information. To minimize your legal fees, prepare in advance of meeting with your attorney.

How to Choose an Accountant for Your Business

Question

Over a year ago I started a small retail store featuring baby furniture. Since I am not a wizard with numbers, I hired a bookkeeper to set up my books, reconcile my bank statement, prepare monthly financial statements, and fill out tax returns. Now I am thinking about expanding and opening another store. How can I find a reputable accountant to help me?

Answer

You need an experienced accountant who specializes in small business and works with other owners like you. As your business grows, the duties of the accountant will become more numerous and demanding and will ultimately involve designing customized accounting systems for your business. This member of your management team should be a good business adviser as well as a skilled tax planner. He or she should understand the importance of building and managing sound cash flow documents, should be able to provide assistance in securing loans, and should become a good source of business contacts as your venture grows.

Shop around for a competent accountant and consultant. This member of your management team will become one of your most trusted and most frequently used advisers. Ask other business owners in the retail trade about accounting people they would recommend. Call your banker, lawyer, or trade association for additional recommendations.

✔ COURTNEY'S SMART TIP
Find an accountant who has experience working with clients in your industry.

If you are planning a significant expansion of your business, seek out an experienced certified public accountant (CPA). If you think you might be a candidate for raising venture capital or going public, contact an accounting firm with an established track record in initial public offerings or private placements. Typically, these firms search for new small ventures that will become the leading businesses of the future. If they are interested in your business, they will most likely charge less than their usual fee until you become more profitable. Then their charges will rise accordingly.

Hiring a nationally recognized firm will lend credibility to your financial statements and enhance your chances of attracting growth capital. Also, major accounting firms have a number of professional manuals, books, and other programs to assist new founders. These materials are usually available free or at very low cost, since accounting firms want your continued business as you grow.

If you do not feel that you need a national accounting firm, look for an experienced independent accountant or retired accountant who could work part-time. Local colleges and universities with accounting departments are another source for referrals. Finally, contact the society of certified public accountants in your state. Most have referral banks.

After collecting a list of potential accountants, interview each one. Check the chemistry and make sure you are compatible. Ask about services and fee structures. Fees will vary significantly according to the experience level of the accounting expert and the size of your venture. As with other members of your infrastructure, do the routine work yourself and use your accountant for professional expertise.

Setting up and maintaining your books at the beginning is critical to successfully managing your venture as it grows. Many entrepreneurs hire bookkeepers to perform the routine accounting work and then utilize a CPA to review their financials on a monthly or quarterly basis.

You need to become familiar with the day-to-day numbers associated with managing your business. Don't just wait for the prepared financial statements at the end of the month or quarter. You must have a feeling for the money going out and the money coming in—your cash flow. Carefully track your sales and expenses, and how much money you are owed and owe. Do not delegate this function to your accountant.

Small-Business Accountant Can Help Lower Corporate Taxes

Question

My corporate taxes have significantly increased this year, which is my second year in business. My bookkeeper and I prepared my corporate tax returns, but I feel I paid too much. What can I do to reduce my tax burden?

Answer

To avoid overpaying your corporate taxes again, find a good small-business tax accountant and immediately schedule a posttax consulting meeting. An experienced small-business tax accountant can find key tax savings to help you better manage your business and, ideally, increase your profitability.

It's imperative for owners to get good tax and accounting advice. As your business grows, use an experienced tax accountant to advise you on tax planning and to act as a member of your management team. To find an accountant who has experience working with clients in your industry, ask other business owners for recommendations. Talk to your banker, lawyer, or trade association for additional recommendations. Look for good credentials or appropriate degrees such as CPA, CMA (certified management accountant), or CPTX (certified practitioner of taxation.) Ask how long this person has worked as an accountant.

After collecting a list of potential accountants, interview each one to determine if you are compatible and have good chemistry. Ask about their services and fee structures. Fees will vary according to the experience level of the accountant and the size and needs of your venture.

After selecting an accountant, set up a tax-planning meeting and bring in your tax returns for the last two years. Ask the accountant to review your deductions. Are they in line with industry averages for like businesses? Look for missed deductions. If you have missed any deductions, the accountant can file an amended return so you can get money back.

Consider the timing of certain business decisions that will either postpone or accelerate income or deductions. Should you wait to invoice customers at the beginning of the new year, or should you render the bills early enough to expect collection during the current year?

Review your corporate entity, which is usually the biggest area for tax savings and where most mistakes occur. If you are filing a Schedule C as a sole proprietor, you may be able to save tax dollars, money on benefits, and social security by incorporating, forming a partnership, or creating a limited liability corporation. An accountant can crunch your numbers to determine which legal entity is best for your business. If you decide to change your legal structure, also seek advice from your attorney before making any changes.

Review your current record-keeping system. Is it adequate? Should it be updated to capture all expenses and income? Do you keep it current? Discuss different accounting software programs to better track your expenses and income. Have your accountant set up your books so you can just fill in the blanks. Setting up and maintaining your books at the beginning is critical to successfully managing your venture as it grows.

Analyze your ledger and identify your best profit centers. Discuss strategies to increase your sales using the 80/20 percent rule, which states that 80% of your business comes from 20% of your customers. Who are your best customers, and how can you encourage them to increase their purchases?

Review your current retirement plan, if you have one. Ask for recommendations to determine if a SEP-IRA, money purchase Keogh, profit-sharing plan, or defined-benefit retirement account is best for your business. Each plan allows for different write-offs and has its own pros and cons depending on whether you have employees, and if you do, how many you have and their ages. Your accountant can show you approximately how much you can shelter annually under each plan. Discuss these recommendations with your insurance broker. Ask your accountant for advice about investing your retirement fund.

Get a jump start on your next year's taxes by planning ahead and using a seasoned tax professional.

How to Find a Reputable Insurance Agent

Question

I have been running a small alterations business from my home for the last 10 years. Because my business has grown steadily, I have decided to move into a neighborhood shopping center. How do I find a good insurance agent to help me buy business insurance, and what kind do I need to obtain?

Answer

Many business owners do not give much thought to risk management until they or one of their friends encounters a disaster. You need to have business insurance to cover unexpected and unpreventable events— fire, theft, lawsuits, severe weather conditions, and so on—whether you operate out of your home or in a separate location. You can work with either an independent agent who represents many different insurers or an agent who represents one company.

To begin, contact your personal insurance agent or company and ask about the types of business insurance available and the costs. Describe your business needs and determine the best form of coverage. Then shop around for both the best price and the best level of service. Select an agent or broker who fits your needs and specializes in your industry or particular type of business. An alterations business has very different needs from a restaurant or construction business.

Ask other business owners who have similar needs to recommend an agent. Contact your local or national trade or professional association for recommendations. Find out if the organization has group insurance arrangements with specialty brokers or insurers. Call your local chamber of commerce as well as your banker, lawyer, and accountant for additional recommendations of agents with experience in your industry.

Interview several agents and ask for their opinion on the kinds of insurance your business needs. Ask what you should do if you need to file a claim. If they respond by giving you the insurance company's telephone number, be wary. The correct response is, "Call me first." Request a list of customers you can call and then contact these references.

Make sure the chemistry is right. It's important that you feel comfortable with an agent and confident that he or she will be there to assist and represent you if a claim must be filed. Ask about the various coverages available and seek out advice in reducing your exposure to potential losses. Effective agents are experienced in risk management. Check to see if your candidates recommend any particular safety devices for theft protection or fire detection, and find out if you can receive credit for installing them.

Before making a final selection, call your state's insurance department to determine if any complaints have been filed against the agent or company you are considering using. Don't make your decision solely on price. Balance that important criterion against the agent's expertise and, once again, the chemistry.

If you determine that your business needs several policies, you might end up with several different agents—one for property or liability insurance, another for benefits coverage, and so on. An excellent resource on this subject is Sean Mooney's *Insuring Your Business*. The book covers property insurance, liability insurance, boiler and machinery coverage, workers' compensation, and other critical areas that business owners need to consider. To order a copy, call 800-331-9146.

How to Select and Use Management Consultants

Question

I am starting a new retail computer-supply business and need assistance in finding a location, negotiating a lease, and setting up my records and book-keeping systems. I do not have the experience to do all this myself, and I am thinking about hiring a consultant. Where should I look for one?

Answer

For many entrepreneurs, consultants are less expensive than hiring staff, especially when a specific problem must be solved or a project calls for expert assistance.

Choosing a consultant is a very important decision that you should make only after carefully researching and interviewing potential consultants. Many skilled consultants can provide invaluable services—if you can find them. Nowhere are the options so abundant and the quality so variable. The price you pay for consulting services varies tremendously. Proceed with caution.

First, consider whether you want a generalist or a specialist. You may need several different consultants to help you. The person with expertise in finding a location for your business most likely will not have the skills you need to set up your books. Be wary of "can do all" types. Second, consider the consultants' track records. Whom else have they worked for and what services did they render? Obtain references from other entrepreneurs so you can verify performance.

The best way to find consultants is through referrals from your banker, lawyer, accountant, and fellow entrepreneurs. The government is also a good resource and sometimes provides consultants at no charge through the Small Business Administration (SBA). Some of these consultants are paid by the government; others volunteer their services. Colleges and universities are a source for both private consultants and those working under federally funded programs. You might also look in the Yellow Pages under management consultants and shop around.

In the beginning, founders are short of cash and often try to find low-cost educational programs or government-funded management-assistance programs such as those offered by the SBA. Typically, independent consultants charge anywhere from $100 to $1,000 a day. Well-known consulting firms usually charge higher fees. Unfortunately, it is difficult to judge consultants solely on the basis of the fees they charge.

Narrow your selection process down to a few consultants and interview them in depth. Ask about their expertise and approaches. Be sure that you are comfortable and can communicate with them. Evaluate their enthusiasm and openness. Try to determine their interest level in your project. Ask for sample proposals based on your needs. Evaluate their proposals by looking for outcomes and objectives they intend to accomplish. Inquire about their fee structure. Is it hourly, daily, or a fixed fee? You want to hire a consultant who works fast but effectively.

✔ COURTNEY'S SMART TIP

When you decide on a consultant, work out a written agreement specifying the consultant's responsibilities, objectives, and compensation.

A good book on hiring consultants is Herman Holtz's *Choosing and Using a Consultant*. Ask your librarian for reference books or articles on consulting. Don't underestimate the amount of time it will take to find a consultant who has the expertise and enthusiasm you need.

Recruiting and Utilizing a Board of Directors

How to Assemble a Board of Directors

Question

I am interested in starting a dry-cleaning business and plan to incorporate. Do I have to have a board of directors for my new company? If so, where do I find people to serve?

Answer

Your decision to incorporate your business is a wise one, especially if financial risk and personal liability are involved. You might look into the possibility of starting your dry-cleaning business as an S corporation. Check with your accountant about the potential tax advantages of this type of corporate structure.

Every corporation is required by law to have a board of directors. Whom you choose for the board is up to you. Many entrepreneurs give little thought to this task. Instead, they take the easy way out and appoint family members just to meet state requirements. Inside boards rarely contribute solid business experience or reliable advice to a venture. Board members should be looked on as resources who can make a significant contribution to the new corporation. They should be able to bring in business, make introductions to potential customers, and influence members of the business community.

✔ COURTNEY'S SMART TIP

An active and effective board of outside directors is one of the greatest resources an entrepreneur can have.

Board members who have extensive entrepreneurial experience, especially with problems similar to yours, can be invaluable. Retired executives make excellent choices, as do influential community or business leaders. They will strengthen the management team as well as impress potential lenders or investors. Most investors and lenders prefer to see outside board members participating—not family members, unless those relatives happen to have direct experience in the industry.

The purpose of a board is to set overall company policy and to ensure that policies are administered by the owners. Board members are responsible to the shareholders and must see that management carries out its responsibilities. The management team should look to board members as in-house consultants. Sometimes management gets too close to the operation, and board members can offer more-objective analyses and place problems in proper perspective. However, the board should not be involved in day-to-day operations.

New entrepreneurs need all the management expertise they can tap into. Most founders appoint at least five board members. A well-qualified board can improve strategy, stimulate planning, and provide emotional support. Often, entrepreneurs flounder around trying to obtain credit from vendors, get goods shipped on time, and so on. One phone call from a board member can accomplish all that in minutes. Board members can act as sounding boards for new ideas and as references for banks, investors, and lawyers.

The downside of appointing an outside board is that busy executives and business leaders may not have sufficient time to devote to your venture. Or they may be reluctant to serve because of the personal liability assumed in becoming board members. Many founders try to secure board liability insurance to protect their members. This is an additional budgetary expense, but in the past few years it has become less costly.

Last, it is a common practice to pay board members a nominal fee for attending monthly meetings—or to compensate them with stock options. Your strategic operating plan will dictate whether appointing an inside board will suffice or whether an outside board would enhance your venture.

Establishing an Advisory Board

Advisory Boards Help Businesses Keep on Track

Question

My business is three years old, and my market is rapidly increasing. My staff and I have different ideas about expanding the company. I definitely don't want to borrow a lot of money or give up ownership control. I hired a consultant to help us who added to our confusion. What else can I do to develop a growth plan that everyone will support?

Answer

Consider establishing an informal advisory board of outside experts to act as your consultants. The beauty of advisory boards is that they have no voting power and, generally speaking, no legal liability to protect shareholder interest.

Therefore, an advisory board is easier to assemble than a board of directors. It is not necessary to obtain liability insurance for board members, which is costly even though it is becoming less expensive to purchase.

Getting input and advice only from your homegrown management team is dangerous to your business's continued growth and prosperity. Likewise, using consultants can also be dangerous. Because of their focused expertise, their recommendations are often slanted. In addition, their services usually bear a higher price tag than that for assembling an advisory board.

It is wise to get new perspectives on how to grow your company and be able to discuss what you don't know with advisory board members. You will enhance your relationship with an advisory board by involving them early in your venture.

Select advisory board members because of their business acumen and their ability to generate new business, make introductions to new customers, and influence business leaders in your industry. Members should have a healthy mix of talent from a variety of disciplines and have related business experience. It's also a good idea to have a strategic planner on your board. Look for potential members who have specific knowledge and skills you lack.

Search for potential advisory board members among retired executives, business-school professors, entrepreneurs who run noncompeting companies, members of your infrastructure, and key customers. Check to ensure that potential members have no ethical or legal conflicts with your business.

Prepare a list of questions to use when interviewing them. Inquire about their past achievements and accomplishments. Ask what role they would like to play, their special expertise, and what they feel they could contribute to your board.

Many entrepreneurs are surprised that few potential candidates will decline to serve on an advisory board, regardless of whether you offer an adviser fee. Instead, advisory board members are sincerely interested in helping companies succeed. They enjoy interacting and networking with other members. You do not have to offer adviser fees. You can show your appreciation by taking members out for a group dinner, providing entertainment tickets, or holding a few of your meetings at vacation resorts.

The primary goal of an advisory board is to provide guidance and feedback about your company's goals and objectives. Members should actively challenge decisions about the directions your venture is taking.

Avoid making your advisory board a rubber-stamp entity. And don't limit membership to insiders and/or relatives. A well-selected advisory board can help you struggle more effectively with the many challenges of growing your venture.

However, an advisory board is not for everyone. You must be willing to seriously consider members' advice and implement their recommendations.

An advisory board will enhance your management team and bring sound business knowledge and expertise to your venture, which can give you an edge over your competition as well as assist in obtaining working capital for expansion. Today, most entrepreneurs cannot afford to operate their ventures without an advisory board. Living in a vacuum when you don't have all the answers is risky to the continued success of your company.

Pitfalls to Avoid

1. Selecting a consultant without interviewing and checking references.

2. Consulting with a business attorney without first preparing for the meeting and completing as much work as you can yourself.

3. Failing to establish an agreed-on price for consultant services.

4. Ignoring the need for business insurance until you are involved in a loss or disaster.

5. Failing to utilize an advisory board for your business.

6. Using family members or friends as directors or advisers when they lack the requisite skills and contacts.

7. Hiring a generalist when you need a specialist.

8. Contacting your local legal society to ask for attorney recommendations.

Today, no owner should be without an advisory board to help chart the future direction of his or her company.

The Good News

Entrepreneurs have many experienced and helpful members of the infrastructure and other professionals to help plan, manage, and operate their ventures. They need to network and balance their team by selecting people who have the expertise they lack.

11
Franchising*

Overview

Franchising is a growing industry and currently accounts for nearly one-third of all retail sales. Approximately 300 businesses are franchised annually. In 1994, there were more than 3,000 franchise companies representing over 270,000 establishments doing over $233 billion in sales. It has been estimated that these companies employ nearly 2 million people.

Franchising is an excellent strategy both for successful entrepreneurs who want to expand their markets and for potential entrepreneurs who are considering purchasing a franchise as a business-entry strategy if there is an innovative, proven business concept and system to replicate it. This chapter addresses the questions from both entrepreneurs who want to purchase a franchise operation and those who are thinking about franchising their business concept.

The reason franchise operations are more successful than new startups is that their concept has been proven and an operating system has been established. Most franchises are designed to be somewhat of a turnkey operation for launching and operating the venture—that is, the owner can begin operation with a complete planning, management control, and operational system in place that includes ongoing support and training. The turnkey concept was developed around the

---

*Note: Ted Rice, cofounder and former chairman of the board of T. J. Cinnamons, contributed many ideas to this chapter, sharing his experiences in building a worldwide franchise of retail and wholesale bakery stores. Ted is currently the CEO of Big Bob's Carpet and is building yet another franchise organization. He is an adjunct professor at Wichita State University and several other colleges and universities in Kansas City (Missouri) teaching entrepreneurship. He is also a Price-Babson College fellow.

idea that the franchisee has only to turn the key in the door to be open for business. In reality, however, the franchisee must undertake much investigation and up-front work, including locating a site, negotiating the lease, finishing the space, obtaining the equipment, and hiring the staff. Potential franchisees who think this is a slam-dunk way of doing business have been misled.

The survival rate of franchised businesses is far superior to that of entrepreneurial ventures. Approximately 4% of franchised businesses fail during the first few crucial years, while other new ventures suffer an 80% failure rate during the crucial period. Because not all franchises are successful, it is imperative that potential franchisees perform due diligence and investigate everything, including the industry, the market customer base, and the track records and background of both the franchisor and other franchisees.

Ask for all information available from the franchiser: the franchise package, year-end financials, a list of existing franchisees, disclosure documents, and so forth. It is also important to determine potential profitability and to consider whether the franchise could reach the financial returns you expect. Unfortunately, most people don't want to spend the time and effort to investigate and make an informed decision.

✔ COURTNEY'S SMART TIP

Potential franchisees need some type of entrepreneurial experience obtained from working, from taking seminars or courses, or both.

Potential franchisees must have sufficient funds to invest in the business and the commitment to run the operation. Entrepreneurs who truly want to be their own bosses may be disappointed with buying a franchise because of the restrictive requirements to follow a standardized operation and use only authorized products. Some franchises are more restrictive than others.

On the other hand, franchising is an excellent expansion strategy for founders who want to grow—provided their product or service is franchisable. Franchising can open the door to low-cost financing not available through traditional money sources. But franchising a new concept takes considerable up-front money that must be spent before you can collect any fees. Whether you are considering franchising your business or purchasing an already established franchise, considerable thought, investigation, and evaluation are essential.

Smart Franchising Strategies

1. Proceed carefully by gathering all available information about franchising opportunities, including the franchiser and a list of the franchisees.

2. Experience the product or service firsthand, if possible.

3. Determine whether there is a continuing market for the franchised product or service.

4. Visit typical franchisees and ask them about the franchiser, profitability, market potential, long-term commitment, and other factors.

5. Ask about the training and support, both initial and ongoing, that the franchiser will provide.

6. Ask the franchiser how many franchises have closed and for what reasons.

7. If you do not have any small-business experience, enroll in a seminar or course on entrepreneurship and running a franchise.

8. Open several locations and evaluate the capability of your business to be franchised to different locations.

9. Determine if you have enough money, patience, and management capability to franchise your concept.

10. Investigate potential franchises, evaluate their entrepreneurial capability, and always look for an owner-operator.

11. Rely on your intuition in deciding whether to become involved with franchising.

12. Franchising can be risky. It requires much research and due diligence.

How to Research and Buy a Franchise Business

Is a Franchise the Right Pick?

Question

I recently retired from the military, and I am thinking about buying a franchise. Is this a good move for me? What kind of franchise should I buy?

Answer

Buying a franchise is a good business opportunity if you can operate under the heavily controlled franchise environment. Choose the right franchise and write a business plan to determine if it could be profitable for you.

The first step is determining whether you are franchise material. Key questions to consider are whether you can work within the franchise structure by following a prescribed way of operating. Are you prepared to work long hours, averaging 60 to 80 hours a week, without staff support? Can you perform routine repetitive tasks day after day?

Are you prepared to take a financial risk and assume a large debt to start the business? Will your family support you? Are you prepared to research the franchise opportunity and write a business plan? Do you have strong sales skills?

Some people retiring from the military have been successful operating a franchise. They are comfortable working within a set system and following detailed procedures. They enjoy the franchise network and support from the franchisers. They are accustomed to receiving training and working in a team environment.

If you think you would be comfortable in a franchise system, the next big step is choosing the right one. First, you must decide whether to purchase a large, established franchise or a smaller, newer franchise. Expect to pay a high entry fee for a large franchise with an established track record, strong name recognition, and instant customers.

Opting to purchase a smaller, newer franchise will give you more location choices but will be riskier. A determining factor is how much you are willing to pay for a franchise. If you are looking for a lower up-front investment, a smaller franchise system may be your only option.

Regardless of how much you budget toward the investment, match the franchise with your skills, background, and experience. For example, avoid purchasing a fast-food franchise if you lack experience in that industry. Stay close to the industries you know well.

Next, decide if you want to operate a franchise from your home with no additional overhead and no salaried employees, or from an office. Some franchises require an office or storefront with support staff.

Because not all franchises are successful, perform due diligence and investigate at least three different franchises that offer the same product or service you have decided on. Research everything, including the growth potential of the industry, the market, the customer base, and the track record of the franchise. Look for franchises that own and operate company stores.

Now you are ready to write a business plan to determine if you can be profitable operating the franchise in the area that you have chosen.

What Would It Take to Open a Franchise, and Where Do I Begin?

Question

I am interested in starting a used-car rental agency like Ugly Duckling or Rent-A-Lemon. What would it take to open a franchise business like this, and where would I begin?

Answer

Purchasing a franchise can be a good entry strategy for entrepreneurs. It eliminates many of the headaches associated with starting a new venture from scratch. It is also an opportunity for you to benefit from the experience, knowledge, expertise, and support from a franchiser who has successfully tested and proven a business concept in the marketplace. Proven franchises offer lower risks of failure than unproven franchises or new start-up businesses.

Often, the franchise offers an established trade name and reputation along with instant recognition in the market area. These favorable aspects will not guarantee success but can certainly give you a head start. For example, *Inc.* magazine recently reported that 38% of start-up businesses fail within the first year compared with fewer than 4% of franchises.

Warning: Considerable due diligence is required before you enter into a franchise agreement. To begin with, ask yourself whether you would enjoy working with a parent company that will most likely require you to follow certain policies and procedures in operating your business. Joining any franchise involves a loss of freedom for entrepreneurs, who must abide by the stipulations contained in the franchise agreement.

Are you willing to pay a franchise fee along with a monthly royalty to the parent company? All franchise companies receive an up-front fee when you sign the franchise agreement and then collect a monthly royalty fee. This fee is based on a percentage of gross sales before taxes, usually 5%. If you feel comfortable with these conditions, then thoroughly investigate the franchise by following these steps:

First, select at least three franchises that offer the same product or service. Before contacting these franchises, visit the business section of your local library. Consult the various franchise handbooks available that contain a variety of different information about existing franchises and their parent companies. Look up any available information that has been written about the franchise in newspapers, journals and the like.

Write for a copy of the *Franchise Opportunity Handbook*, published annually by the Superintendent of Documents, U.S. Government Printing Office in Washington, D.C. It is extremely helpful and probably contains more extensive information on franchises than any other publication. It costs about $10.

Next, ask the librarian to assist you in accessing one of the many available electronic databases that contain financial information and disclosure statements on franchises. It is critical that you evaluate the financial strength of the parent company. These databases contain annual reports, quarterly financial statements, and other detailed financial information.

While at the library, consult INFOTRAC, another database that lists published articles in many different magazines. Get copies of anything written about the franchise. Also, several magazines publish annual listings of franchise opportunities. For example, *Inc.* magazine publishes an annual list of the 100 best franchise opportunities. *Entrepreneur Magazine* publishes an annual list of the franchise superstars.

Visit a couple of franchise locations in your area. Check out the location, examine the exterior and interior, and observe the customers. Try the product or service. Talk to the management and ask about their operations and their relationship with the franchiser. What problems have they encountered with the parent company?

You are now ready to contact the parent company and indicate your interest in joining the franchise. Ask the franchiser if you can come out and visit the corporate headquarters. Inquire as to whether they provide training on how to produce and market their product or service that you may not understand well. Question whether they have established training manuals available for franchisees.

Ask what type of management expertise the franchiser has in production, marketing, and financing the product or service. Ask how many franchises there are in the company and how long they have been in business. How many franchises have closed, and why?

Request that the franchiser send you a disclosure document. It will reveal information about the franchiser, including educational background, experience (what types of businesses he or she has been involved in), and any pending litigation. Sometimes, franchisers are reluctant to provide a disclosure document early on. Be persistent. They are required by law to provide you with a copy. If you are not satisfied with the answers to these questions, pursue other potential franchisers.

How to Evaluate a Franchise Agreement

Question

I am interested in opening up a weight-loss franchise business. The franchiser just sent me the franchise agreement. How do I evaluate it?

Answer

Most franchise agreements are written for five years with an automatic renewal. Determine the exit, or how you can get out of the franchise agreement. Can you sell your franchise, and do the potential buyers have to qualify as franchisees? Under what circumstances can the franchiser terminate the agreement?

What are your obligations to the parent company and the franchiser's to you? How far from your business can another franchise be located? How are royalties determined? Are your royalty payments subject to audit by the franchiser? If yes, how much notice will they give you before the audit?

The franchiser will probably ask you what locations you are considering.

✔ COURTNEY'S SMART TIP

Never lease or rent property until you have signed a franchise agreement.

The franchiser must find out whether the territory you are interested in is available. Most franchisers have site locators that work directly with them and provide the franchisee with considerable location assistance. What, if any, arrangements have you made with the landlord?

During your initial conversations, decide whether you feel comfortable with the franchiser. Buying into a franchise situation is akin to entering into a marriage. There must be good chemistry between both of you, or you'll end up at each other's throats or in court, or both.

If you are still interested in pursuing the franchise opportunity, ask for all the available information about the franchise. Because it costs the franchise about $20 to send out a complete informational kit, it may first try to qualify you as a potential buyer. Usually, the franchiser will send out an initial questionnaire that asks for certain information about your financial condition, including your net worth and your source of money for opening the business.

After receiving the questionnaire, the franchiser will ascertain whether you are capable of purchasing. Then the franchiser will probably send out a formal application package. This package contains detailed information about the company's operations and history, including brochures, flyers, and sample marketing and sales material. Remember, it is the sales tool for the franchiser. Don't take anything at face value; investigate everything. The application packet will ask you to provide biographical data and complete financial information. It will include a copy of the franchise agreement and available territories for purchase.

Consult an attorney who specializes in franchising before signing the franchise agreement to ensure that you fully understand all the terms and conditions of the contract. Guard against having your attorney rewrite the agreement—it is a waste of your money. Instead, ask the attorney to review the franchise agreement and look for any major flaws or inconsistencies. Although most of the terms are standard, you may be able to negotiate some items that are important to you.

Decide whether the franchiser is reputable and whether the required investment will give you the financial returns you are looking for. The franchiser must determine whether you are a viable purchaser and whether you will be able to operate a successful venture. In most instances, the franchiser is looking for an owner/operator rather than an absentee owner.

Finally, it's time to review and evaluate all the information you have gathered. Then, ask the franchiser for high and low financial ratios for the typical franchise operation, including gross revenues and net earning for the franchisees. You might be able to obtain this information from existing franchisees. In general, if the business is a restaurant, ask for the average ticket price. If it is a retail operation, ask for the average sales per square foot.

At each step of your investigation, determine whether the franchiser is fair, honest, and reputable. Will you get the essential assistance you feel is necessary to operate a successful venture? Does the franchiser have related industry experience? What has been its track record to date? Try to visit as many franchise locations as possible.

During the evaluation process, you will most likely eliminate some of the various franchise alternatives. Compare the different front-end fees, royalty payments, expenses, and so on. Franchisers can offer an easier alternative to starting a new business, but entrepreneurs must carefully assess and analyze each opportunity.

Purchasing an International Food Franchise

Question

Since I came back from an overseas vacation, I have been entertaining the idea of opening a specialty restaurant or franchise fast-food business in another country. I feel this could be a good opportunity for a small family enterprise. How can I find the capital needed to start such a venture? What advice would you offer for pursuing this idea?

Answer

Launching a specialty restaurant or fast-food franchise overseas could be difficult, expensive, and time-consuming. In a foreign country it will be easier to open a fast-food franchise, since you will not have all the headaches associated with starting a business from scratch. Not only will the franchiser provide a plan for operating the business, but it also will furnish key management advice, tax information, and other business consulting. An international franchiser has valuable contacts providing expertise on operating a franchise abroad. More important, franchises have an already established name providing immediate recognition and have a proven fast-food concept that has already demonstrated success in the marketplace.

However, there will be some risk involved, since you might not know whether the concept you choose will be successful in another country. The fast-food market may be quite different from its success in the United States. In addition, it will probably be more costly to start a franchise in another country, since the policy of most franchisers is to sell rights to an entire country versus a specific geographic location. Generally, franchisers require a multi-unit commitment to open several locations within a certain period. Usually, they sell the franchise rights to a national of that country.

There are several important factors to consider before becoming involved with an international franchise. First, determine if you can open a business within about 90 days. If it takes longer than that, look for another country. Ask if you are required to make a joint venture with a citizen of that country who must own some percentage of your company. Can you take a profit out of the country? Some franchises require that any money earned must be reinvested in that country. Also ask how much of the raw product or materials must come from that country. Most important, ensure that all money exchanged shall be in U.S. currency at the exchange rate on the first of the month and the fifteenth of the month at 12 noon Greenwich mean time. Last, obtain legal counsel from an attorney in that country to help you understand requirements and customs for conducting business there.

Research which fast-food franchisers have international locations and whether you would be able to purchase the rights to a foreign country. The *World Wide Franchise Directory*, available in most libraries, is a guide to franchise opportunities around the world. The library will also have *Doing Business In . . .* published by Price Waterhouse. This is a series of books focusing on how to operate ventures in many different foreign countries.

While at the library, access the National Trade Data Bank (NTDB) on CD-ROM. This is a database about marketing and doing business abroad developed by the U.S. Commerce Department. Or contact one of the Commerce Department's regional offices or the International Trade Administration for additional information. The office will conduct customized market research for a fee in areas where the government has a foreign office.

Another good source for gathering information concerning international franchises is to attend the annual International Franchise Trade Show sponsored by the International Franchise Association located in Washington, D.C. You can contact the IFA about its shows at 202-628-8000. There are also international franchise fairs held abroad that feature how to start a franchise business in various countries.

As a rule, franchisers do not provide funding for opening a franchise business. They can assist you with leasing agreements for obtaining necessary equipment. Franchisers can also refer you to preferred lenders that they have worked with.

Franchising a Successful Venture

Question

Several years ago I started a fast-food restaurant that sells a new kind of southwestern taco made with a special machine that I designed. Because of its success, I opened another restaurant in January. This restaurant has been equally successful. Several of my friends have suggested that I franchise my business, which I am seriously considering. What is your advice?

Answer

Franchising is a sound business-expansion strategy for you to consider if you have an innovative, proven concept and business system that can be replicated with repeated success. Entrepreneurs have been franchising their ventures at increasing rates for the past decade. Currently franchises account for nearly one-third of all retail sales.

There are a couple of reasons why franchising has been so popular as well as a successful means of expanding a business. It is an excellent way to quickly expand your business, if in fact you can prove that your concept works, your product is widely recognized and accepted, your business has a steady record of success, and you can establish that it could be disseminated to other locations.

The franchiser must provide the franchisee with a predictable way of doing business—that is, a business that is completely assembled so the franchisee can begin operation with complete planning, management control, and operational systems that include ongoing support and training. Facilities are duplicated and equipment is purchased in bulk and installed. Inventory is provided through established procurement systems.

But is this the strategy for you and your business? It is extremely important for you to evaluate whether you should get involved in this expansion strategy. Does it make sense for you to franchise? Do you have the expertise and *capital* to franchise? Will you be getting the value you want from franchising? Are you giving value to potential franchisees through your experience, knowledge, and continual support? To be successful, you must have productive restaurants that provide a steady stream of income to you.

There are several different types of franchises. They include trademark and brand-name franchises, product-distribution franchises, business-format franchises, and affiliate or conversion franchises.

- In a *trademark and brand-name* franchise, the franchisee pays for the right to use the franchiser's established trademark or brand name, usually for marketing purposes. By marketing products or services under a well-known trademark or brand name, the franchisee can gain market visibility and market share more quickly by capitalizing on the credibility and recognition of the franchiser.

- In *product-distribution* franchises, the manufacturer of a product establishes a distribution network by contracting with dealers who distribute the product. The manufacturer stipulates how the franchisee will operate. For example, the distributor may not be allowed to sell competitive products or purchase parts or supplies not expressly authorized by the franchiser. The franchisee receives support in terms of capital, advertising or discounts on purchases, and managerial support.

• In *business-format* franchises, the one you are considering, the franchisee pays a fee and, in most cases, a royalty to receive the entire business format—trademarked products or services, operations systems and manuals, site selection, training, accounting, and other managerial support services. This type of franchise operation is attractive to the individual who is not familiar with business or does not want to take the time to launch a new start-up. It is the fastest-growing segment of the franchise industry today.

• In an *affiliate* or *conversion* franchise, franchisees ally themselves with like ventures. This often occurs in a fragmented industry where there is little opportunity for large-scale visibility. By forming such a system under one name, individual affiliate franchises pool funds for marketing and advertising campaigns that are designed to capture greater consumer attention and recognition for their businesses. Many real estate companies are organized this way.

Pitfalls to Avoid

1. Failing to gather the information needed to make an informed decision before signing a franchise agreement and paying the required fee.

2. Signing up with a franchiser that does not have a track record of multiple locations and a profitable bottom line.

3. Purchasing a franchise that does not complement your skills, work experience, or interests.

4. Thinking that if you purchase a franchise, you will make a lot of money.

5. Thinking that if you franchise your product or service, you can sit back, collect checks, and make a lot of money.

6. Selling a franchise to an absentee owner or letting the owner's family operate the business.

7. Expanding a franchise nationally before successfully penetrating regional markets.

8. Failing to adopt strict quality-control standards and ways to measure them.

9. Franchising an average product or service in a highly competitive industry.

10. Some businesses do not have franchise potential.

The Good News

Franchising can be a smart business strategy that enables you to enter the world of entrepreneurship if you perform due diligence in searching for the right franchise opportunity and thoroughly investigating this business opportunity. It can also be an excellent expansion strategy if you have a proven and innovative concept that can be replicated and enough capital to franchise it.

12

The 10 Questions Entrepreneurs Should Ask But Don't

As you have noticed from reading the previous chapters in this book, I have received many questions from readers across the United States about both starting and growing entrepreneurial ventures. The range of their letters has been varied, indicating that they are groping for basic entrepreneurial knowledge and skills. I have noticed a void—there are certain questions that entrepreneurs are not asking but that are critical to operating and growing successful ventures.

Therefore, I have developed "*The 10 Questions Entrepreneurs Should Ask But Don't*," which should be considered by all business owners. Too often, these questions crop up at later stages in the venture's development when the owner encounters problems. The high failure rate experienced by every type of new venture and typically reported by Dun & Bradstreet illustrates that many of these questions should have been asked at the time of start-up. In 1992, *USA Today* reported that 88% of business failures can be attributed to internal causes such as inadequate leadership, poor business planning, insufficient management experience, and excessive debt.

Since most entrepreneurs experience the same business problems, if these questions had been considered earlier, the novice entrepreneurs could have greatly increased their chances of operating more stable and profitable ventures. This chapter provides important insight into the typical areas overlooked by founders that can jeopardize their chances for success.

The 10 Questions Entrepreneurs Should Ask But Don't

1. How do I go about writing a feasibility plan to determine if my idea for starting a new business could turn into a profitable business venture?

2. What kind of legal structure should I consider for my new business?

3. How do I design a plan for financing my business?

4. How can I put together a budget that will as accurately as possible measure my start-up costs?

5. How can I distinguish my business from others and increase my sales?

6. How do I put together a winning management team when I can't pay high salaries to attract and retain a talented staff?

7. How do I find a corporate strategic partner to assist me in bringing my invention to the marketplace?

8. What kind of business insurance should I get to protect my business?

9. How can I strengthen my sales skills as well as those of my staff?

10. What skills should I develop to keep pace with the growth of my business?

Question #1

How do I go about writing a feasibility plan to determine if my idea for starting a new business could turn into a profitable business venture?

Answer

This is an excellent question that budding entrepreneurs should be asking before investing any money into a new venture. Usually, the opposite is true. The entrepreneur gets all wrapped up and excited about a new venture idea without thoughtful consideration, research, and evaluation of its potential and pitfalls. Several years later, the entrepreneur realizes the idea was sound but finds that the market was saturated, the profit margin was too narrow, the management team was not in place, there was an insufficient amount of capital, or a myriad of other reasons that the venture failed.

If entrepreneurs thoroughly researched new venture ideas and wrote feasibility plans before starting, many failed businesses would never have been launched in the first place. That is one of the fundamental reasons that so many new businesses fail during the first tenuous years of operation. Most statistics show that 40% of new start-ups fail during the first year and, by the fifth year, 80% fail. This failure rate could be significantly reduced if properly structured research and planning was conducted in the beginning.

Starting a new venture takes time, market research, seed capital, financial forecasts, and a sound feasibility plan—all of which entrepreneurs are reluctant to do. Entrepreneurs are doers who want to take their ideas to the marketplace quickly. They know that the window of opportunity will probably be there only for a short time. Consequently, they avoid taking the necessary time to research and strategically plan their ventures, identifying problem areas and formulating plans to prevent potential problems. When this is done, they have time to formulate solutions before encountering problems.

Astute entrepreneurs understand the importance of writing feasibility plans that indicate whether ventures are likely to succeed. While writing the plan, you can identify which areas pose the greatest threats and develop alternative solutions should a problem occur. If the feasibility plan demonstrates that the venture idea has potential, the next step is to write a business plan.

Many entrepreneurs think that if they have a great business opportunity that matches their experience and expertise, the venture will be successful. In reality, finding the right business to start comprises 10% of the work involved before you open up for business. The next step involves writing a feasibility analysis to determine if the venture idea could be profitable. This consists of researching its workability, marketability, and profitability and your capability as well as identifying any potential danger signals.

Writing a feasibility plan forces you to consider every facet of your business opportunity and write the results on paper, where you and others can objectively evaluate its potential. Since every venture has both risks and opportunities, what are the risks compared to the opportunities? What are the potential problems? Could the potential problems be either eliminated or minimized? Developing a feasibility plan addresses these questions and allows for trial-and-error testing before any dollars are spent.

Feasibility plans explore whether venture ideas have the potential to succeed. It is a gateway that must be passed through on the way to developing a detailed business plan to prove the venture idea. There is no reason to waste your efforts on pursuing a business opportunity if it does not have a growing market and the potential to earn a healthy profit.

I suggest that you use the following outline for developing a feasibility plan that specifies the scope of information that should be researched and included in the plan.

Entrepreneur's Feasibility Plan Outline

Executive summary.

Product or service analysis.

Market analysis.

Price and profitability.

Plan for further action.

The *executive summary* is a brief, concise overview of the venture idea and key dimensions contained in each section of the plan. The *product or service analysis* covers the stage of development, limitations, liabilities, proprietary rights, production, and related services and spin-offs. The *market analysis* looks at the size of the market, growth potential, industry trends, customer profile, customer benefits, target markets, and market-penetration methods. The *price and profitability* section measures what customers will pay for the product or service. It is critical that the venture be able to maintain a sufficiently high gross margin to cover expenses and still yield a healthy profit. This section examines the cost of the product or service, sales estimates, gross margin, operating expenses, and start-up costs. The last section, *plan for further action*, focuses on the future, identifies likely pitfalls, strong points, needed capital, license potential, potential corporate partners, infrastructure members, the entrepreneur's role, and whether to proceed with the new venture idea and write a business plan.

Many entrepreneurs use their feasibility plans to show to potential investors, bankers, friends, personal business advisers, and strategic partners. Feedback from these groups will produce useful information and help better focus the venture idea. Remember, the main purpose of writing a feasibility plan is to test the venture idea to determine if it should be further developed. If the answer is yes, you should proceed to write a detailed business plan.

✔ COURTNEY'S SMART TIP

Market research and business planning are critical to launching profitable and successful ventures.

Entrepreneurs who plan carefully are more likely to succeed than those who do not. Planning minimizes risks and gives you better foresight for identifying potential problems. Spending time writing a feasibility plan is time well spent. Writing everything down on paper allows you to encounter and solve many problems before they jeopardize the venture. Business-planning skills will maximize your potential for success and minimize your chance of failure.

Question #2

What kind of legal structure should I consider for my new business?

Answer

Many entrepreneurs just start their ventures without giving any thought to what kind of legal structure would be best for the business and the entrepreneur. Owners discover too late that the legal structure of their ventures is crucial to strategic planning, raising capital, and potential success. When you start a business without declaring a legal structure, the law assumes that your business is a sole proprietorship. This means that you and your venture are legally one and the same. This type of legal structure is usually not the best for ventures, especially those that need to raise outside capital and have high growth potential. Instead, the corporate structure is usually the best legal structure for entrepreneurs.

Before choosing a legal structure, consider tax implications as well as how to limit your business liability. Establishing a sole proprietorship involves only obtaining required local, state, and federal licenses. While there are few formalities and legal restrictions, you have unlimited personal liability. This means you and you alone are responsible for the full amount of your business debts. This liability extends to your home, car, stocks, and other personal possessions. All the profits from the business are yours, but so are all the losses. The only way to limit the liability risk is to obtain proper business insurance.

A sole proprietorship is the most difficult legal structure for raising capital since you and your business are one and the same. If anything jeopardizes your ability to run the business, investors or lenders could lose their investments. There are also some tax drawbacks. Although you avoid the problems of double taxation with the corporate structure, sole proprietors cannot deduct many expenses that corporations can, such as a defined-benefit pension plan, insurance expenses, health benefits, and other corporate expenses.

Overall, the sole proprietorship has some fatal flaws besides personal liability, tax drawbacks, and limited ability to raise capital. First, the life of the business terminates with the life of the proprietor, which poses severe problems to estate planners, not to mention difficulties with the disposition of the business.

Second, existing options are hampered. It is much easier to sell a corporation than a sole proprietorship. Growth is restricted because of financing difficulties. Last, it is more difficult to attract good management and staff to work in a sole proprietorship, which limits growth and performance.

✔ COURTNEY'S SMART TIP

Incorporate your venture to protect against liabilities and to enhance your ability to raise capital.

The corporate shield can protect you personally from creditors' claims except for personal negligence, civil wrongs, or torts—when you are acting as an employee of the corporation. For more detailed information about different legal structures, including partnerships, corporations, S corporations and LLCs refer to Chapter 4, "Legal Structures for Starting a Business."

In summary, when deciding on the legal structure for your venture, consider the cost, stability, risks, liability, and your personal taxation situation. Consult with a small-business attorney and tax accountant for expert advice on legal structure.

Question #3

How do I design a plan for financing my business?

Answer

When starting out, most entrepreneurs neglect designing a plan for financing their ventures through various stages of growth they will encounter. Instead, they search for capital, often not knowing how much money they need, if they can raise it, and how they will use it.

Typically, entrepreneurs contact the wrong money source for financing their ventures. This is evidenced by the many letters I receive from entrepreneurs who ask advice in finding venture capitalists who might provide seed money for new ventures. In the majority of cases, venture capitalists are not an appropriate money source for new start-ups.

From my experience as board director for a Denver bank specializing in small-business and commercial loans, I learned that most entrepreneurs have no idea how much money they will truly need to run their businesses. Few give much thought to how debt and equity financing will affect their business, ownership, profitability, and ability to grow.

Another financial consideration is that the capital you raise must be obtained at a cost that is affordable. One basic entrepreneurial principle to follow is *you cannot make money if you pay too much for what you buy*. Further, your capital structure should be flexible enough so that changes can be easily made to accommodate rapid expansion or contraction of operations. Your capital structure should not block you from pursuing attractive business opportunities. Finally, your legal structure should provide the control you want while giving your investors and lenders the protection they demand. The balance you should maintain between selling equity in your venture and incurring debt will change depending on your stage of growth.

Before designing a financial plan for your venture, use the following checklist to help you formulate your financial strategy:

Entrepreneur's Financial Plan Checklist

1. What stage of development is my business in now?

2. What are my immediate dollar needs?

3. What are my immediate dollar needs in 6 months? 9 months? 12 months?

4. What are my future dollar needs?

5. When will my venture need an injection of capital?

6. How many rounds of financing will I need over the next five years?

7. What type of balance do I want between debt and equity financing?

8. How much debt am I willing to tolerate?

9. How much ownership am I willing to give away for equity financing?

10. What type of financial terms would I be comfortable with and want to negotiate?

Question #4

How can I put together a budget that will as accurately as possible measure my start-up costs?

Answer

One method of determining how much money you will need to start your business is to do a mental walk-through of what your business will look like. Use the following checklist as a basis for estimating your start-up costs:

Entrepreneur's Start-up Cost Checklist

1. Where will the business be located?
2. What size will it be initially?
3. What will the office or retail space look like?
4. What type of walls and fixtures will it have?
5. What type of equipment will I need? (Consider computers, furniture, carpet, copy machine, shelving, etc.)
6. What type of signage will be required?
7. How much of an opening inventory will the business need?
8. How will inventory be paid for?
9. What kind of deposits will I be required to make? (Consider telephone, utilities, rent—first and last month, etc.)
10. What city codes must I comply with, and are there any costs involved?
11. What type of government (local, state, federal) business licenses will be required?
12. What types of supplies will I need? (Consider cleaning, office, shipping, boxes, etc.)
13. What kinds of marketing costs will be incurred before opening? (Consider brochures, advertising, stationery, business cards, etc.)
14. What type of staff training is necessary before opening for business?

When estimating these expenses, be as realistic and accurate as possible. Entrepreneurs always discover hidden costs that are incurred but not planned for. Ask other owners in a similar business what their start-up costs were and how much money they suggest you have in reserve before opening your doors for business.

Most lenders recommend that entrepreneurs plan on having a minimum of three months operating capital on hand. Ideally, they prefer six months of operating capital in the bank. Operating capital is defined as all expenses incurred that will be direct cash outlays during the first 90 to 180 days of operation.

✔ COURTNEY'S SMART TIP
Build some padding into your budget to allow for surprises.

Guard against forcing the budgeting process or trying to underestimate start-up costs. Let the budgeting process indicate how much money the business concept really needs. The purpose of estimating start-up costs is to determine if you can raise enough money to start the venture and if your business opportunity can earn a profit.

For example, one entrepreneur wanted to launch a venture that involved purchasing a submarine and selling underwater ocean tours in the Hawaiian islands. The idea seemed to be feasible. There was a growing market for these types of tours similar to the helicopter rides that tourists purchase on their Hawaiian vacations. At the time, there were no other competitors.

He began his research, analyzed the market, created a market niche, and then located a used 12-seat submarine in Houston, Texas, that he could remodel for the tours. After estimating his start-up budget, he discovered that he needed about $1.2 million for operating capital to launch the venture. He could raise only about $10,000. After estimating start-up costs, he determined there was no way he could start this business himself. Several years later, a couple of other entrepreneurs started the same business and today have a profitable venture.

There is no lack of ideas for launching new companies, but your venture ideas must match your personal and business criteria as well as your pocketbook. You can avoid problems like running out of money or realizing that you cannot raise enough to launch your venture idea by accurately estimating start-up costs and preparing an initial start-up budget. This exercise is one that entrepreneurs cannot neglect before spending more time on a venture idea.

Question #5

How can I distinguish my business from others and increase my sales?

Answer

Many "me-too" or run-of-the-mill businesses fail because they do not distinguish their product or service from those of competitors. Successful ventures carefully carve out a distinctive marketing niche by doing something different. The following checklist will help you design your marketing niche and increase sales.

Each of the preceding tips is discussed below.

Marketing Tips Checklist

1. Know what your customers want.

2. Make your product or service the best it can be.

3. Analyze your competitors and capitalize on their weaknesses.

4. Establish a complete customer profile database.

5. Give your good customers a little extra.

6. Use direct marketing to discover how to improve.

7. Stay in close and constant communication with your customers.

8. Get your customers to sell for you.

1. *Know what your customers want.* When it comes to marketing and distinguishing your product or service, it is vital to know exactly what your customers want and expect. Often their wants are significantly different from what you think they want and expect. One thing you can be assured of—your customers always want more and expect better.

To understand your customers, put yourself in their shoes and see things from their perspective. Look at your venture from their viewpoint and make any changes that are needed. Do whatever it takes to get insights into your customers' thinking. Talk to them often and listen closely to what they say. The most important question you can ask them is "why?" Also listen for what they don't say. Look for patterns and be responsive to their needs and wants.

2. *Make your product or service the best it can be.* Many entrepreneurs think they offer the very best product or service. Just ask them and they'll tell you. Or ask their staff and they'll say the same: "We offer the very best." What makes a difference is when your *customers* tell you that you offer the very best. It is extremely important that you obtain continual customer feedback about quality.

3. *Analyze your competition and capitalize on their weaknesses.* Your competition can provide you with a wealth of information, if you become a good detective. Evaluate your competitors' strengths and weaknesses. Then concentrate on offering what your competitors don't do well. Expand your marketing niche by offering speedy delivery, more

convenience, better service, faster turnaround time, more value, or specialized services that your competitors don't offer. Do whatever you can to rise above your competitors.

4. *Establish a complete customer profile database.* You need good, up-to-date, and accessible customer records that contain information about your customer's business, its history, purchasing habits, special needs, and so forth. A good customer database provides indispensable statistics and patterns that will suggest ways to market your product or service more effectively and at reduced cost.

5. *Give your good customers a little extra.* Have you ever purchased a dozen cookies but instead received 13—the baker's dozen? If so, you will most likely remember that vendor and purchase from it again. Being generous and thoughtful is a wonderful way to show your customers how much you appreciate their business. For example, a very successful neighborhood shoe-repair store gives a sample-size shoe polish with every major repair job; it outsells its competition by two to one. What could you do to give your customers a little extra? Think creatively. Could you offer discounts, small gifts, or extra services to make your best customers feel needed and appreciated?

6. *Use direct marketing to discover how to improve.* Follow up with your customers to find out how their purchase experience went. Call and ask your customers about their purchase experience or send them a short questionnaire on a postcard. Ask them how they liked your product. Ask if it met their expectations. Ask what you could do to improve and do things better next time. Ask if there is anything else that you could offer.

7. *Stay in close and constant communication with your customers.* Keep in close contact with your current and/or prospective customers on a routine basis. Send them an informal newsletter, promotional letter, or a "for your information" memo about industry trends or new products or services you plan to offer. Send a newspaper or magazine article about a new idea or trend to help your customers' business. Send a postcard or fax about a special sale you are running. Keep your customer relationship alive and full of benefits.

8. *Get your customers to sell for you.* Give your customers referral cards and offer them a discount on their next purchase for completing the card. Then thank your customers for having taken the time to do this. Run contests among the staff for those collecting the most customer-referral cards. Ask your customers to write testimonial letters. Feature key statements in your promotional material. Develop a

customer list of your top and most recognizable customers and use it to legitimatize your business and solicit new customers.

Using the preceding checklist will assist you in developing effective marketing strategies. You will be able to better carve your marketing niche and increase sales. It is easy to operate as a "me-too" business, but it takes time, effort, research, and planning to be really effective. Remember, the greatest profits come from the sales you've already made.

Question #6

How do I put together a winning management team when I can't pay high salaries to attract and retain a talented staff?

Answer

Entrepreneurs put together a management team differently from professional managers working in large organizations. Such organizations have the luxury of hiring a multitude of professionals such as lawyers, CPAs, marketing experts, controllers, insurance experts, and other consultants of all types. Entrepreneurs cannot afford such luxury, although they need such highly specialized and technical advice.

Entrepreneurial ventures are a tale of teamwork of key management team members, each of whom plays a critical role in the evolving enterprise. Professional lenders and investors are well aware of the importance of the management team to building a profitable venture. Practically all of them consider your team the most important factor in making a venture profitable. Early in your planning, identify the key management roles and think of what kinds of employees you would like to recruit. Examine your strengths and weaknesses and look for management team members who complement your skills.

One key management trap for entrepreneurs is placing close friends and family in key positions. Generally, this is because you know them, they are convenient to hire, you feel obligated to them, or a combination of these factors. The new-venture graveyard is littered with founders who hired inept friends and relatives.

✔ COURTNEY'S SMART TIP

Team up with only the best-qualified and most highly motivated people who can prove their talents by their track record and who have the training, experience, and skills to do the job you need.

Professional lenders and investors become immediately suspicious when you hire friends and relatives. Be prepared to defend your selection of people who will play key roles in your venture. You should have good reasons to support your selection of each management team member.

Once you determine which positions are critical to your venture, you are ready to assemble your team. There are two ways to put your management team together—contract with professionals or hire staff. The selection of your management team members is of critical importance to your success.

Generally, entrepreneurs are big users of independent professionals to provide technical advice. By contracting with such professionals, you can reduce your labor costs, use only the best, and pay them only when you need them. For further details on the best way to select contract professionals, refer to Chapter 10, "Selecting the Best Business Advisers."

Most entrepreneurs cannot match the pay scales of their larger competitors for members of their management team. As a consequence, you must use tactics other than high wages to compensate your employees, such as establishing a winning incentive program.

Your incentive program could include stock options, stock warrants, phantom stock, profit-sharing programs, deferred-compensation plans, perquisites, time off, and the like. Astute entrepreneurs establish several varied incentive plans for different members of the management team. Be very cautious about the tax aspects of your incentive programs and how employees can eventually cash out.

A creative incentive program is key to motivating your management team. Recognize, praise, and reward their efforts. Share with your people the success they have helped create. The only way to attract and retain highly qualified people is to make it worthwhile for them.

Question #7

How do I find a corporate strategic partner to assist me in bringing my invention to the marketplace?

Answer

Many entrepreneurs do not think about teaming up with a corporate strategic partner to fund their invention or idea and/or to bring it to the marketplace. Today, finding a corporate partner is one of the better ways to tap money sources. A corporate strategic partner can provide the capital resources, credit, management expertise, distribution channels, and/or manufacturing services necessary to successfully market your product or service. A corporate strategic alliance can provide needed funds for research, development, and marketing your product or service.

There are several advantages to partnering with large corporations. First, a corporate partner is usually willing to wait longer to receive a return on its investment than traditional lenders or investors such as bankers or venture capitalists. *The return on the investment is not as important as the potential of establishing new divisions.* If corporate partners are interested in taking an equity position in your business, you probably will give up less ownership than working with a venture capitalist.

Corporate partners can contribute more than capital to your business. They may offer good business advice and moral support and provide state-of-the-art technology. Establishing a corporate strategic alliance can also provide valuable contacts in the business and financial community.

The disadvantages of corporate strategic alliances include loss of control or the risk of the corporate partner making demands that you are opposed to. For example, you could be required to share your research results in exchange for use of its facilities. Also, your affiliation with one corporation may affect your ability to sell your product to its competitors. Or corporate mission and goals could change, causing your corporate partnership to sour.

To identify a potential corporate partner, look for corporations searching for complementary products to distribute through their existing channels. The key is to find a corporation with the resources but not the time, commitment, or creativity to pursue the product or service you provide. Remember, corporations are mainly interested in building and strengthening their basic business. Therefore, your output must fit their mission and goals.

Focus on corporations that are interested in early-stage ventures and have already invested in your industry. Also look for a corporation that might be interested in the right to license your invention.

An excellent resource for structuring corporate strategic alliances is *Winning Combinations* by James W. Botkin and Jana B. Mathews, which highlights the new wave of entrepreneurial partnerships between large and small companies. Refer to Chapter 9 of this book, "Financing Your Venture," for more detailed information on finding and forming corporate strategic alliances.

Question #8

What kind of business insurance should I get to protect my business?

Answer

Business owners are exposed to a number of different risks but rarely seem to think about these risks when starting a venture. There are two major risks that owners need to insure against: property loss and liability for injuries. Entrepreneurial ventures frequently purchase packaged policies that cover both types of exposure.

The most popular package is a *businessowner's policy*, frequently referred to as a BOP, which covers all the major property and liability exposures in a single policy. The biggest advantage of purchasing a BOP is that the founder generally receives broader coverage at a much lower price than if he or she were to buy each type of insurance separately.

Even if you qualify for a BOP package, you may have inadequate coverage for a disaster. For example, loss of business income due to business interruption occurs when vital business equipment or other business property is unusable because of fire, an explosion, or other property peril. If ever there was a case for business-interruption insurance, the explosion in the World Trade Center, forcing nearly 350 companies to conduct business elsewhere, demonstrated its importance. Experts estimate that over 50% of small business owners do not have business-interruption insurance.

Ask your insurance agent about business-interruption insurance coverage. Make sure such coverage covers your company for more than just a few days. Most tenants in the World Trade Center disaster were shut out for at least a month or longer. Depending on your type of business, consider buying *extra expense* insurance to pay for temporary relocation of people and machinery so you can get back in business fast.

✔ COURTNEY'S SMART TIP

The right type and degree of business-interruption insurance can keep your business alive if disaster destroys your company or if thieves walk out the door with your equipment.

You may be able to play the odds and survive without this type of insurance, but you will probably be in debt for a long time. Whether you purchase a BOP or separate policies, it is critical that you adequately cover your disaster-contingency needs. The rule of thumb is to carry enough insurance to get you back into business without impairing your cash flow. This amount is usually equal to what your property is worth.

For further information about business insurance, call the Insurance Information Institute (III) in New York at 800-331-9146. It is a nonprofit educational organization that provides information about the property and casualty insurance business and has many helpful publications. Ask about getting a copy of their publication *Insuring Your Business* by Sean Mooney.

Question #9

How can I strengthen my sales skills as well as those of my staff?

Answer

Most entrepreneurs do not think about the sales function or its importance to their survival. In addition, they often don't think about or practice how to close a sale. Since many entrepreneurs work alone when starting a business, they perform all the jobs themselves and often don't obtain sales training to strengthen their bottom line. However, you don't have a business without customers, and you cannot attract customers without a strong sales effort and plan.

Many owners make the mistake of thinking that because they have a superior product or service, customers will flock to their business and sales will automatically happen. Others do not see themselves as sales people since they may not be directly involved in contacting and selling to their customers.

The truth is that all entrepreneurs are involved in sales from the inception of their business. Entrepreneurs are always selling—themselves, their business, and their products or services. They may infrequently call on customers themselves, but they must continually interact with various members of the infrastructure, such as bankers, accountants, lawyers, and investors, to obtain support and advice for their business. During each contact, owners must constantly sell and resell their venture, its concepts, and its potential.

Developing entrepreneurial sales skills is one of the more neglected areas of operating a business. Entrepreneurs should assess their selling skills and take steps to strengthen them. This is especially true for founders who have not had prior selling experience and formal sales training.

Sales are generally gained or lost in the first minutes of an encounter. Therefore, entrepreneurs must get attention and interest during the first few minutes of the meeting by highlighting captivating or "sexy" features and benefits of your product or service. It is critical for owners to sharpen their sales skills toward becoming expert salespeople. The following are three tips for improving your sales skills.

1. First, recognize that it is not what you say but how you say it. Research has shown that logic, that is, the perceived value of the product or service, does not play as great a role in a persuasion transaction as voice inflection and body language. In fact, body language plays the biggest role and accounts for 55% of the buying decision, followed by voice inflection, which accounts for 38%. Logic accounts for only 7% in making a buying decision. Therefore, it is not what you say, but the way you say it that makes the difference. Both conviction and enthusiasm displayed in body language and voice inflection are critical to making the sale.

2. Second, sales are dependent on relationships. People buy from people they like, know, and respect. Therefore, it is key that entrepreneurs contact customers and establish relationships with them regardless of whether they have their own sales staff.

3. Last, use mental imaging to practice your selling skills. Imagine and then walk yourself through a sales call. See yourself being successful as well as handling resistance—positively comparing your company to your competitors, closing the sale, and the like. This exercise is similar to what successful athletes have done for years to improve their golf swing, pass a football, or land an intricate skating jump.

Assess your sales skills and those of your staff. Provide sales training for your entire team, and especially your sales staff. Everyone in your organization should be constantly selling. The good news is that selling skills can be learned and enhanced if the person has a genuine desire to succeed at selling. It just takes a little time and effort and some sales training.

Question #10

What skills should I develop to keep pace with the growth of my business?

Answer

Often entrepreneurs find out that their business has significantly grown, but their skills haven't. They have not had time to devote to personal professional development. Yet continual enhancement of entrepreneurial and leadership skills is needed. Important entrepreneurial skills to continually develop include business planning, goal setting, problem solving, financial management, marketing, human resource management, and motivational skills. Other important leadership skills are visioning, coaching, influencing, negotiating, delegating, and listening. Both sets of skills are pivotal to the continued success of any venture.

Experts say that more than half of all business problems originate with the perceptions, attitudes, and practices of the owner. The rest come from poor hiring. Both types of problems can be overcome.

It is important to plan how your business will grow, how fast a pace you can handle, and how this growth will affect your staff. Invite your staff to participate in the planning stages rather than hearing about the growth after the fact. Point out areas of vulnerability and develop strategies to strengthen weak areas. Consider what additional skills and training you and your staff will need to prepare for growth.

✔ COURTNEY'S SMART TIP

Success doesn't continue forever—markets will constantly change, making it necessary to develop new strategies and tactics.

Entrepreneurial Resource Checklist

Chapter 1   Overview of Entrepreneurship

References

Patricia and John Naisbitt, *Megatrends 2000*, William Morrow, New York, 1990.

Paul and Sarah Edwards, *The Best Home Businesses for the 90s*, Putnam, New York, 1994.

Charles R. Bevers with Linda G. Christie and Lynn R. Price, *The Entrepreneur's Guide to Doing Business with the Federal Government*, Prentice-Hall, New York, 1989.

Joline Godfrey, *Our Wildest Dreams*, Harper Business, New York, 1992.

Further Reading

Books

Patricia Aburdene and John Naisbitt, *Megatrends for Women*, Villard Books, New York, 1992.

Lynie Arden, *The Work-at-Home Source Book*, Live Oaks Publications, Boulder, Colo. 1992.

Jack Stack, *The Great Game of Business*, Currency Books, New York, 1993.

Jeffrey A. Timmons, *New Business Opportunities*, Brock House, Acton, Mass., 1990.

Gilbert G. Zoghlin, *From Executive to Entrepreneur*, AMACOM, American Management Association, New York, 1991.

Magazines

Home Office Computing
730 Broadway
New York, NY 10003

American Demographics
P.O. Box 68
Ithaca, NY 14851
800-828-1133
http://www.marketingtools.com

Newsletters

Cottage Connection
P.O. Box 14850
Chicago, IL 60614
   This bimonthly newsletter gives information and tips for the home-based entrepreneur.

National Home Business Report
Brabec Productions
P.O. Box 2137
Naperville, IL 60565
This quarterly newsletter offers helpful information for home-based entrepreneurs.

Home Business Directory
Horizon Publications
324 Wright St., 21-202-PR
Lakewood, CO 80228
This quarterly newsletter contains home business information.

Exporting Hotlines

The Department of Commerce's Trade Information Center, 800-USA-TRADE
The center will provide a directory of government export-assistance programs.

Small Business Foundation of America
1155 15th Street, NW
Washington, DC 20005
202-223-1103
Export Opportunities Hotline 800-243-7232
This agency offers market analysis, referrals, trade fair information, and assistance in licensing, customs-distribution options, and other areas. It's free, except for customized services that cost from $15 to $40.

Contacts

American Home Business Association
4505 S. Wasatch
Salt Lake City, UT 84124
800-664-2422
http://www.homebusiness.com
The AHBA is the membership division of the American Home Business Institute, which is a research organization serving home-based entrepreneurs. AHBA publishes a monthly newsletter, *Home Business Line*.

National Association of Home-Based Businesses
10451 Mill Run Circle
Owings, MD 21117
410-363-3698
http://www.usahomebusiness.com
The NAHBB provides seminars and educational materials for home-based entrepreneurs.

National Minority Supplier Development Council
15 West 39th Street
New York, NY 10018
This agency gives information about procurement opportunities.

The National Education Center for Women in Business
Seton Hill College
Greensburg, PA 15601-1599
800-NEC-WB-4-U

NECWB promotes women's ownership of businesses nationwide and offers women-oriented educational programs across the United States, books, videos, and a quarterly magazine.

National Association for Women Business Owners
1100 Wayne Ave., Suite 830
Silver Spring, MD 20910
301-608-2590

NAWBO supports women business owners and has many local chapters throughout the United States.

The American Women's Economic Development Corporation
71 Vanderbilt Ave., 3rd Floor
New York, NY 10169
800-222-AWED

This nonprofit organization assists women in realizing their business potential. It has assisted or trained over 100,000 women during the past 15 years.

The Center for Family Business
P.O. Box 24268
Cleveland, OH 44124
216-442-0800

For more than 120 years, the organization has offered books, seminars, and resources for starting and running a family-owned business.

The Family Firm Institute
12 Harris Street
Brookline, MA 02146
617-738-1591

The Family Firm Institute provides information and support for family-run businesses. It also has a quarterly journal called *Family Business Review*.

Independent Business Institute
3234 South Cleveland-Massillon Road
Norton, OH 44203
216-825-8258

Provides information and consulting services for family-owned businesses. It also publishes books and reports on the subject.

Chapter 2 The 10 Most-Asked Questions from Entrepreneurs

References

Entrepreneur magazine, *Complete Guide to Owning a Home-Based Business*, Bantam, New York, 1990.
Barbara Brabec, *Homemade Money*, Betterman Publications, White Hall, Va., 1992.

Lawrence W. Tuller, *When the Bank Says NO!*, Liberty Hall Press, Blue Ridge Summit, Penn., 1991.

William D. Bygrave and Jeffrey A. Timmons, *Venture Capital at the Crossroads*, Harvard Business School Press, Boston, 1992.

David Pressman, *Patent It Yourself*, Nolo Press, Berkeley, Calif., 1998.

Martha Blue, *Making It Legal*, Northland, Chicago, 1988.

Michael Phillips and Sallie Rasberry, *Marketing Without Advertising*, Nolo Press, Berkeley, Calif., 1997.

Jay Conrad Levinson, *Guerrilla Marketing*, rev. ed., Houghton Mifflin, Boston, 1993.

Further Reading

Books

Lynie Arden, *The Work-at-Home Sourcebook*, Live Oak, Woodland, Calif., 1992.

Irving, Burstiner, *The Small Business Handbook*, Prentice-Hall, Englewood Cliffs, N.J., 1989.

Scott A. Clark, *Beating the Odds*, AMACOM, New York, 1991.

Bob Coleman, *The New Small Business Survival Guide*, W. W. Norton, New York, 1994.

Paul and Sarah Edwards, *The Best Home Business for the 90's*, J. P. Tarcher, Los Angeles, 1991.

Paul and Sarah Edwards, *Making It on Your Own! Surviving and Thriving on the Ups and Downs of Being Your Own Boss*, J. P. Tarcher, Los Angeles, 1991.

Coralee Smith-Kern and Tammara Hoffman Wolfgram, of VGM Career Horizons, *How to Run Your Own Home Business*, NTC, Lincolnwood, Ill., 1990.

Patricia A. Woy, *Small Businesses that Grow and Grow and Grow*, Betterway, Whitehall, Va., 1990.

Magazines

Entrepreneur
2392 Morse Ave.
Irvine, CA 92614
714-261-2325
800-274-6229
E-mail: subscribe@entrepreneurmag.com

Fast Company
The Atlantic Monthly Company
77 N. Washington St.
Boston, MA 02114
800-688-1545

Inc.
488 Madison Ave.
New York, NY 10022
212-326-2600
800-234-0999
E-mail: subscribe@incmag.com

Success
733 Third Ave.
New York, NY 10017
212-883-7100
http://www.successmagazine.com

Contacts

Home-Based Business Information
Association of Home Businesses
6645 SW Terri Court, Suite 240
Portland, OR 97225-1054
   This organization provides support for home-based business owners.

New Mexico Home Business Association
537 Franklin
Santa Fe, NM 87501
   This area-networking group supports education for home-based business owners.

The Association of Home-Based Businesses
P.O. Box 10023
Rockville, MD 20844
   This association serves 90 home-based business owners in Maryland, northern Virginia, and Washington, D.C.

National Association of Small Business Investment Companies (NASBIC)
666 11th St., NW, Suite 750
Washington, DC 20000
202-628-5055
http://www.nasbic.org
   This association, sponsored by the SBA, provides loans to small business.

Procurement Automated Source System (PASS)
Data Management
3225 Jordan Blvd.
Malibar, FL 32950
800-231-7277
   Through this agency, the SBA facilitates and promotes small-business procurement opportunities. It brings together federal agencies, major contractors, and entrepreneurs.

Small Business Administration—Publications
P.O. Box 15434
Fort Worth, TX 76119
817-355-1933
   This organization offers free and low-cost booklets to help entrepreneurs develop budgets, personnel policies, and business plans.

Small Business Innovation Research Program (SBIR)
Office of Technology
Small Business Administration
409 3rd St., SW

Washington, DC 20416
202-205-6450
 This agency provides seed funds for research and development grants.

U.S. Government Printing Office
Superintendent of Documents
Washington, DC 20402
202-512-1800
http://www.access.gpo.gov
 This office prints hundreds of thousands of documents and booklets that help entrepreneurs start and operate their ventures.

National Business Incubation Association
20 East Circle Drive, Suite 190
Athens, OH 45701
740-593-4331
http://www.nbia.org
 This association is a support organization for incubators and publishes an incubation newsletter.

Chapter 3   Starting a Business

References

Gustav Berle, *Do-It-Yourself Business Book,* John Wiley & Sons, New York, 1989.

John Naisbitt and Patricia Aburdene, *Megatrends 2000,* William Morrow, New York, 1990.

Faith Popcorn, *Clicking: 17 Trends that Drive Your Business—and Your Life,* HarperBusiness, New York, 1997.

Kim Long, *The American Forecaster Almanac,* American Demographics Books, Ithaca, N.Y., 1994.

Richard Buskirk, Courtney Price, and Mack Davis, *The Entrepreneur's Planning Handbook,* Entrepreneurial Education Foundation, Denver, 1997.

Joseph R. Mancuso, *How to Prepare and Present a Business Plan,* Prentice-Hall, Englewood Cliffs, N.I. 1983.

Stanley Rich and David Gumpert, *Business Plans that Win $$$,* Harper and Row, New York, 1985.

Daniel H. Bangs, Jr., *Business Planning Guide,* Upstart, Portsmouth, N.H., 1992.

Robert Morris Studies, Robert Morris Associates, Philadelphia (published annually).

Further Reading

Books
Scott A. Clark, *Beating the Odds,* AMACOM, New York, 1991.

Paul and Sarah Edwards, *Making It on Your Own!: Surviving and Thriving on the Ups and Downs of Being Your Own Boss,* J. P. Tarcher, Los Angeles, 1991.

Entrepreneur magazine, *Complete Guide to Owning a Home Based Business,* Bantam, New York, 1990.

Jay Conrad Levinson, *555 Ways to Earn Extra Money,* Holt, Rinehart and Winston, New York, 1991.

Courtney Price, Richard Buskirk, and Mack Davis, *Program for Writing Winning Business Plans,* 2d ed., Premier Entrepreneur Programs, Denver, 1991.

Magazines

American Demographics
P.O. Box 68
Ithaca, NY 14851
800-828-1133
http://www.marketingtools.com

Home Office Computing
730 Broadway
New York, NY 10003

Cottage Connection
P.O. Box 14460
Chicago, IL 60614

National Home Business Report
P.O. Box 2137
Naperville, IL 60567

Contacts

Small Business Administration (SBA)
409 3rd Street, SW
Washington, DC 20416
800-827-5722
http://www.sbaonline.sba.gov
Or contact the SBA office in your area to receive a list of government agencies, trade associations, chambers of commerce, or other professionals or counselors.

Small-Business Development Centers (SBDC)
Contact one of the small-business development centers (SBDCs) in your area to assist you in starting a new venture. SBDCs are university-affiliated advisory centers located in more than 500 cities and are a partnership of the SBA, the local university, and the local state government. SBDCs provide many free management-consulting services to existing and new business owners. They also offer training workshops and have business-information resource services. Counselors will match your needs with existing resources and identify both fee-paid consultants and volunteers who have expertise in your specialty area.

Small Business Institutes (SBI)
The SBA operates small business institutes on about 500 college campuses in every state. SBIs are staffed by instructors and students trained to provide counseling to entrepreneurs. Call the SBA's toll-free answer desk at 800-827-5722 to find the SBI nearest you.

Service Corps of Retired Executives (SCORE)
http://www.score.org
SCORE provides free, confidential counseling for entrepreneurs. SCORE has about 385 offices and an equal number of satellite or branch offices. It also offers small-business workshops for a nominal fee. Local SCORE offices are listed in the blue government pages of the phone book, or under the Small Business Administration listing, or call 800-827-5722 for the chapter nearest you.

National Association for the Cottage Industry (NACI)
P.O. Box 14850
Chicago, IL 60614
312-472-8116
NACI supports home-based entrepreneurs with specialized information and resources. Members receive its newsletter, *Cottage Connection,* about new industry trends and techniques. For newsletter information, contact P.O. Box 14460, Chicago, IL 60614.

National Home Business Report
Barbara Brabec Productions
P.O. Box 2137
Naperville, IL 60567
This quarterly home-business publication is dedicated to helping small home businesses grow and prosper.

Local Colleges and Universities
Many colleges and universities offer entrepreneurial courses or workshops on writing a business plan. Ask about business plan–writing courses or workshops.

Chambers of Commerce
Many local chambers of commerce offer workshops and/or seminars on how to write a plan. Call the chamber in your area.

National Business Incubation Association
20 East Circle Drive, Suite 190
Athens, Ohio 45701
740-593-4331
http://www.nbia.org
The National Business Incubation Association can provide information and resources about any type of business incubator located in the United States. The association also publishes a useful newsletter.

Census of Business
Federal Office Building, #3D
Washington, DC 29233
301-763-4100

Census of Population
U.S. Census of the Population
Washington, DC 20233

National Association of Small Business Investment Companies (NASBIC)
666 11th Street, NW, Suite 750
Washington, DC 20000
202-628-5055
http://www.nasbic.org
This association, sponsored by the SBA, provides loans to small businesses.

Procurement Automated Source System (PASS)
Data Management
3225 Jordan Blvd.
Malibar, FL 32950
800-231-7277

Through this agency, the SBA facilitates and promotes small-business procurement opportunities. It brings together federal agencies, major contractors, and entrepreneurs.

Small Business Administration—Publications
P.O. Box 15434
Fort Worth, TX 76119
817-355-1933
This organization offers both free and low-cost budgeting booklets to help entrepreneurs develop budgets, personnel policies, and business plans.

Small Business Innovation Research Program (SBIR)
Office of Technology
Small Business Administration
409 3rd Street, SW
Washington, DC 20416
202-205-6450
This agency provides seed funds for research and development grants.

U.S. Government Printing Office
Superintendent of Documents
Washington, DC 20402
202-512-1800
http://www.access.gpo.gov
This office prints hundreds of thousands of documents and booklets that help entrepreneurs start and operate their ventures.

Sourcebooks, Inc.
P.O. Box 372
Naperville, IL 60566
708-961-3900
Sourcebooks, Inc. is a publisher of various books on small-business topics. Call or write for a catalog. All titles are available at your local bookstore.

Chapter 4 Legal Structures for Starting a Business

References

S. J. T. Enterprises, *Do-It-Yourself Incorporation Kit*, Lakewood, Ohio, 1991.
Michael Seltzer, *Securing Your Organization's Future, A Complete Guide to Fundraising Strategies*, Foundation Center, New York, 1987.

Further Reading

Books
John Cotton Howell, *Forming Corporations and Partnerships*, 2nd. ed., Liberty Hall Press, Blue Ridge Summit, Pa. 1991.
Judith McQuoum, *Inc. Yourself*, Harper Business, New York, 1992.

Ted Nicholas, *How to Form Your Own Corporation Without a Lawyer for Under $75.00*, Enterprise/Dearborn, Chicago, 1992.

PSI Successful Business Library, *The Essential Corporate Handbook—For Small Business Corporations*, Oasis Press, Grants Pass, Ore., 1992.

Steve Sanderson, *Standard Legal Forms and Agreements for Small Business*, Self-Counsel Press, Bellingham, Wash., 1990.

Daniel Sitarz, *The Complete Book of Small Business Legal Forms*, Nova, Carbondale, Ill., 1991.

Magazines

Chronicle of Philanthropy
P.O. Box 1989
Marion, OH, 43306
800-347-6969

A newspaper focusing on the nonprofit sector, including fund-raising and grant distribution.

Contacts

State Department of Revenue
Register your company's trade name with your state department of revenue.

Secretary of State
File articles of incorporation, limited partnerships, and limited liability companies (LLC) with the state secretary of state.

Internal Revenue Service
All forms of legal structure, except sole proprietorships with no employees, must obtain a Federal Employer Identification Number (FEIN), which becomes your federal tax ID number. If you are a sole proprietorship with no employees, your federal ID number is your Social Security number.

Start-up Kits
Many states have small-business start-up kits that contain all the necessary information you need to start your venture. Check with your secretary of state.

Council of Foundations
1828 L. Street NW, Suite 300
Washington, DC 20036
.202-466-6512

This organization has publications, information, referral services, and workshops for nonprofit organizations and grant makers. Check to see if your state has a council of foundations listing nonprofit support organizations in your area.

Nonprofit Management Association (NMA)
315 W. 9th Street, Suite 1100
Los Angeles, CA 90015
213-623-7080

This association is dedicated to the improvement of management of nonprofit organizations. It sponsors annual conferences and offers a variety of other services to its members.

Corporate Agents, Inc.
P.O. Box 1281
1013 Center Road
Wilmington, DE 19805
302-998-0598
This organization provides information on how to incorporate a business.

Sourcebooks, Inc
P.O. Box 372
Naperville, IL 60566
708-961-3900
Publications: *The Small Business Legal Guide,* by Lynne Ann Frasier, Esq.; *The Small Business Start-Up Guide,* by Hal Root and Steve Koenig.

The *Small Business Legal Guide* offers legal advice and explanations on the legal aspects of starting a business. This publication also provides forms and agreements that may be imitated. *The Small Business Start-Up Guide* discusses the forms of business that one can take and the requirements for each individual state. Each book costs around $10 and is available at your local bookstore.

Chapter 5   Buying a Business

References

C. D. Peterson, *How to Leave Your Job and Buy a Business of Your Own,* McGraw-Hill, New York, 1992.

Further Reading

Books

Arnold Goldstein, *The Complete Guide to Buying and Selling a Business,* John Wiley & Sons, New York, 1993.

Brian Knight and the Associates of County Business, Inc., *Buying the Right Business at the Right Price,* Upstart, Portsmouth, N.H., 1990.

Joseph R. Mancuso and Douglas D. Germann, Sr., *Buying a Business for Very Little Cash,* Prentice-Hall, Englewood Cliffs, N.J., 1991.

L. Tuller, *Buying In: A Complete Guide to Acquiring a Business or Professional Practice,* McGraw-Hill, New York, 1990.

Magazines

The National Review of Corporate Acquisitions
Tweed Publishing Co.
23 Main Street
Tuburon, CA 94920
415-435-2175

Business Ventures Magazine
Elsevier Science Publishing Co., Inc.
655 Avenue of the Americas
New York, NY 10020
212-989-5000

Contacts

International Association of Business Brokers
P.O. Box 704
Concord, MA 01742
617-369-5254

This association provides lists of business brokers who have been certified as business intermediaries and belong to their association.

First National Bank of Maryland
800-842-BANK

The corporate finance division of this bank publishes a quarterly list of companies that are up for sale and provides a listing of financing sources for about $350 a year.

World M&A Network
717 D Street NW
Washington, DC 20004
202-628-6900

This organization publishes *The Network*, a 100-page magazine that includes a listing of sellers, buyers, and financing information for about $335 a year.

Annual Statement Studies
Robert Morris Associates
1650 Market St., Suite 2300
Philadelphia, PA 19103
800-677-7621

A valuable source of industry statistics and financial ratios on every industry. Available in most libraries.

Geneva Companies, Inc.
5 Park Plaza
Irvine, CA 92714
714-756-2200

Provides information on buying and selling businesses.

Chapter 6 Commercializing Technology and Protecting Intellectual Property

References

Courtney Price, Richard Buskirk, and Mack Davis, *Entrepreneur's Resource Handbook*, 2d ed., Entrepreneurial Education Foundation, Denver, 1996.

David Pressman, *Patent It Yourself*, Nolo Press, Berkeley, Calif., 1998.

Thomas Register of American Manufacturers. Lists who manufactures what products and where manufacturer is located. Available in most libraries.

Trade Names Dictionary and International Trade Names Dictionary, Gale Research Inc., Detroit, Mich.

Richard Buskirk, Courtney Price, and Mack Davis, *Program for Writing Winning Business Plans*, 2d ed., Primier Entrepreneur Programs, Denver, 1992.

Intellas, Inc., *The Complete Copyright Protection Kit: Information and Legal Forms You Need to Protect What You Create*, Denver, 1992.

Dun & Bradstreet, *Reference Book of Corporate Management: American Corporate Leaders*, Information Services Staff, New York, 1993.

Ted Nicholas, *The Complete Guide to Business Agreements*, Enterprise/Dearborn, Chicago, 1992.

Don Debelak, *Bringing Your Product to Market*, John Wiley & Sons, New York, 1997.

Further Reading

Pamphlets

General Information Concerning Patents, U.S. Government Printing Office, Washington, DC 20402, 202-783-3238.

Basic Facts about Trademarks, Patent and Copyright Office, Washington, DC 20231, 703-557-3158.

Contacts

Better Business Bureau

Contact your local Better Business Bureau's consumer fraud division to determine if an invention-marketing company has been involved in any cases of fraud.

Registrar of Copyrights
U.S. Copyright Office
The Library of Congress
101 Independence Avenue SE
Washington, DC 20540
http://www.lcweb.loc.gov/copyright

Contact this agency to register copyrights. Or call the Copyright Office hotline at 202-707-3000.

U.S. Patent and Trademark Office
Commissioner of Patents and Trademarks
P.O. Box 9
Washington, DC 20231
800-786-9199
http://www.uspto.gov

Contact this agency to find out information about patents and trademarks and to register them, or call the Patent Office Status Branch hotline at 703-308-7704 to check on the status of your patent application.

Licensing Industry Merchandisers' Association
350 5th Ave., Suite 2309
New York, NY 10118
212-244-1944
http://www.licensing.org

This organization provides information about licensing agreements and licensing issues.

Rocky Mountain Inventors Congress
P.O. Box 36233
Denver, CO 80236-0233
303-670-3760

This association of inventors, innovators, and entrepreneurs provides information and education to its members in the Rocky Mountain region on organizing, developing, protecting, and/or producing and commercializing their ideas.

National Association of Small Business Investment Companies (NASBIC)
666 11th Street NW Suite 750
Washington, DC 20000
202-628-5055
http://www.nasbic.org
Firms licensed as small-business investment companies (SBICs) under the Small Business Investment Act.

National Venture Capital Association
1655 N. Fort Myer Drive, Suite 850
Arlington, VA 22209
703-524-2549
http://www.nvca.org
The NVCA publishes an up-to-date directory of its members. It will send out a copy of its directory of 200 members when requested in writing to the above address.

National Technical Information Service Center
Center for the Utilization of Federal Technology
U.S. Department of Commerce
5285 Court Royal Road
P.O. Box 1423
Springfield, VA 22151
707-487-4600
This agency provides support for negotiating licenses to commercialize inventions at various federal laboratories and government agencies.

NASA Tech Briefs
Associated Business Publications, Inc.
317 Madison Avenue
New York, NY 10017
212-490-3999
This organization publishes information about NASA's inventions available for licensing.

Chapter 7   Marketing Analysis and Planning

References

Encyclopedia of Associations, Vol. 1, Gale Research Inc., Detroit, Mich. This reference lists national organizations, including trade, business, and commercial.

Karl Albrecht and Ron Zemke, *Service America: Doing Business in the New Economy*, Dow Jones-Irwin, New York, 1985.

Karl Albrecht, *The Only Thing That Matters*, Harper Business, New York, 1992.

Karl Albrecht, *Service Within*, Business One Irwin, New York, 1990.

Kristin Anderson and Ron Zemke, *Delivering Knock Your Socks Off Service*, American Management Association, New York, 1991.

Courtney Price, Richard Buskirk, and Mack Davis, *Program for Writing Winning Business Plans*, Premier Entrepreneur Programs, Denver, 1991.

Marilyn and Tom Ross, *Big Ideas for Small Service Businesses: How to Successfully Advertise, Publicize, and Maximize Your Business or Professional Practice*, Communication Creativity, Buena Vista, Colo., 1994.

Harvey Mackay, *Swim With the Sharks Without Being Eaten Alive*, Morrow, New York, 1988.

Further Reading

Books

William A. Cohen, *The Entrepreneur and Small Business Marketing*, John Wiley & Sons, New York, 1991.

Kenneth Cook, *AMA Complete Guide to Small Business Marketing*, AMACOM, New York, 1991.

T. Scott Gross, *Positively Outrageous Service*, Mastermedia, New York, 1991.

Michael Phillips and Salli Raspberry, *Marketing Without Advertising*, Nolo Press, Berkeley, Calif., 1997.

Anthony O. Putnam, *Marketing Your Services*, John Wiley & Sons, New York, 1990.

Computer Databases

Dow Jones News Retrieval Services
Compact Disclosures
INFOTRAC

Magazines

Sales and Marketing Management
Bill Communications Inc.
355 Park Avenue South
New York, NY 10010
www.salesandmarketing.com
800-821-6897

Advertising Age
Crain Communications
740 N. Rush Street
Chicago, IL 60611
800-722-6658

Contacts

American Business Card Club
303-690-6496
This association is a worldwide network for exchanging business card designs and ideas.

Simmons Market Research Bureau
900 N. Michigan Ave.
Chicago, IL 60611-1542
312-951-4400
The bureau lists product categories and demographic characteristics for varying levels of consumption.

Mediamark Research, Inc.
708 Third Ave., 8th Floor
New York, NY 10017
800-310-3305
   This research group lists product categories and demographic characteristics for varying levels of consumption.

Information Industry Association
1625 Massachusetts Avenue NW, Suite 700
Washington, DC 20036
202-986-0280
   This association is involved with the creation and distribution of information services and publishes a free two-page brochure, "Customer Service Guide for 900 Programs."

Trade Show Information
   Three organizations publish various books about trade shows: *Tradeshow Week Data Book*, 800-521-8100; *Trade Show & Exhibit Schedules*, 800-253-6708; and *Trade Shows Worldwide*, 800-877-4253. You should be able to find these publications in your local library.

Trade Show Bureau
Denver, Colorado
303-860-7626
   This national bureau is the industry's resource center, providing information about the latest industry trends, successful practices, and hot topics of interest. An extensive catalog of publications assists entrepreneurs with exhibiting at trade shows.

U.S. Department of Commerce
http://www.doc.gov
   The department publishes extensive data and demographics on various industries.

Chapter 8   Market-Penetration Strategies

References

Jeffrey Price, *Yellow Pages Advertising: How to Get the Greatest Return on Your Investment*, Idlewood, Pacific Palisades, Calif., 1991.

Barry Maher, *Getting the Most from Your Yellow Pages Advertising*, Aegis, Newport, R.I., 1997.

H. Gordon Lewis, *How to Handle Your Own Public Relations*, Nelson-Hall, Chicago, 1977.

Robert Mestin, *How to Succeed with Your Own 900 Business*, Aegis, Newport, R.I., 1993.

Tradeshow Week Data Book, New York, published weekly.

Chapter 9   Financing Your Venture

References

Venture Capital at the Crossroads, Harvard Business School Press, Boston, 1992.

Robert J. Gatson, *Finding Private Venture Capital for Your Firm*, John Wiley & Sons, New York, 1989.

Gerald A. Benjamin, *Finding Your Wings: How to Locate Private Investors to Fund Your Venture*, John Wiley & Sons, 1996.

Dun & Bradstreet's Reference Book of Corporation Management, Dun & Bradstreet, New York, 1993.

Standard & Poor's Register of Corporations, Directors, and Executives (check your local library).

Million Dollar Directory, Dun & Bradstreet, Parsippany, N.J., 1993.

Middle Market Directory, Dun & Bradstreet, Parsippany, N.J., 1993.

James W. Botkin and Jana B. Mathews, *Winning Combinations*, John Wiley & Sons, New York, 1992.

Laurie Blum, *Free Money for Small Businesses and Entrepreneurs*, John Wiley & Sons, 1992.

James M. Hardy, *Developing Dynamic Boards*, Essex Press, 1990.

Further Reading

Books

William Alaird, *Money Sources for Small Business*, Puma, Santa Monica, Calif., 1991.

Bruce Blechman and Jay Conrad Levinson, *Guerilla Financing*, Houghton-Mifflin, Boston, 1991.

George M. Dawson, *Borrowing for Your Business*, Upstart, Portsmouth, N.H., 1991.

Jennifer Lindsey, *Start-Up Money*, John Wiley & Sons, New York, 1989.

Ted Nicholas, *43 Proven Ways to Raise Capital for Your Small Business*, Enterprise, Wilmington, Del., 1991.

Jeffrey Sieglin, *Financing Your Small Business*, McGraw-Hill, New York, 1990.

Lawrence A. Tuller, *When the Bank Says No!*, Liberty Hall Press, Blue Ridge Summit, Pa. 1991.

Magazines

The Chronicle of Philanthropy
1255 Twenty-Third St. NW
Washington, DC 20037
800-347-6969

Venture Capital Journal
Venture Economics
75 Second Ave.
Needham, MA 02194

Contacts

Directory of Venture Capital Clubs
P.O. Box 1333
Stamford, CT 06904

The National Venture Capital Association (NVCA)
1655 N. Fort Meyer Drive, Suite 850
Arlington, VA 22209
703-524-2549
http://www.nvca.org
   Ask for a copy of its 200-member directory.

Western Association of Venture Capitalists (WAVE)
3000 Sand Hill Road, #1-90
Menlo Park, CA 94025
415-854-1322

Association of Venture Capital Clubs
P.O. Box 3358
Salt Lake City, UT 84110
801-364-1100
   Ask for a list of venture clubs.

National Association of Small Business Investment Corporations
666 11th Street, NW, Suite 750
Washington, DC 20000
202-628-5055
http://www.nasbic.org
   The association provides information about securing financing from SBICs.

National Technical Information Services (NITS)
5285 Court Royal Road
P.O. Box 1423
Springfield, VA 22151
703-487-4600
   You can locate government inventions with specific commercial value and then negotiate a license with the agency.

National Executive Service Corps (NESC)
257 Park Avenue South
New York, NY 10010
212-259-6660
   This network of national organizations provides management assistance and coaching to nonprofit organizations through retired executives.

Small Business Administration (SBA)
409 3rd Street SW
Washington, DC 20416
800-827-5722
http://www.sbaonline.sba.gov
   You can contact your local office to receive information about funding assistance for entrepreneurs as well as publications, seminars, and workshops. Ask for the brochure "Business Loans from the SBA."

The Foundation Center in New York
79 Fifth Avenue
New York, NY 10003-3076
212-620-4230
   The center collects, organizes, and disseminates data on foundations and corporate philanthropy.

Council on Foundations
1828 L Street NW, Suite 300
Washington, DC 20036
202-466-6512
    Call or write for information on grant-making foundations and corporations.

Securities and Exchange Commission
450 5th Street NW
Washington, DC 20549
202-272-3607
    Write the Commission for a copy of Regulation D governing private placements.

Forum Publishing
383 Main Street
Centerport, NY 11721
516-754-5000
Publication: *Venture Capital Directory*
    This publication includes over 400 members of the Small Business Administration and small-business investment companies that provide funding for small and minority-owned businesses.

Venture Economics
Wellsley Hills, MA
Stanley Pratt, author
Publication: *Pratt's Guide to Venture Capital Sources*
75 Second Ave., Suite 700
Needham, MA 02194
    This publication contains information on more than 700 venture-capital companies and lists the type of companies in which they invest.

Bankers Systems, Inc.
P.O. Box 1457
St. Cloud, MN 56302
612-251-3060
    Bankers Systems, Inc. provides the Robert Morris Projection of Financial Statements form. This form is very useful in preparing financial statements for business plans.

Veribank
P.O. Box 461
Wakefield, MA 01880
617-245-8370
    Veribank offers information on banking to small-business owners. Veribank is also a resource for checking on the financial health of your bank and the banks recommended by the SBA Preferred Lenders Program hotline, 800-827-5722.

Sourcebooks, Inc.
P.O. Box 372
Naperville, IL 60566
708-961-3900
Publication: *How to Get a Loan of Line of Credit* by Brian Milling
    Bryan Milling is a banker, and his book is a good source describing what bankers would like to see in the loan process. The book costs around $10.

Institute of Management Consultants
521 5th Avenue, 35th Floor
New York, NY 10175
800-221-2557
   This organization provides professional management help and consulting directories.

Chapter 10   Selecting the Best Business Advisers

References

Krasnow and Conrad, *100 Ways to Cut Legal Fees and Manage Your Lawyer*, National Legislation Center, Washington, D.C., 1988.
Ted Nicholas, *Complete Book of Corporate Forms*, Finance Dearborn, Chicago, 1994.
Sean Mooney, *Insuring Your Business*, Insurance Information Institute Press, New York, 1992.
Herman Holtz, *Choosing and Using a Consultant*, John Wiley & Sons, New York, 1989.
John Ward, *Creating Effective Boards for Private Enterprise*, Jossey-Bass, San Francisco, 1992.

Library Reading

Martindale-Hubbell Law Directory.
The Lawyer's Register by Specialties and Fields of Law.
Attorney's Register.
U.S. Lawyer's Referral Directory.
Directory of the Legal Profession.

Contacts

Society of Certified Public Accountants
   Check with your state society of certified public accountants for referrals to accountants who specialize in small businesses, or contact the American Institute of CPAs in New York at 212-596-6200.

National Association for the Self-Employed
P.O. Box 612067
DFW Airport
Dallas, TX 75261-2067
800-232-6273
http://www.nase.org
   The self-employed members of this association have access to a business-consultant hotline. Group health and disability insurance is also available.

Young Presidents Organization
451 S. Decker Dr., #200
Irving, TX 75062
972-541-1044
http://www.ypo.org
   This is an international group of presidents with strong local chapters. It has strict age requirements and company qualifications for membership.

U.S. Chamber of Commerce
Center for Small Business
1615 H Street, NW
Washington, DC 20062-2000
202-659-6000
800-649-9719
http://www.uschamber.org
    The Center for Small Business is actively involved in representing small-business concerns before our government. It also provides issue reports, *The Small Business Update*, and other publications.

Service Corps of Retired Executives (SCORE)
409 Third Street SW, 6th Floor
Washington, DC 20024
800-634-0245
800-827-5722 Answer Desk
http://www.score.org
    SCORE, part of the SBA, is an organization of retired businesspeople who provide free advice to entrepreneurs. The answer desk provides information on all government agencies.

Chapter 11   Franchising

References

Franchise Opportunity Handbook, published annually by the Superintendent of Documents, U.S. Government Printing Office, Washington, DC 20402-9325.
The World Wide Franchise Directory, Gale Research, Detroit.
Doing Business In . . ., published by Price Waterhouse, New York, is a series of books focusing on how to operate ventures in many different foreign countries.

Further Reading

Books
Robert E. Bond, *The Source Book of Franchise Opportunities*, Business One Irwin, Homewood, Ill., 1995.
Evaluating Franchise Opportunities, Small Business Administration, publication MP 26.
National Trade Data Bank (NTDB) a CD-ROM database about marketing and doing business abroad developed by the U.S. Commerce Department.
Andrew Sherman, *Franchising and Licensing: Two Ways to Build Your Business*, AMACOM, New York 1991.
Starting and Managing a Small Business of Your Own, Vol. 1, available from the Superintendent of Documents, U.S. Government Printing Office, Washington, DC 20402-9325.

Magazines
Nation's Business, Inc.
1615 H. Street NW
Washington, DC 20062
202-463-5650

Entrepreneur Magazine
2392 Morse Avenue
Irvine, CA 92714
714-261-2325
http://www.entrepreneurmag.com

Contacts

American Franchise Association (AFA)
53 W. Jackson Blvd., Suite 205
Chicago, IL 60604
800-334-4232
    This is a national organization aimed at improving the investment climate for potential as well as existing franchisees. AFA publishes a quarterly newsletter.

International Franchise Association
1350 New York Avenue, Suite 900
Washington, DC 20005
202-628-8000
800-543-1038
    This association is one of the best sources for gathering information concerning international franchises. Ask about the $15 *Franchise Opportunities Guide* as well as other books and tapes. Attend the annual International Fanchise Trade Show.

U.S. Commerce Department's regional offices of the International Trade Administration
    This association conducts customized market research for a fee in areas where the government has a foreign office.

Program Advisor
Franchise and Business Opportunities Program
Federal Trade Commission
Washington, DC 20580
202-326-3128
    This agency provides information to people who are considering investing in franchise businesses.

Pilot Books
103 Cooper Street
Babylon, NY 11702
516-422-2225
Publication: *Directory of Franchising Organizations and Franchising Investigation and Contract Negotiation*
    This source supplies a list of titles on franchising.

Entrepreneur magazine
2392 Morse Avenue
Irvine, CA 92714
714-261-2325
http://www.entrepreneurmag.com
Publication: *Franchising Directory*
    The publication of this organization is an annual directory of franchises.

Franchise Index/Profile: A Franchise Evaluation Process
Small Business Management Series no. 35
Small Business Administration
Washington, DC 20416
800-827-5722
Publication: *The Franchise Index/Profile*
   This is a guidebook for those considering buying a franchise. It also contains a series of questions to be asked for the franchisers.

Index

A

Aburdene, Patricia, 8
Accountants:
  as business adviser, 232
  certified public accountant,
    232–233
  firms, 232–233
  tax planner, 232–235
Advertising:
  magazines, 159–160
  marketing strategy, 33
  radio, 160–162
  yellow pages, 157–158
Albrecht, Karl, 128
American Business Card
  Club, 154
American Home-Based
  Business Association, 8
Angels, business, 178, 209–210
  (*see also* investors)
Association of Venture Capital
  Clubs, 195, 209
Attorneys:
  finding, 227–229
  firms, 227
  legal expenses, 228–231
  See also intellectual property

B

Banks:
  banker's lending checklist, 26
  questions to ask bankers, 27
  investment, 201–202
  loans, 182–187
  guaranty, 190–191
  process, 182–187
  revolving, 189–190
  merchant, 209
  See also line of credit
Benjamin, Gerald A., 210
Better Business Bureau, 19, 49
Biotechnology, 2, 4
Blue, Martha, 30
Botkin, James W., 212, 269
Brabec, Barbara, 25
Business brokers, 207
Business cards, 152–154
Business incubator, 37–38,
  54–56
Business plan, 6, 38, 53–54,
  184–185
Buyout agreement. *See* Buy-sell
  agreement
Buyout entrepreneur, 80
Buy-sell agreements:
  death of partner, 71
  shoot-out clause, 71
Bygrave, William D., 28

C

Catering, 50–51
Certified development
  companies (CDC), 216
Charitable organization. *See*
  Nonprofit organization
Children's products/services, 3–5
Company name. *See* Trade
  business name
Computer business
  opportunities, xii, 3–4

Confidential disclosure
  agreement, 96, 103
Consignment goods, 170–172
Consultants:
  business plan, 38
  financial, 210
  management, 236–238
  small-business, 50
Copyright, 29–30, 93, 100
Corporate venturing:
  strategic alliance, 211–212,
    268–269
  trend, xii
Corporation:
  form of structure, 65, 260–261
  registration, 45
  See also S corporation
Council on Foundations, 16, 222
Credit cards:
  financing option, 178, 181,
    212–214
  merchant's credit, 191–193
Customers:
  lists, 94
  marketing tips, 32
  See also trade secrets

D
Debelak, Don, 188
Defense Logistics Agency, 11
Delivery services, 2–6
Direct mail:
  list brokers, 152
  lists, 150–152
  mailings, 149
  newsletters, 150
  postcards, 150
Direct Marketing
  Association, 151
Direct Selling Association, 50

Disabled Businesspersons
  Association (DBA), 16
Disabled entrepreneurs, 2–3
Disadvantaged business
  enterprise (DBE):
  certification, 13–14
  opportunities, 2, 12–13
  qualifications, 13
Displaced executives, 2–3,
  15–16

E
E-commerce, xiii
8(a) certification, 12
800 numbers. See telemarketing
E-mail, 154–155
Economic development area, 17
Edwards, Paul and Sarah, 8
Employment agreement:
  ownership rights, 111
  technology agreement,
    111–112
  See also trade secrets
Entrepreneurial Education
  Foundation, 6
Entrepreneurial growth skills,
  272–273
Entrepreneurial history, xi
Entrepreneurial myths, 41
Entrepreneurial reasoning, xii
Ethnic markets:
  medicine, 4
  opportunities, 9
  products/services, 2–4
Executive entrepreneurs, 17
Exporting, xii, 3

F
Factoring, 178, 219–222
Failure rate, 256–257

FastTrac, 6, 54
Feasibility plan, 257–260
Federal Aviation
    Administration, 12
Federal Highway
    Administration, 12
Federal Trade Commission
    (FTC), 31, 49–50
Federal Transit
    Administration, 12
Federal Laboratory Consortium
    (FLC), 217
Finance companies, 183, 206
Financial plan, 261
Financing strategies, 178–179
501(c)(3). See Nonprofit
    organization
Focus groups, 125–127
Food products, 45–47, 52
Foundation Center, 16, 222
Franchising:
    agreement, 249–250
    entry strategy, 35–36, 247
    expansion strategy, 244,
        252–254
    fees, 247
    international, 251–252
    research, 244–248
    site locators, 249
    trend, 2, 243
    turnkey operation, 243
Friendly money, 178–179,
    180–182
Fund-raisers, 206–208
Fund raising. See Nonprofit
    organizations

G
General Agreement on Tariffs
    and Trade (GATT), 1

Global entrepreneurism, xii, 1
    (see also International
    opportunities)
Godfrey, Joline, 15
Goodwill, 193–194
Government bidder's list, 3, 11

H
Handicapped Assistance
    Loan, 16
Hardy, James, 223
Holtz, Herman, 238
Home-based business:
    number of, xii, 2, 7
    opportunities, 7–8
    profit trend, 3
    quiz, 23
Home employment scheme, 39,
    47–50
Home Shopping Network, 138

I
IBM Special Needs Information
    Referral Center, 16
Imitator, creative, 38–39
Incorporation, 56–57, 72
Information Industry
    Association, 170
Information superhighway. See
    Internet
INFO-TRAC, 122, 248
Initial public offering (IPO),
    184, 200–202
Innovator, 39
Insurance:
    business interruption
        coverage, 270
    businessowner's policy, 270
    finding agent, 236
    types of coverage, 235

Insurance Information
    Institute, 271
Intellectual property, 29
Internal Revenue Service, 73
International Franchise
    Association, 252
International opportunities,
    8–9
Internet:
    marketing, xiii, 155–157
    opportunities, 3–4
    trends, 43
    World Wide Web, xii
Intrapreneurship. See Corporate
    venturing
Invention marketing
    companies, 30–31, 92,
    112–115
Investors, 209

K
Kaiser, Leland, 5

L
Law of Landlords, 60
Leadership skills, 272–273
Lease, 61–63
Leasing companies, 183
Levinson, Jay Conrad, 34
Licensing agreement, 103–106
Licensing Industry
    Merchandisers
    Association, 105
Licensing rights, 94
Life extension, 5
Life-style ventures, xiii
Limited liability company
    (LLC), 65–66, 76–77
Limited Partnership, 65
Line of credit, 187–188

M
Maher, Barry, 158
Management team:
    advisory board, 225,
        239–241
    board of directors, 225,
        238–239
    importance, 196
    infrastructure, 225
    selecting, 267–268
Marcus, Claudio, 142
Margolis, Don, 92
Marketing:
    database, 140–142
    key contacts, 117
    mix, 131
    niche, 264
    penetration, 131, 134–135
    plan, 33–35, 118, 130–132
    strategies, 143–144
    targets, 34, 118, 142
    tips, 265–276
Marketing tools:
    audiocassettes, 145
    coupons, 148–149
    flyers, 146–148
    videocassettes, 146
    See also direct mail
Market research, 121–123 (see
    also focus groups, trade
    associations)
Mathews, Jana B., 212, 269
Media, 164–167
Mestin, Robert, 170
Microenterprises, 17
Microlenders, 16
Minority entrepreneurs:
    government contracts, 10
    growth, 2
Mirares, Urban, 16

Money sources, alternatives:
  commercial finance
    companies, 206
  hard-asset lenders, 206
  sale of distribution
    rights, 205
  suppliers, 205
  options, 183
Mooney, Sean, 236, 271
Multilevel marketing. *See*
  Network marketing
Mystery shoppers, 127–130

N
Naisbitt, John, 8
National Association for the
  Specialty Food Trade
  (NASFT), 52
National Association of Small
  Business Investment
  Companies (NASBIC),
  105, 217
National Association of Women
  Business Owners, 15
National Business Incubation
  Association, 52, 56
National Consumers League, 50
National Education Center for
  Women in Business
  (NECWB), 15
National Executive Service
  Corps (NESC), 223
National Factoring
  Services, 222
National Fraud Information
  Center (NFIC), 50
National Minority Supplier
  Development Council, 14
National Technical Information
  Services (NTIS), 217

National Trade Data Bank
  (NTDB), 252
National Venture Capital
  Association, 28, 105, 195
Network marketing, 18
Newberg, Jay, 142
900 telephone numbers. *See*
  telemarketing
Nondisclosure agreement. *See*
  Trade secret
Nonprofit organization:
  501(c)(3), 66, 78
  forming, 78
  funding, 78, 222–223
North American Free Trade
  Agreement (NAFTA), 9
Novelty search, 94

P
Partnerships:
  finding/selecting, 68–69
  general partners, 66,
    69–70
  incorporation, 70
  key-partner life insurance,
    66, 71
  limited, 65, 69–70
  types, 65–66
Patent, 29, 92, 95–98
Personal services, 5
Pet services, 2–4
Physically disabled
  entrepreneurs. *See* Disabled
  entrepreneurs
Prentice-Hall Legal and
  Financial Service, 19
Pressman, David, 29
Price, Jeffrey, 158
Private placement, 184,
  196–199

Procurement contracts, 11–12
Procurement Technical
    Assistance Centers
    (PTAC), 11
Public relations program, 166
Publicity:
    media coverage, 164
    reprints, 164–165
    speaking opportunities, 165
Publicly held company,
    199–202
Purchasing a business:
    checklist, 89–91
    finding, 87–89
    pros/cons, 82–87
    selling price, 83

R
Retail stores, 56–63
Retiree entrepreneurs, 2, 8,
    17–18
Rice, Ted, 243
Right stuff, 39

S
S corporation:
    articles of incorporation, 75
    common stock, 74
    different from regular
        corporation, 74
    double taxation, 74
Sales:
    brochure, 145–146
    forecast, 134–135
    referrals, 139–140
    skills, 271–272
    strategies, 132–134
    See also Marketing
Sales representatives, 172–174
Second careers, xii, 2

Securities & Exchange
    Commission (SEC), 197,
    200–203
Seed capital, 180–183, 206–208
Self-employment, 1
Seltzer, Michael, 78
Service business, 136
Service mark, 29
Shopping channel, xiii, 137–138
S.J.T. Enterprises, 73
Small Business Administration:
    consultants, 237
    Contract Finance Program, 216
    Cooperative Research and
        Development Agreement
        (CRADA), 217
    hotline, 17
    international expertise, 10–11
    job creation, xi
    loans, 177, 183, 185,
        214–216, 218
Small Business Advocate,
    xii, 210
Small Business Equity
    Enhancement Act of
    1992, 218
Small Business Foundation of
    America, 10
Small Business Innovation
    Research program (SBIR),
    216–217
Small Business Investment
    Centers (SBIC), 10–11, 17
Small Corporate Offering
    Registration (SCOR), 179,
    184, 203–204
Software programs, 29, 116–117
Sole proprietorship, 65, 67–68,
    72, 260–261
Specialty boutiques, 3, 5

Start-up:
    costs, 262–264
    issues, 38
    number of, xi–xii
Subcontractors, 125

T
Technology agreement. *See*
    Employment agreement
Technology-based product,
    115–117
Telemarketing, 167–170
Testimonials, 162–164
Timmons, Jeff, xii, 28
Trade associations, 123–124
Trade business name, 44–45
Trade Information Center, 10
Trademark, 29, 93, 98–100
Trade secret:
    customer lists, 108–109
    definition, 30, 93
    different from copyright, 106
    law, 107
    nondisclosure agreement,
        110–111
    process, 106–107
    protection, 110–111
Trade show, 3, 43, 174–175
Transporting services, 2–6
Trend spotter, 39
Tuller, Lawrence W., 28
Turnaround artist, 81

U
Underground business
    economy, xii
U.S. Copyright Office, 30,
    93, 102
U.S. Department of Commerce,
    10, 29–30
U.S. Department of
    Transportation (DOT),
    12–14
U.S. Government Printing
    Office, 36
U.S. Patent and Trademark
    Office, 45, 92, 97
U.S. Postal Service, 50

V
Venture capital, 28, 178, 184,
    194–196
Venture checklist, 23
Venture opportunities, 2–3
Virtual companies, 1–2

W
Women:
    disparity with men, 14–15
    government contracts, 11
    growth, xiii, 2, 14

Y
Yellow pages. *See* Advertising